ॐ

Eating Sugarcane

A Spiritual Journey

SitaLakshmi
Clasina van Bemmel

Library and Archives Canada Cataloguing in Publication
Van Bemmel, Clasina, 1944-
Eating sugarcane : a spiritual journey / Clasina van Bemmel.
ISBN 978-0-9784689-0-3
1. Van Bemmel, Clasina, 1944-.
2. Spirituality.
3. Amritanandamayi, Mata, 1953-.
4. Spiritual biography--British Columbia.
5. Businesswomen--British Columbia--Biography.
I. Title.
BL73.V36A3 2007   204.092   C2007-906023-4

First printing: October 2007.

Paperback ISBN-13: 978-0-9784689-0-3

Book and cover design: Marcela Noriega.
All photographs from the Author's archive.

Printed and bound in Canada by Friesens.

Distributed by:
Dempsey - Your Distributor, Inc.
www.dempseycanada.com
Vancouver area (604)708-1081 or (800)667-3399

Only Love can heal the wounds of the world.
Amma

This book is dedicated to my spiritual teacher Amma

Foreword

Like millions of people in this world, I have wondered for decades what my life was really all about. Why do certain things happen to me and not to others around me? Do I deserve the good and bad experiences that happen to me? Is my path in this lifetime shaped by my karma?

Sometimes, I haven't even wanted to be part of this world. I used to ask myself, "Why am I here? What is my purpose?" Life seemed full of unnecessary struggles and unfairness and yet, at other times, experiences of abundance, wealth and beauty.

So much violence, greed, and waste have become part of the world we live in today. So many people live in unbelievable wealth and abundance, while others do not have even the very basics of life. We think we are an evolved species, but while we are able to envision offering sightseeing journeys to other planets, we do not even know how to feed and clothe most of the human race. Has there ever been one day, just one day of peace in this world? The plethora of scientific knowledge we have uncovered is astounding, yet our new technologies baffle our minds and most of us have trouble keeping up with the overload of information thrust at us day and night. Our pace of life is so much faster than it was in the past, but although we have created many "time-saving" devices, have we really created more time for ourselves? The Western world has gradually come to this: the faster we go, the less time we have.

Not long ago, books on spirituality, having been loaned to me, were put aside and then returned without being read. I thought that I was the most unlikely person to read, talk, or even write about spirituality or Divine grace. My own life had been a struggle, and I believed that the atrocities occurring elsewhere in the world wouldn't continue to happen if there were really a God.

Even wars have been fought in the name of religion for as long as I can remember. It made no sense to me.

However, it is true that when one continues to question and reflect on spiritual issues, the answers will come when one is truly ready to hear, see, and experience. When I was finally ready, I had an experience that transformed my life. I met someone who helped me make sense of my questions about everything—in short, someone who helped me explain my own life. Nothing would be the same for me again.

It was not my intention ever to write a book, although several close friends suggested over the years that I ought to. They believed that my experiences in overcoming the many struggles I faced and my thoughts on how I finally came to understand "why I am here on this earth" would be interesting to others and might even give some hope and meaning to their lives. But it only became possible for me to start to explore these issues and process them through writing after I met Amma during a visit to India in January of 2002.

Amma, Mother, or Ammachi, is a small, dark, Indian saint whose humility and compassion for humanity touched me so deeply that every confusing, inexplicable thing that had ever happened in my life gradually began to make sense.

This story of my life is written from my heart without any reservation about how things should be said. The events are woven into a narrative that describes how my life has come full circle.

In India I often watched small children sucking and chewing on small sticks of sugarcane and then spitting out the inedible fibres. They knew how to enjoy the best part of the sugarcane, obtaining energy from the sweet juice and spitting out the rest. I look at my life that way.

Prologue

When I was a child I often asked my mother if this angry man living with us was my real father. Truth be told, I desperately wanted him to be a different one. The baker, I thought, would have been perfect, as we were hungry most of the time and he was always kind. During those days, in our small village, the baker still delivered the loaves of bread house to house with a push wagon on three wheels. I could see and smell the flour on his clothes when he was standing in the doorway talking to my mother. But each time I asked, she would say, "My dear, the one you have is your father."

Later in life, three different astrologers told me that indeed I had chosen this family, father and all, because only through the painful experiences of my childhood would I learn the opposite of what was given to me from them. They went on to tell me that we also choose our friends, and the people with whom we surround ourselves. They all somehow come into our lives to teach us what we need to know during our life on this school of earth. The sooner we become conscious of this, it seems the faster we learn. True or not, when I finally thought about this much later in life, it became easier to forgive. One astrologer said that already by the age of four I knew subconsciously that one of my life's tasks was to break the cycle of violence in which I had been raised. I was here to be responsible for directing my own life, just as my parents were for their lives.

The same astrologer also told me that my soul was in a hurry to be reborn. It brought with it a special strength with some good karma ready to do some hard work. Anxiety had already been given to me in the womb—as if through an addicted mother—for I was born seven months before the liberation of my country during WW II. After nearly five years of the German invasion of Holland, my country was plundered, millions of people were killed, and millions more died of starvation. My family had also suffered greatly, and it was repeated to anyone in the village who wanted to listen they certainly did not want anymore children; I was simply called "an accident."

Part I

One

I was born in 1944 in Vleuten, a small village of nearly 700 people, close to the big city of Utrecht in the Netherlands. As was the custom in my country, I was named Clasina, after my mother and grandmother. The world was at war and Europe was in chaos.

While my mother was preparing to give birth to me, she ran from one room to the other trying to figure out which would provide the safest place to deliver. Our house, part of a row of houses rented from the city, was half a block away from the railway station—a prime target for bombing raids—and so the house was not particularly safe. The bombs often fell so close that after the noise settled down my young brothers would ask my mother, "Are we dead now?"

My father was "in hiding" in the polders* with other men from our village. At that time all the younger men were regularly rounded up and deported to Germany to work in the camps. The German soldiers would storm into the village houses at any time of night or day, shoot through the floors in case someone was hiding there, kick in walls and doors, and then walk out. No one could predict when they would appear again. Often my mother simply didn't know where my father was, so it wasn't necessary for her to lie when the house was searched and she was interrogated.

At that time everyone in our village was poor. The long war had taken its toll and food was scarce. My mother's youngest sister, a teenager and too young to live on her own, had moved in with us for a while when their 46-year-old mother—my grandmother—died of breast cancer. Now and then, at the

---

* areas of reclaimed land that were once part of the sea bed in the Netherlands.

most desperate times, my aunt would leave and push an old pram 127 kilometres each way to and from a farm in the North of Holland to get extra food from some people my parents knew. It was not only a courageous thing to do; it was very dangerous. Often on her walk German soldiers accosted her, and she was forced to beg them to leave her alone. She was always very quiet about what happened on those trips. Sometimes she would arrive home with only half of the food she had been given because on her way back other hungry people would beg from her or force her to give them food.

The children in my family included the boys, Jan and Dirk, and my sister, Willie, and me. Many times during my younger years my parents made it very clear to me that an "extra eater" wasn't wanted. One daughter had been more than enough. My brothers, Jan and Dirk, were already "farmed out" on a daily basis to a local farmer for two meals a day; there simply wasn't enough food for all of us.

For many years, well into my adult life, I would become anxious when I did not have a fridge full of food.

I remember very well that before beginning to attend school, I had just one dress. At night after dinner this dress was washed and put close to the stove to dry. After it was ironed the next morning I would wear it again. My mother used to say, "Perhaps there is a good reason why people are poor, but I know of no good reason why people should be dirty." Around the age of four I also wore wooden shoes. They were, of course, cheaper than regular shoes. During the winter I wore them with old newspapers as insoles to keep my feet warm. Although I was poked fun at many times by other children for wearing them, I still remember the comfort I felt wearing those old-fashioned wooden shoes.

I adored my older sister. She was my friend, my playmate, my hero, and the light of my life. Our favourite games were jumping on our bed and playing hide and seek. We built tents on our bed with the sheets and sat inside for hours, hiding, especially from the German soldiers. We sometimes giggled a little, but mostly we were very scared. We had learned to be scared. Our parents talked about the war incessantly.

I would watch my sister sitting at the table, decorating postcards with ribbons. Willie sewed the outlines of flowers and buildings into them with all kinds of different coloured threads. Sitting in my chair with my head on my hands and arms, I leaned on the table and watched her for hours.

By then Willie had also learned how to read. She would read to me about the old windmill owner who headed home from work late at night. When he passed by the river he noticed a child's wooden shoe drifting along. He panicked, for it was already dark, and wondered where the other little wooden shoe was. Though his wife was waiting for him, he still felt he had to go around the village from house to house to see if all the children were accounted for. Where was the child who was wearing the other wooden shoe? I couldn't get enough of this story; every time I heard it I would become anxious and want to know where that child could be. Was he or she lost, drowned in the river, or at home in bed? Willie always made me wait as long as possible to hear the re-

With my father and big sister. She was the light and tragedy of my childhood.

mainder of the story, which I liked the most. The child was finally found asleep in the mayor's horse barn. Afterward, when all the tears were dried, everyone celebrated and ate warm apple fritters. Those apple fritters did it; I can still taste them.

Life continued in this way and seemed unremarkable until I was four and I lost Willie. I remember seeing her pale, sad face when we picked her up from the hospital. We had come in a taxi, the only taxi in the entire village. It was green, a colour I liked at that time. Willie stood beside the car, waiting to be helped in. Her face was pale and drawn. Although it was warm, she had her winter hat and coat on. When I realized she could not talk, I knew instinctively that something was terribly wrong. Due to complications following a tonsillectomy (apparently she had the beginnings of chicken pox), fluid had built up in her lungs. Within a few days of her return home, Willie died. She was only six. Suddenly, my life seemed over as well.

My parents were absolutely devastated. Years before, my mother had lost her first child a few days after it was born, and now, after losing a second child, she was overcome by such profound grief that she had to be sedated and hospitalized for some time.

I remember vividly Willie in her coffin near the window in our home. I was not allowed to touch her, but I did anyway, trying to wake her up when no one was looking. She was cold and wouldn't move. I pushed her, begged her, cried and even got angry with her. She looked beautiful, her long blonde hair wreathed by little white flowers. A great many people, all in black clothes, sat around the coffin for three days, crying and mourning. There was no way anyone could tear me away from my sister; I fervently hung onto her little coffin.

Finally it was time for Willie's funeral. The little boys from our neighbourhood arrived in their black suits, while the little girls wore white dresses and crowns of flowers on their heads, just like my sister in her coffin. It became clear to me that I would not be allowed to accompany them, wherever they were going. In those days, a four-year-old child didn't belong at a funeral. After much thrashing and biting, I was finally torn away from the coffin and taken upstairs. I looked through the window and saw Willie's funeral procession walk around the corner. From that moment on, I stopped talking and eating.

Overwhelmed by grief, my parents didn't notice for a long time that their other little girl was literally wasting away. It seemed that for them time didn't exist anymore, and that there was no life left in them.

Some time after the funeral, some of our neighbours finally noticed that something was wrong with me. I would sit on the floor where Willie's coffin had been and just stare. I had lost so much weight that I was hospitalized. When they couldn't find anything physically wrong, I was taken to a child therapist. That was very unusual in those days. He was a large, tall, dark man in a white coat. He invited me for a walk in the garden. My mother wanted to come too, but he told her to watch us from the window. I have vague memories of walking in the garden, but no recollection of what was said.

Immediately upon my return home, I was taken to Gerrit's bike shop, a "one-man-in-a-wheelchair business" next to the train station. We lived close to the station, so we knew Gerrit very well; he often came over to our house for tea. I often wandered over to visit him, too. My father asked him to put a scooter together for me. In those days people never considered buying anything new— there just wasn't enough money. Instead, they put things together.

I was given the most beautiful bright red scooter I had ever seen. It had cold steel handles and the tires were huge to my eyes, but those things did not matter. Like a crazed child, I started racing through the village on this new toy, gathering scars on my knees that would last a lifetime and tasting a freedom I had never known. Soon I was eating and talking again.

I had been told that my sister had gone to heaven, and that she was now a star in the sky. As soon as I was taken to bed at night, I would get up and stand in front of the window, no matter how cold the floor was, and wait for the first star. A star would always come. Later on I was shown where Willie was buried, right next to the Protestant Church where we were all baptized, and near my elementary school. Sometimes my father and I would plant some flowers at her grave. I went to that school for six years and not a day went by that I didn't talk to my sister Willie through the tall, black iron gate.

I now understand that for some reason my sister was meant to have a short life. Why she came into this world I do not know; however, her beautiful spirit was close to me during my difficult childhood and has stayed with me throughout my entire adult life. In my most desperate moments, I have heard her voice giving me direction, new hope, and strength. She has remained an integral part of me over the years and I still miss her very much.

* * *

I've often heard about parents divorcing after the death of one of their children. In those days, however, no matter how much fighting or abuse went on in a home, people did not divorce. They stayed together for the children and that was that; there were few alternatives. Where would they go when the marriage ended?

I now feel this is a grave mistake. Children are much better off living with one parent in harmony, even if that means living in poverty, than with two parents who fight all the time or who abuse the children and each other.

My grandfather had beaten his sons when they were children, a thing they said was normal in those days. Whether a beating was deserved or not wasn't important; parents were simply allowed to beat their children. A man could physically harm his wife or throw her out of the house. There were no social workers, the police didn't want to hear about it, and neither did the neighbours or the teachers at school. It was no one's business what happened in other people's homes.

My father had been an angry man for some time and he dealt out a daily quota of beatings. I really became aware of it after my sister died and my little brother Cor was born. It was rumoured that my youngest brother was not really my father's child, and it was true that my mother had not been faithful to my father for some time. On the other hand, my father was not an angel either. He was not only physically violent; he was also sexually abusing my mother's teenaged sister, who was living with us. It was not a pretty picture all around.

One problem with living in row housing was that the noise and screaming from the beatings could be heard easily by all the neighbours. But they would simply close their windows and pretend nothing was happening. I was told that every house had to carry its own cross; all of our neighbours probably had their own problems. But ours were loud and therefore obviously known in the community. Later on, that fact meant the girls from my neighbourhood shunned me and would not wait to accompany me to school. They just did not associate with "those kind of people."

On one occasion, I was able to run out of the house to get help from a police officer who lived in the next block. He was home and ran back to my house with me, but by the time we got there, my father was sitting quietly in his chair, as if nothing had happened. We had bruises and swollen lips, but he wasn't caught in the act of beating us, so the police could therefore do nothing. When the policeman left, my father made sure that I understood not ever to do that again.

My mother had been working at cleaning jobs, bringing in a little extra money, and then she got her own large newspaper and magazine route in our village and the surrounding villages. My brothers and I would distribute the papers to our own village, and my mother, her bike laden with large, heavy bags and my younger brother in his little seat on her handle bars, delivered papers to different communities. My father was not happy about my mother going that far away from the house, but somehow she stood her ground, insisting that we desperately needed the money. However, her work brought much extra trouble and anguish into our family. It was on her delivery outings that she met her "other" men. Sometimes she brought some of her male "friends" home. They carried bags full of food and hard liquor into the house, and kicked us children out when they settled in to drink. My father would join them after work and enjoy the free booze he would not buy himself. He was just too cheap, and besides, we could not afford it.

One day during the wintertime, my mother arrived home early. Upon my return home from school I was thrilled to see her and naïvely thought that perhaps my family's problems would suddenly all disappear. But she announced that it was too cold to deliver the newspapers and magazines on her bike and that her ears had frozen. She was so tired that day, that out of desperation and on the spur of the moment, she had dumped all her deliveries into the canal close to the Catholic church. "Go and look for yourself, if you don't believe me," was her comment. I ran as quickly as I could and, lo and behold, there they were: newspapers and magazines floating everywhere close to the bridge where the water hadn't yet frozen. We were all terrified she would lose her job, but somehow the company forgave her and so did her customers.

Since my mother was away so much, and because I was now the only girl in the family, before I was six years old I knew how to cook, clean the house, and iron clothes. We ate potatoes every day; I learned how to peel them fast and perfectly with very little waste. I was good at cooking the vegetables. We didn't have any meat until I was a teenager; we simply could not afford it.

I became an expert at washing windows and scrubbing the path and sidewalk in front of our house. This was the weekly thing to do in our village; every Saturday morning the houses were cleaned from top to bottom including changing all the bedclothes. Everyone else in our row of low-rental housing performed these weekly chores, so my father insisted we had to do so as well. What that really meant was that I had to. Somehow, boys were not supposed to do any housework, so my brothers were spared.

At the age of seven, I was allowed to go to school. Since my birthday is in October and school started in September, I missed out on one entire year. Kindergarten didn't exist at that time, so I had not developed any reading or writing skills. School terrified me. I couldn't even hold a pencil properly. We sat in pairs on a bench at a table. I watched as the little blonde girl next to me made perfect zeros. I couldn't make the shape properly, and so, frustrated, I made the table wobble with my knees so that my table-mate would have trouble, too. She started to scream. The teacher asked me why I was shaking the table, and I told her I couldn't stand having my classmate do it right while I was having so much trouble. She smiled and came over to help me. I still remember that teacher's name.

I want to say thank you to all the teachers out there. Do you have any idea how important you are in the lives of the children in your classes? That first-grade teacher's attention, patience, and warm smiles made me trust all my teachers for as long as I attended school.

I always worked hard in school, but I couldn't wait to get out and was always in a frenzy to get home because I was responsible for all the household duties. When school ended at four o'clock, I would rush home and try to prepare everything before six when my father arrived home from work. Food had to be on the table as soon as he entered the house. Since he worked in the furniture factory right across the street, I could see him coming. How many times did I walk from one window to the next, praying that my mother would arrive just before my father did? Not finding her at home ahead of him made him angry and volatile. I was always in a waiting mode—what was going to happen next? But no matter how much or how fervently I prayed, she was invariably late.

Even if his food was ready on the table, my father would find something to be angry about. The slightest little thing—a thing that often made no sense to the rest of us—could set him off. His face would turn shades of red and then blue and his veins would swell up. He would spit profanities and then his fists hit whatever they landed on. He would grab anything within reach, be it a chair or simply a loaf of bread from the table, and he would throw it any direction—usually ours. I can still picture him throwing a glass container of mustard at me, but it missed and shattered against the wall behind me. In retrospect, it was funny—watching the mustard dripping down the wallpaper. But at the time it was terrible. Often he wouldn't even take the time to remove his wooden shoes, instead kicking us with them while he punched us at the same time. He would look like a wild, rabid animal. My father was a very sick man, emotionally distant and completely unpredictable.

Many people who were abused as children will tell you that there comes a point when we simply do not scream or cry anymore, and that is true. Gradually I learned to tune out the pain, pretending I was somewhere else. I seemed to move naturally into

11

this kind of survival mode. I let the hitting happen and simply waited for it to stop. The worst part was not knowing when it was going to happen.

My mother, brothers, and I carried this anxiety with us, day in and day out. There would be a little relief for a few days afterward, but it always began again. Sometimes his beatings were so bad that my father, afraid of the damage he had inflicted, would check our breathing just to make sure he hadn't killed one of us yet.

I was only seven or eight years old when one evening there were no vegetables in the house, so I could only prepare the potatoes. I was frantic because my mother wasn't home yet. My father rummaged around in the drawers and found a few onions that he told me to cook right away. I had no idea how to prepare them, and I told him so, my body shaking heavily. In an instant, he went absolutely berserk. He still had his wooden shoes on when he threw me against the kitchen wall and kicked me onto the floor. He continued to kick and kick with no indication he was going to stop. It occurred to me that he was going to beat me until I died, that he would go on until nothing was left of me. With that realization came a feeling that my own death was welcome.

I let go. Then something happened that I still remember so vividly that it might have been yesterday. The very moment I let go, I felt a sense of peace flowing through my body. Suddenly I knew that I had something in me that could never die. I had no understanding of what it was, but somehow I connected with some knowing. Calmness set in and I was able to move out of my body to a place where there was no pain. I could see my body from above and observe what was going on. After that experience, during periods of extreme pain when I was beaten, this "letting go" became easier and easier to do. I didn't know what it was, of course, but years later this knowing would again become a precious gift.

Two

My eldest brother Jan was a tall, skinny fellow; he and I and our mother were the focus of my father's abuse. For some reason he avoided my brother Dirk, who was born with a disability in his legs. Dirk was "a cripple," they said. There was a rumour in the family that he had been born that way because my father had kicked mother around so badly during her pregnancy. I can remember with clarity that Dirk was always wearing braces on his legs, trying to lengthen the tendons behind his knees. He cried constantly, especially during the night when they pulled it an extra notch. My mother carried Dirk everywhere until he was 11 years old. I cannot remember my father ever carrying him. There was no money for a wheelchair. By then, Dirk wasn't around our house much; he was semi-adopted by some neighbours a few houses down the block. My youngest brother Cor, born with spina bifida and crossed eyes, wasn't home much either, as he accompanied my mother on her paper route and while she cleaned houses.

As time went on, my older brothers were at home less often. They found any excuse to be away and only came home at mealtimes and to go to bed. My eldest brother, Jan, was a handy fellow and started working at all kinds of small jobs in a garage in the village. He also learned how to do small electrical jobs. One day as he was attaching an electrical cord to the wall in my parents' bedroom my father flew into a rage, grabbing Jan's hammer out of his hands and hitting him on his back with it. That was the moment Jan reached the end of his tolerance and finally stood up to our father. He grabbed the hammer from Father's hands and stood poised to hit him, screaming, "Don't you ever touch me again or I will kill you!" For a long time he just stood there, shaking violently, hammer in the air and ready to strike. Jan was the first of us to leave the house for good.

Cor was the first one my mother would grab when my father threw her out of the house, which happened regularly. Often she would leave on her bicycle, in just her dress and without a coat, and ride seven kilometres to the next town, where her brother lived with his family. She dropped off the child there and then hid in a home she had discovered on her paper route.

One day when I was 11 or 12 years old, after she had made another escape, I was taken out of class and summoned to the director's office. My mother was on the phone. She would not be coming home anymore, she said, and she needed some clothes. I was told to go home, climb up into the attic and retrieve the wooden suitcase, fill it up with her clothes, put it on the back of my bike and deliver it to a transport company in the village. She gave me the address of her hiding place and warned me that under no circumstances was I to tell my father where she was. I was petrified.

Whenever he threw my mother out of the house, my father locked all the doors and cupboards. In order to start the cooking and cleaning and the family's washing and ironing, I would have to pick up the keys from him as soon as I arrived home from school. That day I trembled all the way home, worried about getting the keys and the logistics of her request. I had to figure out how to get this massive, cumbersome suitcase from the attic, pack her belongings, take it to the transport company, and get the food on the table by six o'clock. My father was busy in the factory when I went to pick up the keys and he did not notice me shaking.

When I returned home after delivering the suitcase full of her clothing, I was late, and utterly exhausted and frightened. I rode my bike up and down the street several times, too afraid to enter the house. Dinner was not on the table. Finally I had to go in. My father was waiting for me. He was beside himself with rage; spit and foam erupted from his mouth. He hissed and blew and was barely coherent. First, he wanted to know where my mother was hiding. I could not talk; I could not move. But I would not speak to him, not a word. He was not able to kick it out of me. I silently endured his abuse and waited for the rage to pass. At the end I felt a sense of pride for withholding my mother's whereabouts from him. I recognized a tenacity in myself already at that young age that served me well in my future struggles.

Subsequently, mother took a job in a big hotel in town; she worked in the kitchen checking all the food orders before they were served. At the time, my youngest brother lived at my uncle's house, and I was the only one at home with my father. The house became quiet, and I knew my father was trying to get my mother back. He could be a sweet-talker when he wanted to be. He pleaded with my uncle, assuring him he would never beat any of us again. "A wife needs to be with her husband and the children," he said earnestly. This time, however, he was having a hard time getting her back and his options were running out. Suddenly it occurred to him to involve the minister of our church, although he had not been to church for many years. Perhaps the minister could be persuaded to talk her into returning to us. The minister finally did go and talk to my mother, with big promises of no more disturbances, and home she came. One morning I awoke to find my mother was back in her bedroom. I felt betrayed.

Yes, my father could be a sweet-talker. He was a model workman in the factory, where he received nothing but praise. Despite all the stories of abuse going around in the village, many people saw him as a kind man. When in a good mood, my father was friendly to the neighbours' children and would give them a few coins for their birthdays, yet none of his own children ever received a birthday or Christmas gift. I cannot remember ever receiving a dime or a hug from my father.

One day, my father decided not to give my mother any more household money. She was not spending his hard-earned money to his liking. As a result of his decision, after his prayer one night at the dinner table, my father opened the lid of the dish on the table to find only boiling water in it. My mother said, "No money, no food." We went without dinner that night. But he got the message.

My mother had already known that my father was withholding a part of his salary, but she had no idea what he was doing with the money. She finally found his stash of cash hidden in the back wall of the linen closet. I had no idea she had found it until one day when I returned home from school. I ran inside, and confused, ran out again, because I thought for certain I had gone into the wrong house. All the furniture, including the carpets and curtains, had changed. Mother must have planned this well, because it had all been done within the time my father was at work across the street. Without cooking anything, I wandered the streets until it was dark. From a safe distance I saw my father going home, then my mother's entrance, but I stayed away. I was too scared to go home again that day. In the end, he had no choice: the furniture was there to stay.

My father's appeal to the minister and his connection to the church were little more than a joke. My father was the only one who prayed over his food before dinner. We would all stare at him while his lips moved. Somewhere in the middle of his prayer, he often opened his eyes and swore. Then, unprovoked, he would turn to my brother Jan and strike him on the side of his head. If my mother dared to ask him why he had done that, he would say, "Well, just in case he was going to do something." Now 68 years old, my brother still leans to one side when he sits at the table for a meal, as if anticipating a blow.

Every Sunday at lunchtime, my father read to us out of the Bible. We were to be thankful for all that we had. While he read we didn't move an inch and we didn't say a word. We knew that if by any chance there was a God, He certainly wasn't visiting our house, no matter how much my father might pray. And the rest of us were certainly not going to pray. I had lost confidence in God since the loss of my sister. The doctors and the minister had said, "It was God's will." Whenever anything went terribly wrong it was always "God's will."

At the age of five, I had gone to Sunday school, but I didn't last there very long. When the Sunday school teacher told us children about how wonderful Jesus was I jumped up and screamed, "It isn't true! He took my sister!" I finally had to be taken home.

My father wasn't only cruel to his wife and children but also to the animals we brought home. One day, a girl in my second-grade class offered me one of her pet rabbits. Without asking my parents, after school I went to her home with an empty shoebox to pick up the rabbit. To my surprise, my father said nothing when I brought it home. After seeing my rabbit, my little brother wanted one too and off we went to get another. Their owners were glad to get rid of them. I was now in charge of the two rabbits. I loved them. I cleaned their cage every week, found them clover and healthy grass, and stole carrots out of the gardens for them because they loved them so much. While feeding them, I would confide in them and caress their soft fur. They were my silent friends.

One day when I got up to feed them they were gone, the door of their cage still open. I sped around the village on my bicycle, asking everyone if they had been seen. No such luck—they seemed to have disappeared for good. I could not get over it; I cried and cried. Finally, my father grew tired of my "whining." He grabbed my arm and pulled me into the kitchen. Taking the lid off the cooking pot, he said, "Here they are—now shut up." That night I was obliged to sit at the table, nauseated, while my family ate my rabbits.

I found two abandoned puppies but my father drowned each one of them in the sewage tank behind our house. "We don't need any extra eaters," he said. I still do not trust people who do not like animals.

Somewhat ironically, one day a fish nearly killed my father. He enjoyed fishing in the Old Rhine Canal. We were all so relieved when he took his fishing rod and went out. He would not throw away anything he caught, not even the smallest fish. When he got home he would bake them in the frying pan, and then eat them by himself. At one time there was just the three of us at home—my father, my little brother Cor, and myself. Cor—who with his crossed eyes could barely look over the table—and I, watched as my father choked on his fish bones one evening. He started coughing and began to choke. It went on and on. He turned red and blue and began gasping for air. Both of us just stared, helpless, and then my dear little brother started waving goodbye to him. I remained frozen in my chair. We didn't know what to do—we were so young and we had no phone. And my father was in his long underwear. It was a comical sight to see this little boy with crossed eyes waving goodbye, and today I can still laugh about it. My father finally ran out the door to the neighbours and got help. Out of sheer helplessness, I think, we would have just let him perish.

.

Three

I managed to make it to the seventh grade in school. The teachers liked me all right, and said so. They could see that I tried hard. That is one thing I've always given myself credit for. I have always tried hard at everything I attempted, and I still do. But in school I had trouble concentrating because of all the tension, anger, and violence at home.

The teachers could see very well the damage being done to me. My nails bled all the time because I bit them to the quick. When they walked past my desk, they could see wounds on my skull, often open and bleeding from my constant nervous scratching. I was always anxious to get home to get my chores done and dinner ready on time. For years, when there was any trouble in the classroom, every student had to stay after the regular four o'clock dismissal as punishment. I was the only one allowed to go at the proper time. Focused and absorbed with trying to get home as fast as I could, it never dawned on me that the other children remained silent about why I was singled out.

In my teen years I badly wanted to go to prison. I imagined that I would be fed and put in a room by myself where I could relish the quiet, sleep and read, and finally be safe. At home I was sometimes able to escape to the attic when my father went into a rage. To reach the attic I had to get into my room, pull the ladder down, and climb up. Once up, I could either pull the ladder up or use it to block the bedroom door, but his anger was often so violent and out of control that I thought he would break the door down. At night I slept with a hammer under my pillow in case my father got into my room and I wasn't able to make it up the ladder into the attic before he reached me. And as a last resort, although my room was on the upper floor, I had often contemplated jumping out of my window. I'm sure that at the very least I would have broken my legs, and far worse could have happened. But at those times my fear was so intense I could not think straight. Prison seemed like a positive alternative. Little did I know at that time that one day I would be severely tested. Had things turned out differently I might have had to spend many years of my life in prison.

In my early teens I got into trouble a few times, mainly with the girls in my class. They often made funny remarks about my clothes and my family situation. Our village was small, and everyone knew what was going on in our house.

Children at school were cruel and called me and my siblings and parents terrible names. After repeatedly turning the other cheek I finally lost my temper one day when two sisters from my class called my mother a whore. Enraged and charged with adrenaline, I jumped at them, got them on the ground, and beat their heads together. After I released them I stood and shook uncontrollably for a long time. I looked down at my hands and saw that I was holding clumps of their hair. The girls ran home crying their eyes out. Soon afterward I was called into the director's office, where they sat with their father, who held his daughters' hands as they moaned. I was asked to explain my side of the situation. I told the adults that my classmates had called my mother a whore. The sisters confirmed my story by nodding their heads and I was told to go back to my classroom. My outburst went unpunished and the name-calling in school finally came to a stop.

No matter how much grief my mother caused by being late, spending time with other men, and leaving me behind when she was kicked out of the house, I still loved her and admired her in many ways. In her absence, as the only female, I naturally took on a protective role. I cooked, cleaned and often spoke up to defend her when anyone bad-mouthed her. It was a tiring role with no rewards. Over and over, I thought that if I could just get it right, if I could just plan ahead and be obedient, perhaps things would change. Perhaps someday we would have some happy, peaceful moments. But it never happened. A continual feeling of nervous apprehension always permeated our household. It still chokes me up when I think of that little girl, myself, trying in vain for years to achieve some semblance of a peaceful childhood.

* * *

My earliest recollection of meeting an "ordinary" family happened when an Indonesian girl named Judith joined our class in Grade 4. We had never had a classmate from a different country, especially one with a different skin colour. I liked her right away. Judith was more delicately built than the rest of us and had a gentle disposition and a warm shy smile for everyone. When she spoke, her voice was soft and tender.

She happened to live at the end of our street, and each time I saw her pass our house on her way home from school, I wished fervently that I was her sister and could go home with her. One weekend day she invited me to her house to play and meet her family. She had four sisters and three brothers. I had never met such a large family. Her father was a slender, short, dark man with beaming eyes, and her mother was a large, tall woman who smiled broadly and hugged me when I arrived.

Awestruck, I watched this family and their friends interact with each other in good humour, without any tension. They were having fun. They had a small living/dining room similar to ours, and some of the children were doing their homework on the floor or at the table. Some played the guitar and sang, some read, and others just sat around engrossed in laughter and conversation. I was shown the kitchen, where a large pot of rice, meat, and vegetables was being kept warm on the stove for anyone to help themselves when they got hungry. After eating, each person washed and put away his or her own plate and utensils. Spending just one day with this generous, loving family made an important and lasting impression on me. I had seen with my own eyes that a family could live harmoniously, enjoy life, and express love for one another. I didn't have it, but I could strive for it.

* * *

One of Mother's "friends," a wealthy man who owned a car, often bribed me with money to entice me to leave the house when he visited. With his money I bought my first seven paper-back dictionaries: one Dutch, two English, two French, and two German, and a world map that I put on the wall of my room. I dreamed of all the places where I would travel as soon as I could get away.

When I announced I was leaving school at the age of 14, the director summoned me to his office. He was a friendly man. He asked me what my parents thought about me leaving school and what was I going to do without any education. In truth, my parents didn't care one way or the other. They thought girls were not sup-posed to be educated anyway. In a brave voice, I told him I was going to learn languages and travel the world. He wished me well.

Although I was only 14, I had to leave school to find a job and earn money. My parents promised that I could keep 25 cents out of every guilder (Dutch dollar) I earned; the rest would have to be contributed to the household. I found my first job at a fac-tory that manufactured cardboard picture frames in the big city of Utrecht, a seven-kilometer bike ride from our village. I worked at a long table with other people gluing picture frames. It was a sticky, dirty job and indescribably tedious.

I began to learn about what could happen in the world out-side the confines of my little village. The factory employed the most interesting people I had ever met: prostitutes, people from the welfare rolls, handicapped people, and seniors—people of all ages, ethnicities, and socio-economic classes. I had never been exposed to such diversity. The women wore colourful clothes and make-up and their language was filled with the obscenities my father used regularly. They were experts at name-calling; of course none of these words or phrases could be found in a dictionary. There were fights daily, but that didn't faze me in the least. I was able to stand my ground, and I let them know I would not let them touch me. When the same person stole my lunch a second time, that was enough for me. I pulled her over the table by her shirt and demand-ed my lunch back. Soon the boss stood in front of me.

I was moved to a different job that involved working with machinery, not people. Now I stood behind an enormous, noisy machine that opened and closed automatically. Two hinged plates, one with a steel relief of a picture frame and the other bare, came together to cut cardboard for the frames. I had to put a piece of cardboard in between the steel plates and then take it out when they opened to produce a newly formed picture frame. After a few days of doing the same thing I became restless and began to experiment by not putting anything into the machine when it closed. Nothing terrible happened.

I complained to my supervisor that my job was boring and, as a result, was promised an office job if I learned how to type. So off I went to typing school at night after work. I learned how to type on one of those old-fashioned typewriters you see in old movies. It was hard to stand at the stamping machine all day and then hammer on this old thing at night. But I was determined to learn how to type so I could get a better job.

After receiving my typing diploma, for some reason I was not given the promised office job. One day in the middle of the week, I walked out of the factory while the machine went on opening and closing. My mother was not happy that I had walked off the job and took me back. However, I threatened to walk off again and again, until she finally gave in and agreed that I wouldn't have to return. My father thought he could beat me until I agreed to go back to the factory, but that didn't work either.

I soon took a job as a typist with an insurance company. Within only a few weeks I figured out that the owner of the company enjoyed looking up the women's skirts while they were bending over the filing cabinets. My colleagues knew about his "hobby," but kept their mouths shut and put up with it. But I wouldn't tolerate it—I left and was out of a job again.

Getting out of the house—even to work at a miserable job—had its advantages. Then I discovered recreation. Once I got to know the city a little, I joined a women's handball team. Secretly, I also signed up for judo classes and became a soccer player. During a handball tournament, the coach of the national women's soccer team saw me kicking the ball around during the intermission and invited me to join his team. At 14, I became the youngest female national soccer player in the Netherlands. And by the age of 15, I had my brown belt in judo.

At this time, I learned to drive a car. In Holland the legal driving age was 18. You acquired a proper driver's licence (learners' licences did not exist) after taking lessons from a certified driving school. It was strictly forbidden for anyone else to teach you how to drive. However, my mother's latest boyfriend had an old clunker he was trying to fix up, and he offered to teach me how to double shift with the clutch. The car didn't have a floor, just two bars across, but that hardly mattered—I just had to be sure to keep my feet up while the bare ground rushed by below. I had scarcely learned the shifting when this car decided it didn't want to go forward anymore, it only worked in reverse. We drove it backward through the village for several days before the police finally knocked on our door.

* * *

My eldest brother Jan had been working as a plumber and electrician for some time. He began to date and was seldom seen around the house. As soon as he started making a decent salary, he got married, and moved into a boarding house with his new wife in Utrecht. My handicapped brother Dirk had found work in a cardboard factory. Because Dirk was not able to stand even for a few minutes, he spent his days sitting at a table cutting and gluing pieces of cardboard. One day upon his return home, he complained to my mother that the other men at his table produced less work than he did, but he was paid less because he was handicapped. My mother, with me in tow, went to the factory and demanded to speak to the manager. It was true—handicapped people were paid less simply because they were handicapped; it didn't matter if they worked harder. When it became clear to my mother that the conversation wasn't going anywhere, she walked into the factory, went straight to the long table where Dirk and others were working, and told him to get up. She pulled him by his arm out of that factory, saying loudly to everyone in earshot, "My son is as good as anyone else."

In awe, I watched this as she confronted the manager and then pulled my brother from his workbench. There were many more instances where I observed my mother standing up for her beliefs at critical times. She had her own spontaneous, innovative, brave, and somewhat eccentric style. She never did fit the average housewife's role. Over time, in my own life, I would often find myself reacting in similar ways when pushed into a corner or confronted with a moral dilemma.

Since Dirk hadn't attended school beyond the sixth grade, my mother had him tested by the Handicapped Association to assess his skill levels. Although his physical handicap prevented him from walking normally, he had a flair for conversation and it was thought that he had some potential skill in sales. With the assistance of the Handicapped Association, Dirk got a three-wheeled ice-cream bike. He got a vendor's permit and every day we helped him load up the ice chest with the boxes of ice cream. Then off he went pedalling through the surrounding villages. He quickly learned how to handle the unwieldy bike and became fitter than he had ever been. Being out on the road all day, chatting with people, and selling his packaged ice cream, Dirk began to blossom. He had a smile for everyone and joked with the children. People got to know him and supported his desire to work like everyone else despite his handicap.

Dirk's ice cream sales did well in the summer, but what was he to do during the cold winter months? Once again, my resourceful mother found the answer when she saw a second-hand catering truck for sale. It had two large propane-fuelled hot oil vats to make hot snacks: meatballs, hamburgers, hot dogs, french fries, croquettes, and space to store ice cream and candy. My father thought that everyone had gone crazy and said, "It is never going to work," but my grandparents—who had previously not been involved in this business venture—suddenly offered the down payment of 1,200 guilders to buy it. The main obstacle was obtaining a permit from our town hall to operate this new venture. Our household, being part of the Protestant Church—although we rarely attended—needed a permit from the mayor and councillors, who were Catholics. In a small village of 700 people that was not easy. The permit was refused twice. My mother finally resorted to contacting the Catholic priest. Several years previously, she had gone to see this priest in connection with our neighbours. A very large Catholic family next door was so poor that the children were severely under-nourished. She told him that if the Catholic Church was promoting large families, they also had an obligation to look after them. The priest was so impressed that my Protestant mother had the nerve to bring this to his attention that he told her, "If you ever need me for anything, just let me know." Well, this was the moment. He remembered her well, and with his influence we soon had the desired permit.

My mother got her driver's licence in order to drive the truck. Acquiring that truck licence was no small feat for a woman at that time. To obtain a normal driver's licence was extremely difficult, and the requirements to drive a larger vehicle were much more stringent.

Because I had quit my job at the insurance company, my mother put me to work in the snack truck. Dirk took the passenger's seat as I stood in the centre aisle, gripping the candy shelves and avoiding splashes from the hot oil vats while Mother drove the truck through the bumpy streets of the village. At the same time, I rang an old sailing-ship's bell to let people know of our arrival.

We did well, and I got my first lessons in running a business. My mother had a gift for it, but neither she nor I knew it at the time. Our little venture was run by pure instinct, as my mother had no formal education. She had gone to school until the age of 11, and then went to live and work on a farm quite a distance from home. She was given room and board in exchange for milking the cows and helping with the cleaning. She was also physically harassed by the farmer. That's just the way it was; one didn't question things like that in those days.

Mother was adamant about scrubbing the old beat-up truck every day, inside and out. The vegetable oil was kept scrupulously clean and the food we cooked was bought fresh each day. We worked until everything was sold, even if that meant waiting next to a café in the middle of the night for the drunks to buy a hot snack at closing time. One day the truck broke down when we were already loaded up to go. No one was able to fix it that day, so my mother had Dirk sit behind the wheel, put the transmission into neutral and steer it, while she and I, with the help of some neighbourhood kids, pushed the truck through the village until everything was sold. It was an embarrassing day for me. People laughed and joked, and although I didn't want to be seen, I had nowhere else to go or hide.

We would keep cooking and selling our snacks even during the biggest thunderstorms, while lightning strikes were killing cows in the fields. My mother laid down the strict rule: we were not going home until all the food was sold, period. The most frightening times were when we visited the gypsy sites on the outskirts of the city. According to local gossip and prejudice, these were potentially dangerous people: thieves, con artists, and troublemakers who often carried knives and guns. But my mother had discovered they were good clients when times were tough. Just in case someone physically threatened us, my mother had given me instructions to douse the assailant with a ladleful of hot oil.

Mother was never afraid of the competition and stood her ground firmly when she believed her way was right. One day, to our surprise, a beautiful new truck showed up immediately ahead of us on our normal route. We watched as "our" clients lined up in front of the new truck to buy their snacks. "Sorry," we were told by our regular customers, "their prices are cheaper." My brother and I froze, unsure of what to do next, but my mother stayed calm. She inquired about the prices offered by the operator of the new truck, and then said, "We will see you again soon." Then she turned toward us and explained that our competitor would not be able to keep his lower prices for long. She said that with his low prices he must be losing money. After the purchase of that new truck he would have a heavy debt to pay off. Our prices would stay the way they were, she said, otherwise we would lose money. We just needed to work harder for a while.

When an old customer left our competitor's truck, my mother approached him and asked to taste his french fries. After sampling this product, she noted the competitor was using a lower-quality cooking oil than we did. She also noted that their food must have been cooked at too high a temperature, thus burning the oil quicker and giving it an unclean look and acrid taste.

We continued on our route as usual, keeping the same times and stops, no matter whether we sold anything. Mother would say, "People like to know that we will show up. They need to be able to count on us. They want good, clean, reliable service and quality food." It didn't take long for the new competitor's prices to go up and our old clients to return to us.

Mother and Dirk adhered to the same simple business rules for the next 30 years: providing the best products available, keeping everything scrupulously clean, charging fair prices, being dependable, and working day and night. They kept their goals in mind—mainly keeping their clients happy and paying off the debts—and continued working toward these goals with passion and tenacity. Who would guess that many years later I would draw upon the same successful techniques to use in business myself?

* * *

I knew that my future did not lie in selling french fries day in and day out for such long hours and so little pocket money. My family situation was still almost unendurable, and soon after my 16th birthday I decided to prepare for my departure. I began to read the newspaper every day and found an ad placed by an employment agency that provided families abroad with Dutch au pairs*. I wrote them a letter, enclosed a picture of myself, and soon received a reply. A British family with two young children was interested in hiring me. I told my parents about the offer, but they would not hear of it. I was to continue working for my brother's little snack truck business. Girls were meant to stay home until they were married.

I needed a passport in order to leave for England and my parents refused to sign any of the papers I required. Without their help I would have had to wait until I was 18 years old—an alternative that was just not acceptable to me. I decided to stop working, eating, and talking—to go "on strike." Being beaten up didn't help as I was long inured to it. Being sent to my room was a pleasure. Not eating was difficult. Not talking wasn't a problem—I was not a talkative

* live-in nannies.

28

person. At the beginning of my strike, my family made fun of me, then they ignored me, and eventually they became angry.

I finally got help from my grandfather on my father's side. He kept telling my parents to let me go, reassuring them that I would be fine in England. I am not even sure he knew where England was. Because they were getting increasingly fed up with me, my parents finally signed the papers and I was told to "get out!" My mother drove me in her old Opel to the city of Hoek van Holland, where the ships left for England. She uttered little during the drive, and when she did speak, she said sarcastically, "We'll see how quickly you will come running back." With me I had one suitcase that held my few clothes, my dictionaries, and some 45 rpm records. I was barely 16 years of age, but I was ready and eager—to stand on my own two feet.

Four

It was January 1961 when I left Holland by boat from Hoek van Holland bound for Dover, England. I was apprehensive and on guard, but relieved and looking forward to my new life away from home. It was a night passage and the sea was very rough. On the bunk bed below me my cabin-mate was terribly sick, likely because she was very drunk. When the ship docked in Dover, I boarded a train for London. I finally arrived at Victoria Station and patiently waited for Mr. Campbell, my new employer, to pick me up. He had been given a photo of me but I had no idea what he looked like.

My English was minimal, but good enough to make it clear to him when he arrived that I wanted to see some proof of his identity. I said, "See your picture and name?" He understood and smiled. After producing his identification, he loaded me and my luggage into his fancy dark green Jaguar and we drove South, in the direction of Surrey. There was very little conversation because my English was so poor, but he seemed a nice man. I also noted that with this kind of car, these were not ordinary people.

After driving for several hours we arrived at the Campbell's home, a large estate. As we drove up the lane toward the house, their dogs, two beautiful golden retrievers, gave me a great welcome as soon as I stepped out of the car. Finally, there would be some animals in my life!

Mr. Campbell took me through the kitchen and into the living room, where I was introduced to Mrs. Campbell and Alison, their four-year-old daughter. Next, we went into the garden, where a pram held the sleeping form of Alistair, their baby boy. I had never taken care of children before, but my job would prove to be uncomplicated. I was to take care of the children's needs, which included cooking for them, cleaning their rooms and bathroom, and laundering their clothes.

I would walk Alison to a local private nursery in the morning, where she played and had lunch before I picked her up again. I would eat my breakfasts and dinners with her, bathe her and put her to bed. When Alison was at the nursery, I stayed busy with the baby. Alistair was either in bed, in his pram in the garden, or in his playpen. I fed him, bathed him, and played with him. I fell in love with that little fellow immediately.

When the children and I ate alone together, we took our meals in the kitchen. When both parents were home, I was expected to eat with them in the large dining hall. At home I had been served my vegetables on top of my potatoes, making one pile that was then mashed together and eaten with a fork. At the Campbell's, I was surprised when I was served my first meal—the food was divided into separate areas on our plates and eaten delicately, a bite from each food group at a time. It was there that I learned how to eat properly with a knife and fork.

The Campbell's house was vast, and I had my own bedroom and a sitting room with my own television. I shared a bathroom with the children. Each morning around seven I would quietly peek into Alistair's room and watch him peacefully babbling to himself, playing with his little hands, or kicking the mobile above him while he waited for me. When he discovered me peeking around the corner he would give me the most beautiful smile. He just knew that I would be coming. It was such a wonderful way to start my day. When Mrs. Campbell was not home I would go into the sitting room and play my Harry Belafonte and Mahalia Jackson records. Dancing around the room with Alistair in my arms, I would sing, "Nobody knows the trouble I've seen, nobody knows my sorrow…" We bonded very quickly. Without knowing it, during my time with Alistair I was giving myself the nurturing I had never received, and beginning to heal some of the painful wounds of my childhood.

Alison was a little more demanding. She knew how to talk well, and I had trouble following her continual chatter. My inability to understand her was difficult for her. She knew her bedtime storybooks by heart and would "read" them to me rather than having me read to her. This suited me well as I had trouble reading to her in my broken English.

The Campbells, married and having children late in life, related to each other in a way I had never witnessed before. When Mr. Campbell arrived home at the end of the day, he greeted us all with a big smile on his face and even asked how our day had gone.

Mrs. Campbell was friendly and easy to be with. She loved her children dearly, but was in some odd way uneasy with them. They had to be fed and well rested before I could turn them over to her. When one of them cried for one reason or another she was quick to hand them back to me. On Thursdays, my day off, it was difficult for her to care for them all day.

Sometimes Mrs. Campbell needed to ring up one of her friends, who also employed a Dutch au pair, in order to have her requests translated for me. Thus I was introduced over the phone to Dickie, also an au pair, about two years older than me. She helped me to get Thursdays off work. She also took me into the town of Guildford in the evening to attend school so I could improve my English. In order to reach the town we walked or cycled to the bus stop and then rode the bus in.

Dickie also took care of two children who were the same age as my charges, as well as two dogs. Because we lived in the country just over the hill from each other, we decided to meet for daily walks in the afternoons after the children's rest period. We gathered with the four kids, two in prams, and the four dogs. Dickie was amiable and wonderful company. Fortunately for me, she did most of the talking.

During our walks on the "common," Dickie and I, the children, and the dogs always had a great time. The two girls played together, the four dogs ran about and got completely filthy, and the two baby boys watched all the commotion, fascinated. It wasn't easy to push the prams on the dirt paths; nevertheless, the time flew. Up to that point, I had never enjoyed life more.

* * *

Dickie came from a close family and was very fond of her three sisters and her parents, and much of her talk included stories about them. One day she broached the subject of my reticence in talking about myself. She said, "It doesn't really matter to me that

32

you don't talk very much, but if it's because of a situation you've left behind in Holland, don't forget that you have now embarked on your own journey. You're so young and this is a new life for you, and whatever you do, it will be for you. If you try to do well in this world for yourself and others, you'll have a good life, but if you keep worrying about everything that might be happening at home, you'll have a miserable life." Then she changed the subject. After we parted ways for the day and went home, I could not help but think about what Dickie had said. I slowly began to confide in her and we became, and still are, best friends.

On my days off I travelled into town to meet with the other European au pairs I had met at school. Because we all made very little money, we exchanged clothes with each other so we would occasionally have something different to wear. At Marks and Spencer, we gazed longingly at the things we could not afford to buy. After a matinée movie, we finished the day with something hot to drink at a small coffeehouse. We had some good laughs sharing tales about the families with whom we lived before we headed home to them.

On one of those Thursday afternoons we had just settled into a movie when suddenly I began to feel very anxious and uncomfortable. I had a strong urge to go home. It suddenly felt as though I had consumed 10 cups of coffee, one after the other. I told my friends I had to leave. They tried to persuade me to stay, but after a few minutes I couldn't bear my anxiety any longer and left in a hurry. I ran to the bus stop, where I waited with extreme difficulty for the bus to arrive. Once on board the bus I paced back and forth; it just wasn't going fast enough. My anxiety was becoming stronger and stronger. I didn't question why—I just knew I had to get home. When I got off the bus and reached my bike, I had trouble getting the lock freed up because my hands were shaking so badly. I raced home, not even sitting on my saddle so I could pedal faster.

I tore into the house and found Alistair on the living room floor, choking. He was not moving. His little face was blue and a small sound came from his mouth. I grabbed him by his tiny legs to hold him upside down and slapped him on his back. A hard cookie came out of his mouth. My whole body was shaking and we were both crying. Not knowing what to do, I paced the living room, holding Alistair gently in my arms and attempting to calm us both down. After some time I began to wonder where Mrs. Campbell was. We walked around the house and found her upstairs in the bathroom giving Alison a bath. Strangely, she wasn't surprised to see me. I told her that Alistair had been choking on a cookie and handed her the baby. She turned to her daughter and said, "Alison, you should not leave any cookies on the floor." I was dumbfounded, and silently retreated to my room. I could not fully comprehend what had just happened, and it was not mentioned again.

Dickie returned to Holland in May. The Campbells and I went for a holiday on the seaside and then they took me with them to Scotland, where they had a summer home. I loved Scotland, although I could not understand a word anyone said. On my days off, the postman took me through the countryside in his jeep to deliver mail, bread, milk, and other items people had asked him to deliver. The people on his route lived in small stone houses in remote areas surrounded by incredible beauty. I had never before seen a landscape such as this, mountainous and rough, interspersed with glistening green lakes. People kept chickens and gardens and lived independently—there were no shops or businesses. It was a healing time and life was treating me well.

Once back in Surrey, Mr. and Mrs. Campbell announced they were going on a month-long safari in South Africa. During their absence a certified nanny would move into the house to supervise all of us. The nanny, who wore a uniform, was a very nice woman and we got along fine. She was so well organized that our own household duties were done by eleven in the morning. She also helped me a great deal with my schoolwork; as a result my English improved immensely.

By now Alistair could crawl and he was learning how to walk and use the potty. One day he was so pleased to have something in the potty that he pulled me toward it and proudly said, "Look!" He loved looking at picture books of animals. This fascination led to a moment of embarrassment when his mother came home from the safari. When she walked into the house, I said to Alistair, "Look who's here." He looked at her and said, "Monkey!" His mother was so dark from her time in the sun that he did not recognize her.

I had now been with the Campbells for well over one year and it was time for me to move on. With the little money I had saved I bought a small gift for everyone in my family. With the very last of my savings I bought a deluxe new razor as a present for my father. Mr. Campbell generously paid for my trip back to Holland.

Living at a distance from my disturbed family life, in a different country and surrounded by people who functioned without violence in their daily lives, had been a very healing experience for me. I was proud of myself for not getting into any trouble, for getting a letter of recommendation from the family who had employed me, for learning to speak a different language, and for managing to buy small presents with my hard-earned money.

My mother picked me up at the airport and drove me home. Dickie was there with my family to welcome me. I was optimistic and excited about my future. After I had distributed all the gifts, my father asked, "So how much have you saved over this past year?" I was taken by surprise, but replied that my new bank account statement read, "Speaks English Fluently" and that I could always withdraw from this account without losing anything. Dickie gave me a big smile; at least she understood what I was talking about.

Five

My next goal was to learn to speak German. While I looked for an appropriate family, I worked in the snack truck again.

My mother had new plans. She and my brother had seen a house with a hair salon for sale in a village about 40 minutes' drive away, and wanted to buy it and renovate it into a snack bar. My father, of course, would not hear of it. He informed her once again that she had lost her mind. But Mother was serious. She countered by stating that when the deal was done the rest of us would move without him. I was plunged right back into the same dismal situation I had left.

Once I had settled into my old room, I noticed a number of cartons had been stored under my bed. My mother had already figured out what to leave my father: a table, a chair, and one of each item of basic furniture. Everything else was to be loaded into the food truck; then we would simply leave without telling him. The tension was terrible. I had trouble swallowing and my stomach was in a knot. We were all afraid that my father would discover my mother's plans and somehow physically prevent us from leaving.

Before I could get away from all this, my mother announced that we were ready to move. The day of departure arrived, and as soon as my father left for work we began to load the truck. The neighbours were watching and asked us what we were up to. Their questions fell on deaf ears—we were in a terrible hurry, racing in and out of the house not inclined to say anything. Anyway, wasn't it obvious we were leaving for good? Our anxiety was almost unbearable. Finally, everything was packed and ready to go. My mother had one of her "friends" ready to drive us to the new location.

The truck refused to start. We were already drenched in sweat and this turn of events made our physical discomfort even worse.

Neighbourhood kids offered to push us and even offered to get my father from his job across the street to help push the truck. It was a terrible situation. We were just preparing to unload the truck's entire contents again when the engine suddenly started. We clambered onto the furniture and could not have made a quicker exit.

When we arrived at the new house we quickly unloaded everything and locked the door behind us. We all knew that my father would find us and show up that evening. Exhausted from the move and all the tension, we turned off all the lights and pretended we weren't there.

My father arrived exactly as we had anticipated. He pounded on the door and yelled and swore outside the windows for quite some time before leaving in frustration. The neighbours knew right away what kind of people had moved in.

A few weeks later, I could scarcely believe it when, despite the fact that she had promised never to do so, my mother allowed my father to move in with us. My brothers and I had thought that we would finally be on our own with the peace we had longed for, but our dream was sadly short-lived.

Meanwhile, a Dutch au pair agency provided me with an address not far over the German border, where an elderly German-English couple sought someone in their house for small cleanup jobs and a little cooking. The wife also wanted a companion because her husband travelled a lot. I visited the Grundels overnight and we appeared to be a good fit. I arranged to move in with them within a week.

My family had now moved into the new house, and my mother had transformed the hair salon on the ground floor into a snack bar. The living quarters on the upper level included a living room, a kitchen, one bedroom, and a bathroom. There were two more small bedrooms on the third floor. When I arrived home from my short trip to Germany, my family was in the living room watching television. No lights were on—at that time people watched television in the dark. I had no interest in the show so I offered to prepare coffee for everyone. A short time later, I walked back into the living room with a tray of coffee, cups, cake, and a knife. While I switched on the light, trying not to spill any coffee on the tablecloth, my father suddenly jumped up and kicked me before I could react. I dropped everything and ran out the door and through the hallway, heading for the staircase. Swearing and yelling, my father came after me and kicked me in the head—with his shoes on—as I stumbled down the stairs. At that moment, I finally lost any semblance of control I might have possessed. A powerful adrenaline rush charged through my body and—I do not know how—I pulled myself back up the stairs and pushed him through the hallway and back into the living room. I grabbed him, threw him over the table, and then pushed him against the wall. I still held the cake knife in my hand and I was about to stab him when my mother and my aunt, who was visiting, grabbed hold of my arm. I screamed over and over, "Don't you ever touch me again or I'll kill you!" until I had exhausted myself. I knew then that if I had been alone with him, I really might have killed my father. Later on I thought, "Well, I once wanted to go to prison. My wish almost became a reality."

For many years I had been pushed beyond my level of tolerance. As a result, this one moment when I lost complete control could easily have been fatal for my father, not to mention disastrous for me. After this incident I knew that I would never let my father touch me again. But, astonishingly, he never tried.

When I read or hear news about children who kill their abusive parents, I surmise that they probably suffered at the hands of those parents for a long time. It is very difficult for a judge and jury to have any idea for how long and in what manner these children are slowly "killed" themselves by abuse before they finally lose their sanity—if only momentarily—and kill their parents. Often, children from this kind of background become extremely self-destructive by using drugs and alcohol or engaging in prostitution. They may become destructive to others by joining gangs or becoming violent with their own spouses and children. It is a vicious cycle. It is a cycle that I understand very well and can recognize clearly in abused people. After that incident, I made a promise to myself that I was not going to follow in my parents' footsteps. I already knew there was a better world out there. I had seen glimpses of it and I was never going to settle for less.

Six

Mr. and Mrs. Grundel seemed like a kind couple. They were in their early sixties and childless. He was a consultant; his wife was an English-German translator at important government functions. I discovered after a short time that they were really just looking for companionship for Mrs. Grundel when her husband was out of town on business. They might have looked for someone closer to her own age, but chose me instead. I was glad to have a roof over my head and determined to make the best of it.

I could see that Mrs. Grundel was used to moving around in high society. She was always impeccably dressed and made up even if she had nowhere to go. She was the first woman I'd ever encountered who smoked long cigarillos. While it didn't bother me terribly, I thought Mrs. Grundel's ever-present cigarillo tarnished her otherwise distinguished image. She smoked even while she was cooking. I often watched apprehensively as the long ash grew on her cigarillo, afraid that it might fall into the food and spoil the meal.

Because there wasn't much for me to do in their household, I was asked to type Mr. Grundel's business reports, which was fine with me. I could practice typing and improve my German. Mrs. Grundel and I both cooked, and I did all the cleaning. On Sundays I was expected to join them for their weekly lunch at some of the finer restaurants in town. Afterward, we would sit in their fancy car on the well-known Konings Allee, a main shopping street in Düsseldorf. There we watched people before driving home.

It didn't take me long to figure out that Mrs. Grundel was taking prescription drugs and drinking too much alcohol, although she tried to be sober when her husband was expected home. I had spent my lifetime around people who drank, and although I had never been around people who took drugs, her use of them was fairly obvious from her demeanour. During her spells of over-indulgence she said things that she soon forgot, and thus I found out that Mr. Grundel was taking his secretary on his business trips. That explained why Mr. Grundel was always so nice and a little awkward with his wife when he came home. He was full of guilt.

One day when his wife was out on a translating job, Mr. Grundel offered to take me for lunch, and I used the opportunity to ask him about his trips with his secretary. He smiled in some embarrassment, saying he couldn't help it. Then he told me I was attractive and put his arm around my shoulders. I pushed his arm away, warning him not to get any ideas. I stated emphatically that I intended to tell his wife about his overture and that I would leave his household. He apologized and told me it would not happen again. It was a sad situation, and it taught me that although they might have different problems from the poor, people living in luxury and high society had their own struggles.

On my days off, I went for long walks near the river Rhine. I loved to walk and cycle and could be away for hours surrounded by nature. Since I was getting private German lessons from Mrs. Grundel, I did not go to school. To meet some people my own age, I decided to check out a club for immigrants I found in the newspaper. A guest speaker was scheduled for the advertised meeting, after which there would be dinner and dancing for those interested. I felt a little intimidated attending such a gathering on my own, but I had to do something to get out of the house.

The guest speaker focused on current happenings in the world and talked about shuttles going into space and the competition between the Americans and the Russians. He threw a question out to the audience, inquiring about the distance from earth to one of the planets. The answer didn't mean much to me and I tuned out a little, but came to attention when I heard a voice behind me say something so outrageous that people in the audience began laughing. The guest speaker started laughing as well. I had no idea what the correct answer was, but somehow I knew that what this man had just said was right. When I turned around to look at him, he returned my gaze and smiled. It turned out that the answer he had given was correct.

When dinner was served he approached and asked if he could join me at my table. His name was Hayati. Born and raised in Turkey, he was an engineer by trade and was in Germany building bridges. I asked him how a Turkish man came to have blue eyes, and he explained that his parents were originally from Czechoslovakia. We talked some more and he invited me to dance. Soon we found it too noisy and crowded to talk in the hall and he suggested we go for a walk.

For the next several months, Hayati and I went for long walks following the paths of the Rhine River. He had an easy smile and infectious laugh that made me laugh in response. Hayati was charming, educated, cultivated, and easy to talk to—an ease that was unusual for me. Best of all, he was very respectful and made no advances or attempts to touch me, and slowly I began to trust him. He didn't criticize or interrupt me even when I caught myself saying silly things. He was my first male friend.

One day I accidentally ran into him in town. He was carrying two bunches of flowers. When I asked him, "What's up?" he answered, "I'm on my way to say goodbye to two lady friends. I need to tell them that I can't see them anymore because I want to spend more time with one special lady I recently met." "That's nice," I said sincerely, not realizing that the special person he was talking about was me.

After our long walks we went out for tea. Hayati always seemed to know out-of-the-way places where piano concerts were performed while we sat, sipped, and chatted. When it rained we returned to his rented room to listen to operas. I had never been exposed to classical music, let alone opera, but Hayati had a way of making me feel comfortable with it. He read the stories of the operas to me and then we listened to his records. When he saw my growing pleasure, he surprised me with tickets to performances at the Düsseldorf Opera House.

It was during one of our visits to the Opera House, six months after we met, that I reached out to hold his hand and kiss him. At eighteen years old, I had fallen in love for the first time.

In the meantime, Mr. and Mrs. Grundel were becoming very curious about whom I was spending so much time with. As

I was still young and innocent, they felt rather protective of me. Eventually I told them about the wonderful Turkish man I had met, but as soon as I mentioned the word "Turkish," a look of horror appeared on their faces. They wanted details, but after I told them about our outings and the time we spent in Hayati's room, they only looked further horrified. Expressing doubt and concern, they asked me to invite him over for dinner so they could talk to him themselves. Hayati was very willing and a date was set. Since he and Mr. Grundel were both engineers, I was sure they would at least have some common, work-related interests.

Hayati arrived with a beautiful bouquet of flowers for Mrs. Grundel and another for me. The evening seemed to go splendidly. I was proud of how Hayati handled their questions. There was even some laughter. When I showed him to the door at the evening's end, I gave Hayati a gentle push, whispering, "You did really well."

By the time I walked back into the kitchen, the flowers that Hayati had given Mrs. Grundel were already in the garbage can. I was stunned; without knowing what to think, I took them out to put them in my own room. In the days that followed, the atmosphere in the apartment became intolerable. The Grundels informed me they did not believe a word of what we had told them and I was not to see Hayati again. No good would become of this relationship, they warned, and we must stop seeing each other before it was too late.

The Grundels explained that they wanted to adopt me and give me a good future. They would introduce me to some German friends because it seemed evident that I desired a boyfriend. I was shocked. First, I told them that I was going to continue seeing Hayati whether they liked it or not. Next, I assured them we had told no lies about the time we spent together, and the fact that Hayati was Turkish made no difference to me. Finally, I said that I did not want to be adopted by anyone as I already had parents. In reality, I did not wish to have any parents. My birth parents were still an onerous burden.

Some time passed, but the atmosphere in the apartment remained heavy, cool, and distant. Perhaps the Grundels thought I would change my mind and choose not to see Hayati anymore. Hayati was calm about it, telling me only that if the situation became intolerable to call him at his office. He would move into the YMCA so that I could have his room. Eventually, that is what happened.

One evening while Mrs. Grundel was out, her husband, quite a large man, approached me with unpleasant intentions and pushed me into my room. I fought him off, pushing and yelling that I would report him to the police. I grabbed any furniture I could get hold of and threw it at him. The fight became more intense, but I was strong and angry and he finally backed off, totally out of breath. As soon as his wife came home I told her about his advances and that I was packing.

Hayati moved into the YMCA and I stayed in his room. I worked for an airline in the reservation office for a while, and we had a wonderful time getting to know each other. Often he came by the office for lunch—the separation until the end of the day just seemed too long. Our days together were filled with long walks, belly laughs, classical music, and opera. To this day I still cherish my relationship with Hayati. Just thinking of him makes me smile. But I had one more goal. I was now fluent in German and Hayati supported my decision to learn one more language—French. We promised each other to keep in touch by phone and letter writing, and to visit each other as much as possible.

* * *

In the meantime, back in Holland, my father's parents had died and my parents had moved into their house. My mother continued to make her daily trips to the snack bar, which now belonged to Dirk. So when I returned to Holland to prepare for my next trip, I just moved in with my brother to prepare for my next adventure.

Soon after this, my mother announced her intention of training to obtain a special diploma for a liquor licence for the snack bar, which would allow them to make more money. It was a very courageous thing to do, as she had attended school only until the age of 11 and it was known that this diploma was difficult to get.

I thought it was a great idea and offered to help out while she was going to school in Amsterdam, an hour's drive away. The rest of the family, as well as many of our clients, scoffed at her new idea. Oblivious to any negativity, off she went anyway. She failed her first exam after six months of schooling and heard a lot of "I told you so's."

I was going to be leaving soon for a new au pair job in Switzerland, but while I worked in the snack bar, Hayati regularly visited me. I introduced him to my parents and to my great surprise they liked him immediately. During his visits, Hayati and I spent time together at a youth hostel in Noordwijk aan Zee, a small village on the North Sea beaches. On those memorable days, we would walk in the dunes and along the beaches, watching the thrashing ocean and just talking. Hayati used to love running after the surf that was created by the rough ocean waves and heavy winds. Then on one of his visits, he told me that he intended to return to Turkey soon as his work in Germany was complete. As a student he had received several scholarships, and he now felt obligated to return to his native country to repay this "debt" in some measure. In order for him to finish his studies and gain experience in his field, the Turkish government had allowed him to postpone his army duties for several years, and it was also time to fulfill that obligation. Before leaving, he asked my parents' permission to invite me to his home country for a visit in the near future.

My mother, meanwhile, ignored everyone and returned to school but failed her liquor licence exam for the second time. My dear mother persisted in continuing her schooling, copying her textbooks word by word (this was the only way she knew how to study) while the piles of notebooks kept mounting. After she failed for the fifth time, people told her it was ludicrous to try again. But she did. And not only did she study hard, she also worked in the snack bar six days a week from 11 a.m. until often after midnight. After she wrote the exam for the seventh time, she received a phone call from the secretary of the school she had attended. This woman was in tears as she said, "Mrs. van Bemmel, I'm not allowed to tell you this because you're supposed to wait for the results by mail. But I've seen you going through these exams so many times, and I'm so excited for you that you've finally passed that I could not help calling you." Again, my mother had beat the odds. I recognized this stubbornness and tenacity in myself. We both seemed to have this endless natural thirst for learning. My mother was inquisitive about everything until the day she died. In the seniors' home where she lived out the last few months of her life, she stood up to many of the rules and often accused the authorities of numbing the old people's minds. She categorically refused to participate in their childlike activities, such as cutting little animals out of paper. She would insist on being wheeled outside so she could watch the trees and the birds instead. When she died, all I wanted to inherit was her diploma.

Seven

My new family lived in Vevey, Switzerland. This time I was to look after two very young children belonging to the daughter of a well-known Dutch industrialist. The van Vliet family's modest, cozy villa was perched high on a hill in an upscale neighbourhood overlooking Lake Geneva. They were a young, energetic family trying to raise their children in a healthy way. They took great care with their nutrition and they treated each other and me well.

The van Vliets were very anxious for me to watch their children at all times while I was on duty. At first I thought they were simply very protective of their children until one night, while looking in their family photo albums, I discovered to whom they were connected in the Netherlands. The pictures showed the children's mother with members of the Dutch Royal family, including the Queen and her husband.

Life was easy with this family. The children were small and adorable and I got along well with their parents. The single flaw in this arrangement was that only Dutch was spoken at home, and my French was not improving very fast from going to night school just a few times a week.

The van Vliets were planning a long trip to the USA with her mother's parents, during which time their children and I would move to the Netherlands. I had no objections, although I regretfully told them I was going to look for a French-speaking family upon their return. They expressed their disappointment but respected my decision.

I returned to Holland and settled into the residence of the paternal grandparents of the two children, a well-off and famous family. Their estate was surrounded by a vast park and employed staff to look after the cooking, cleaning, gardening, and driving. I had never dreamed of living on such an enormous estate, but that is where I found myself. A governess looked after the daily affairs of running the estate, managing the staff—including me—and the children.

I had my own room but spent most of my time outside in the garden and forest with the children or in the staff sitting room next to the kitchen. The staff room was furnished with a couch, coffee table, television, and fridge. It was a comfortable and cozy place for any of us while off-duty or on a break.

The youngest daughter of the family was about my age, and when she was not at school or studying she spent most of her time in the staff room socializing and playing with her little niece and nephew. We had a lot of fun together and my friendship with her is still intact after all these years.

My time with the van Vliet family came to an end after they returned from the USA. I returned to Switzerland to join a French-speaking family, who lived in a beautiful mansion in La Tour de Paix, not far from where I had lived with the van Vliets.

I arrived in the middle of winter after a long train ride. It had been a cold and tiring journey. Upon my arrival I was led into the kitchen. Mr. and Mrs. Neumann were eating their lunch in the dining room and I couldn't see the children. While I waited to meet my employers, a bell rang. As I wasn't familiar with anything yet, I did not move. A few minutes later the bell rang again, and then again. I thought, "Well, this is a busy household!" After a little while, Mrs. Neumann came into the kitchen and asked if I had heard the bell. "Yes," I replied. Apparently she had been ringing the bell in the dining room because she needed a serving spoon. "That is not the job of an au pair," I thought with foreboding.

After their lunch was finished, Mrs. Neumann returned to the kitchen, placing a dish with a little bit of cold, leftover food in front of me before she rejoined her husband for tea. It was such an unwelcoming gesture. After Mr. Neumann, an executive at the famous Nestlé Corporation in Vevey, had returned to work—without introducing himself—Mrs. Neumann came back into the kitchen. Without any greeting or mention of the inadequate cold lunch, she requested that I do the dishes. She also instructed me on how to dry them, pointing to a rack with six tea towels. One towel was designated for glasses, one for plates, one for serving plates, one for forks and knives, one for cooking utensils, and one for pots and pans. She then showed me the rest of the house. All of her instructions were about cleaning and maintaining the rooms. I learned that their three children were in a private school in Montreux and only came home on weekends.

When she showed me the small table at which I would sit for my meals, away from the dining table where the family sat, I finally told her that she needed a cleaning lady and not an au pair, and that I was not going to stay. She suggested I was probably tired and should have a rest, offering to show me to my bedroom. She informed me that after her husband got home, he would have a talk with me.

When I walked into my room, the strong smell of stale cigarettes hit me. An old, squeaky metal bed was situated next to the wall that separated the house from the main street. I was appalled, scarcely believing that this beautiful, luxurious home on the border of the scenic lake had such an unsightly, smelly, noisy room hidden away. I had no idea where I would go next, but I was not going to stay there, that was for certain. Later that evening, Mr. Neumann asked me to give his family a fair try, while putting contract papers in French in front of me to sign. I simply sat in silence, knowing very well what these papers were all about.

During my time in England, Germany, and Switzerland, it had been easy to meet other au pairs at the language classes in night school. We shared stories about our employers, the problems we had with our families, and the work we were given beyond our child-care duties. We even helped each other relocate to different families when bad situations became intolerable. There was a great deal of mistreatment going on; young girls, far from home and often unable to speak the native language properly, were often too shy to report the abuse. Although I could not read Mr. Neumann's papers, I knew if I signed them I would not be able to work anywhere else in Switzerland for the next six months. What a dirty trick! I refused to sign them, of course. I felt angry and betrayed.

Afterward, I took a long shower; I had no idea where or when I would have my next one. With the constant traffic zooming by my window, I didn't sleep very well. It was freezing and I felt terribly lonely. The following morning, no one was up when I entered the kitchen, so I served myself some breakfast. Then, picking up my suitcase, I walked through the front door into the snow and wind without saying goodbye. Where to go next? I decided to take the first bus that came by, wherever that bus was going, just to be out of the cold. I had about 50 Swiss francs, not enough money to return home or stay in a hotel. I did not own a credit card. The thought of seeing my parents again held no appeal for me anyway.

I boarded the first bus that arrived, which was heading to Vevey, where I had lived before. When I arrived at the railway station, I put my suitcase into the luggage storage and found a coffee shop. After drinking some coffee I still did not know where to go or what to do. I decided to walk; perhaps an answer would come to me. I was just happy to be away from that demanding family and out of that smelly room. There were not a lot of options but I knew that something would come up—it always did.

Suddenly I saw a familiar face. Outside a Chinese grocery store stood a girl I knew named Renate filling up cartons of vegetables on the sidewalk. She was the German au pair who had worked for the van Vliet family before me. We hugged and laughed and quickly exchanged news. Renate invited me to share her small room above the grocery store where she was working. She gave me her key and returned to work. I found her tiny room. It had a sink and just enough space for a single bed and one chair but it was cozy and warm.

When Renate arrived that evening, we had a great time eating pizza and sharing the stories we had accumulated since we'd last seen each other. There was no space in the room to move about at the same time so the next morning I waited until Renate had left for work before I arose.

I decided to visit the agency, also located in Vevey, that had provided me with the address of the Nestlé executive and inform them that this was not a good place to send any au pairs, that they really needed cleaning people instead.

When I walked into the agency, the woman in charge was talking on the phone. She recognized me from the picture on my application and motioned for me to sit down. She was speaking in French so I could not understand what she was saying to the person on the phone. Then she put one hand over the mouthpiece and said in German, "Would you like to go to Leysin up in the mountains? A French family needs an au pair immediately for their four-year-old girl." I nodded affirmatively. After a little discussion, arrangements were made for me to take the train and attend an interview at lunchtime that day. The Neumann family had already advised the agency that I had left, and I was promised that no other au pairs would be sent to their address.

I took the train to Aigle and then up the mountain to Leysin, where Mrs. Caubel and her daughter Sandrine waited for me at the station with Jolie, their German shepherd. What I did not know at the time was that it was Jolie the dog that would decide whether I was hired. If she allowed me to touch Sandrine at the station, I was hired. Unaware of this, I approached Sandrine, greeted her in French, and told her what a beautiful dog she had brought along to greet me. She proudly went over to the dog and hugged her. Unbeknownst to me, I had passed the test.

Mrs. Caubel took me to the hotel where they lived and invited me to lunch. Her husband joined us, along with a German-speaking family friend who translated our conversation. Mr. and Mrs. Caubel told me that they managed the hotel, which was one of three in Leysin owned by a French organization called Club Méditerranée. This tourist organization had many hotels in different countries.

Both Mr. and Mrs. Caubel were busy with tourists day and night, and it was difficult for them to give their little girl and the dog the attention they needed. The previous au pair had not been reliable and Sandrine was often still in her pyjamas at 11 in the morning. I got the message. After I'd answered a few questions, Mr. Caubel told me I was hired and offered to take me back down to Vevey to pick up my suitcase.

Sandrine was a delightful little girl; I bonded quickly with her and with Jolie, her dog. Sandrine and I shared a room and she taught me how to speak French. With endless patience she moved about the room and showed me things, asking me to repeat their names in French. When she played with her little friends at the hotel, they often couldn't understand me; she ordered them to hush up and explained that it was her duty to teach me French.

Sandrine and I quickly settled into a routine. This time, I didn't have to cook any meals or clean the dishes because we often joined the family table in the hotel restaurant. In the event that I wanted us to eat in our room I simply went into the hotel kitchen and was given anything I asked for.

We spent our mornings doing kindergarten activities, and after Sandrine's afternoon nap we went for walks, played in the snow, or went skiing. Sandrine was too small to use the T-bars to go up the mountain so she would stand in front of me and I would guide her up between my legs. She was a fearless little thing heading down the mountain without any ski poles, her thin legs ending in a pair of big ski boots.

Au pair in Switzerland with Sandrine and Emmanuelle.

The dog was part of our small team and followed us everywhere. Jolie also joined me on my days off when I went hiking in the mountains. She would sit next to my pack and boots as if to say, "I know that you're going, and I'm coming with you." She was a wonderful companion.

Sandrine's parents were very supportive of how I looked after my young charge. They never interfered in front of the child, but at times told me gently in private that she was allowed to do certain things that I had refused her.

At the end of winter we moved to a hotel in Misurina, in the North of Italy, for the summer season. Climbers from all over the world stayed in our hotel when they came to scale the famous Dolomite Mountains. Anytime climbers did not return on the day or time they had specified, all the hotel guests would stare through their binoculars at the mountains for hours until they finally spotted the missing climbers making their way back.

After the summer in Italy we all moved back to Paris. Mrs. Caubel was about to give birth to another baby. As the family awaited the new arrival, I returned to Holland to visit my family and prepare for a trip to Turkey to visit Hayati.

Eight

It hadn't been easy for Hayati to tell his parents he was dating someone from the Netherlands and that he intended to ask me to marry him. Aware of neither his intentions nor the difficulties they had created, I was rather puzzled when I was not greeted with much enthusiasm upon my arrival. His parents had refused to allow me to stay in their home, so I moved in with his friends, a young family. Hayati, now a soldier, visited me on his days off and took great care to make me feel at home in Turkey. We visited many interesting places and he introduced me to his friends and extended family. Only his parents did not warm up to our relationship.

Hayati asked me to marry him and promised that we would live in our own home rather than with his parents, as was the custom in Turkey. However, I got the feeling that I was too independent to live with the many restrictions placed upon Turkish women—married or unmarried. I suggested that we consider moving to another country in Europe; that way, we'd have a fresh beginning to start a family. But for the moment he needed to finish his tour of duty in the army and I needed to return to my au pair job with my French family.

I left Istanbul with a heavy heart, wondering if we would ever see each other again. During the long train ride, over and over I relived my time with him in Turkey. It was a sad journey home.

Nine

Emmanuelle Caubel was born in Paris and soon afterward the family returned to Leysin for another winter season. Mrs. Caubel went back to work and I took care of Emmanuelle from the outset. Life was easy and it was a happy time for me. I was treated with kindness and respect by the entire family. I took care of feeding and bathing the children, as well as cleaning their clothes and our room. We went for walks, skied, played, danced, and read stories. We did all the things children do. Taking care of the girls gave me an opportunity to live the joyful childhood I had never had. I learned how to ski and climb mountains, and my knowledge of the French language was improving.

In the evenings Jolie guarded the children while I had my dinner with the guests and socialized a little. One evening a hotel guest accidentally walked into our room. Upon my return I found him standing against the wall with Jolie growling at his feet. He had been waiting for nearly an hour for someone to rescue him from our faithful, protective dog.

I stayed with the Caubels for over two years. At the end of the fourth tourist season, I knew it was time for me to move on, as normally au pairs do not stay with a family for longer than one year.

Mr. and Mrs. Caubel thanked me for taking such good care of their children and for being a part of their family for so long. Mr. Caubel asked me if there was anything he could do for me in terms of future employment; he said that the Club Méditerranée often employed multilingual people. By now, I could speak four languages fluently. I told him that over the past two years I had seen the hotel's tour guides taking people on all kinds of excursions and that I would love to be trained to become a guide. Executives from the club's head office in Paris would soon be attending a meeting at our hotel, and Mr. Caubel promised to introduce me to the person who hired for this area.

Now that I had accomplished my goal of speaking four languages, Hayati asked me again to return to Istanbul to marry him. I told him again that it was difficult for me to imagine living in his country and starting a family. I had become used to being independent after all my years away from home. I also remembered well the time I had spent in Turkey and the difficulties Hayati and I constantly faced due to his family's unwillingness to support our relationship. I recalled the time I'd spent waiting for him to return from his duties in the army. It had been impossible for me to leave the house on my own and a friend or family member had to join me each time I wanted to go out. On the few occasions I had ventured out on my own a little, men harassed me constantly. Having blonde hair and blue eyes didn't help. After some deep consideration, Hayati regretfully decided that it was not possible for him to leave his country. With heavy hearts we realized we had to separate.

As I look back on this period in my life, it surprises me that I was able to pay such close attention and listen to my inner voice. My instincts warned me to be alert to the things that were not working between Hayati and me. I took some time to ponder my own needs and I listened to the people closest to me. I knew how much was at stake and wanted to make a good choice for myself, even at that young age. Although I truly loved Hayati and wanted to start a family with him, I vividly remembered how restricted I had felt when visiting him. I had become too independent and I knew instinctively that our love for each other would not be enough to help us survive a marriage in a country such as Turkey.

Ten

Now, at the age of 22, I was offered my first real job, working for Club Méditerranée in Cefalu, Sicily, Italy. I felt excited and proud that I had accomplished my long-term goal of speaking four languages. I finally felt like an adult—whatever that meant. I also felt that I had distanced myself another great step from my negative past.

The club's tourist village in Cefalu was right on the shore of the Tyrrhenian and Mediterranean Seas, and housed about 800 guests and 60 staff. Everything in the self-contained village was within walking distance: the restaurant, the beach, huts for the clients, and all the activity areas. My colleagues on staff came from all over Europe and I shared the top floor of a large building with some German women. Directly downstairs was the excursion office, so work was just a flight of stairs away. Trains arriving weekly from Paris carried special cars full of club members heading for the club's village of Cefalu; they also transported huge freezers filled with French delicacies intended for our consumption. The French chefs were first-class cooks. Staff were expected to eat with the guests and encouraged to join any activities the club offered, including sailing, diving, and horseback riding.

It was my job to sell tours of Sicily and excursions to the outer islands to our European guests. My fluency in other languages was greatly appreciated when I gave slide presentations and in my direct contact with our foreign guests. Together with my colleagues, I accompanied the guests to make sure the tours were presented as advertised and the Italian guides did a good job of interpreting the local history at each destination. The salary wasn't terribly high, but I did not have to pay for my meals, accommodation, or travelling expenses, and I was enjoying life immensely.

Shortly after beginning my job in Sicily, I met my new love, Alex, the resort's German chef de cuisine. He was a good-looking, athletic man with bright blue eyes. Soon we were spending all our free time together, and he had me taste his fanciest dishes before he put them on the menu. On our days off we hiked and toured the island in his funky old car. We roamed the streets of Palermo, the city of the infamous Mafia. He taught me how to scuba dive and we explored the coast. Sometimes when clients were looking for us, our colleagues pointed at the bubbles on the water. At night we danced until our legs couldn't carry us anymore. Life was fun and carefree.

Then something happened that changed my life. One afternoon while I was in the office typing a long list of participants due to leave on a boat trip, I heard a female voice with a French accent joking with my Italian colleague. They were talking about ice cream. Still half-focused on my work and without looking up, I said, "Could you bring me one, too?" and heard the response, "Of course." I looked up and saw Martine. At first all I saw was a smile that radiated across her entire face as she flirted a little with my colleague. He surely was enjoying the attention. When our eyes met, she became more reserved and shyly said, "I'll be back soon." Martine returned with ice cream for all three of us. While we enjoyed our treats she invited me and Alex to have lunch with her and her boyfriend, Patrick. The four of us spent several weeks socializing and exploring together.

The day arrived when Martine was supposed to leave on the boat trip she had signed up for on the day we met. It was my job to organize the departure. I had to make sure the tour members showed up for lunch and their bags were ready for pickup before I accompanied them to the boat that left from our village. At lunch, Martine took me to the side and said she didn't want to go on the trip anymore. We looked at each other. I knew I did not want her to leave, either. I couldn't name the reason, though, so I attended to duty and told her the Eolian Islands were fabulous, assuring her that she and Patrick would really enjoy them. I walked away to take care of my other clients. After I had escorted them all to the boat, they made their final preparations to leave. As the boat slowly pulled away from the dock, Martine looked at me and called out, "I can still jump into the water and swim to shore." I responded, "You'll have a great time." After they were gone, I slowly walked up to the highest point in the village, where I watched the boat grow smaller in the distance until it totally disappeared.

While Martine was gone, I missed her terribly and realized that I had special feelings for her. I was confused and needed to spend some time alone. Gently I told Alex that our relationship was over without telling him what was really going on. How could I explain that I was falling in love with a woman? I didn't know what was going on myself, and I was also uncertain of Martine's feelings.

With anticipation I awaited her return. I watched the ship from far away as it approached the resort. After it docked, I greeted the guests and ensured that everyone had made it back safely. Then I saw Patrick disembark and head to the cabins by himself; Martine trailed behind. When she reached me, we embraced, and she whispered that her relationship with Patrick was over. During dinner together that evening I told her I had left Alex and moved back into the main building with my other female colleagues. We did not discuss why we had each left our boyfriends.

Martine was scheduled to leave for Paris in two days. We spent the intervening time sunbathing, swimming, and walking the beaches. Fortunately it was my duty to organize the departure of the train that would carry Martine to Paris. I was very busy and pretended not to be nervous, but inside I was a wreck. In a way I was glad she was leaving; I would get over this strange phase and get on with my life. I wasn't sure I would even hear from her again. People on holidays make all kinds of promises. I had seen enough colleagues become heartbroken when no word was heard back from their affairs.

However, when the next group of club guests arrived from Paris a week after Martine's departure, the guide handed me a package from her. It included several letters and two books from our favourite poet, Jacques Prevert. I was surprised and overwhelmed with joy. We corresponded faithfully until the end of the season but said no word about our feelings for each other.

When the summer season ended and our work contracts were finished, all the staff and the remaining guests boarded the old steam train heading for France. When we finally pulled into the Gare du Nord in Paris, Martine was there waiting for me. During my first night in the city I stayed in a hotel, but the next day she insisted that I come to meet her parents and stay at her house. Martine took several days off from her job and we hit the streets of Paris in a way one can do only when one is in love.

When we finally admitted our feelings for each other, we cried a great deal and were at a loss as to what to do or say. Neither one of us had ever been in this kind of situation or met any other women with "romantic" feelings for one another. At times things felt terribly awkward.

When I picked up my last paycheck at the club's head office, I was congratulated on my work performance and offered my choice of position in any of the club's villages around the world. I chose Egypt. It was hard to leave Martine and Paris, but I needed a job. My new contract would be for six months but it felt like I was signing up for a lifetime.

Eleven

When I arrived in Egypt, the club was in the process of opening a new resort. My job consisted of looking after guest arrivals and departures, the reception desk, maintaining the books, and promoting and guiding the tours.

The club's hotel was located in the Mocatam Mountains just outside Cairo. I arrived late at night and will never forget opening the curtains in the morning and seeing the desert for the first time. The famous pyramids and the city of Cairo loomed majestically in the distance.

The hotel had been a casino until very recently and the renovations were hardly finished. Because the owners of Club Méditerranée were Jewish, the company operated under the name Connaissance du Monde in Egypt. Israel and Egypt were not on good terms and the word "Jewish" was not to be mentioned at any time.

Our staff of 14 worked together to prepare the hotel for our first guests. We had to teach the local staff to make beds and clean the rooms. Some of them had never made a bed with sheets, and the work ethic seemed almost non-existent. Teaching them was challenging, to say the least, because as soon as we left them alone to do their jobs, they would stop working.

Foreign staff had to obtain a visiting permit from the government office in Cairo. To qualify for the permit we each needed to show that we had enough money to stay in Egypt for six months. It was quite comical to see us all sitting in a row in the hallway of the immigration office, pretending we did not know one another. One at a time we filed into the office, signed papers, showed a large bundle of cash, and walked out with stamped papers on our way to pass the same bundle of money to the next person in line.

Going into Cairo for business or pleasure, even moving around outside our hotel perimeter alone, was not possible for the women in our group. I was assigned a bodyguard and given a handgun. When I drove I was told not to stop en route for any reason, even if people tried to stop me. I expect that tourists can freely move around in Egypt these days, but that was not the case in 1967. However, accompanying our guests on excursions was not a problem as we had several Egyptian tour guides along with us. I was the liaison between these guides and our clients on trips by train to Luxor and Aswan, boat trips on the Nile, and bus tours to various cities and, of course, the pyramids.

Because I had already lived and travelled in Turkey for several months, life in Egypt was not completely foreign to me, and I thoroughly enjoyed it. I will always remember the long walks outside the hotel into the desert, and the incredibly bright colours of the sky at the end of the day. Under the evening light the scenery changed every few minutes. Sometimes the pyramids and buildings in the far distance looked as though they were on fire. I grew to love the quiet stillness of the desert.

I had been working at the hotel for about four months when I became very ill from eating contaminated meat. In Egypt, all meat was painted or dyed red with a product that protected it from rot and fly infestation. I was unconscious for a time; all I remember is awakening to find an Egyptian and a French doctor sitting at my bedside. It took several weeks for me to recover. While I recuperated in bed, I learned that our butcher had been fined and ordered to go to jail because he had purchased unpainted meat. However, he had avoided incarceration by sending one of his kitchen staff in his place after offering him a watch for his trouble.

Suddenly we received news from the club's head office in Paris that no more guests would arrive in Egypt as the country was now at war with Israel. All of the guests and staff were to evacuate as quickly as possible. We caught the last plane out of Cairo before the airport closed.

I was very happy to return to Paris and join Martine again. Our separation had been hard on both of us. I'd had trouble recuperating from my illness without the proper medication and my body was not happy with the intense heat. After a short and sweet rest in Paris and in Holland to visit my family, the club sent me off to a different country.

Twelve

My next assignment was to another new hotel, this time in the middle of the Moroccan desert. The club already had two hotel villages in Morocco, one in Agadir and one in Al Hoceima. The new hotel in Ouarzazate would serve as an excursion destination for very privileged guests. It was beautifully built and painted in the colours of the desert. It had a restaurant with a large window looking onto the swimming pool, and the roof had a garden and space to sunbathe.

The entire complex overlooked the desert and a large structure called a kashba. Hundreds of people lived together in these kashbas, each family in its own little house and the houses all attached together. People could walk from one house into another without going outside. The kashba had a large courtyard for the children to play in, or for weddings or other festivities. Many of the people from the kashba came to work in our hotel, and in this way I gradually met the locals and was invited into the kashba on different occasions.

As in Egypt, the staff was required to do a bit of everything until the hotel opened for business. Everything was luxuriously appointed: beds, linens, tables, and even kitchen utensils were flown in from Paris. I was assigned many different tasks, one of which was to help buy food in the local markets and take care of the local staff. When the hotel opened, I was assigned to welcome our guests. I soon learned that most of the people interested in coming to our resort were wealthy and often well known. They were seeking something different to do and an opportunity to be away from everything. Many television commercials and print ads were made in our little paradise, the skinny models showing off the latest swimwear and summer clothing. Film stars finally had a little place to hide at Ouarzazate. Accompanied by guides from the Moroccan army, they took off exploring the desert with our Land Rovers. Some didn't want to spend days driving in order to reach the hotel, so they flew in and out. Their small planes landed behind the hotel, bringing not only the guests but also the most delectable food from the club's two other resorts.

Although we had the most exquisite housing, food, and entertainment in this small paradise hotel, people reacted differently to the tranquility of the setting. Or perhaps it was the sudden change from a very busy lifestyle to arriving in the desert where there was relatively little to do. The desert can be completely still and soundless, and after a short while some people could not bear the stillness. Upon their arrival, clients often told me that they were desperately looking forward to being away from everything. However, after they had spent a few days in our hotel, boredom would set in. Some guests left earlier than they originally intended, although there were enough simple things to do such as yoga, reading, walking, horseback riding, or swimming. Some flew off to the club's village in Agadir on the coast to party for a few days before they returned to Ouarzazate.

In this unusually quiet setting, people sometimes got bizarre ideas—or perhaps they were somewhat disturbed to begin with. One day, a very famous guest dressed up for lunch in a tuxedo, which was a bit eccentric. After the rest of the guests had gone for their afternoon siesta, he proceeded to climb down the ladder into the swimming pool. He remained completely clothed, even wearing his shoes and socks. The barman and myself glanced at each other and then back at the pool. We saw his hat float on the surface as he went under. When we suddenly realized that he couldn't swim, we rushed to get him out of the pool. This guest's behaviour became increasingly bizarre so that our hotel director finally had him flown back to Agadir.

I also noticed that many of my colleagues began to drink excessively, use drugs, and stay up all night. Of course on the mornings after their excesses they were hung-over. They would work only a little, which was fine as there wasn't really much for us to do, and repeat the whole process that evening. The staff became bored, particularly when there were no guests, which was quite often.

I realized that if I was going to survive the season in one piece, I would have to keep myself as busy as possible. Instead of napping in the afternoons, I chose to take long walks and went swimming so I could sleep well at night.

After dinner in the evenings I would discreetly disappear into my room or spend time on the roof. I was not a drinker, nor did I smoke, and the other staff members quickly noticed that I did not intend to participate in their lifestyle. At first they taunted me verbally, and then they resorted to sneaking into my room in the middle of the night. One night, they picked up my mattress while I slept, but I managed to jump off while they headed for the door to dump it into the swimming pool. The second time they pulled this prank they also took all my clothes out of the closet and threw them into the water. I thought it best to stay silent, so I simply went to another room to sleep and had the local staff wash and iron my clothes.

One day a film crew arrived with plans to film some nomads and small villages situated a few days' drive into the barren desert, close to the Algerian border. I was invited to join the group, and eventually eight of us plus our two driver guides from the Moroccan army left in two Land Rovers. The vehicles also carried several coolers full of food and water.

The hotel director had joined our party with the intention of visiting a French doctor he knew in a little village along the way. I had no idea how our drivers knew how to find this village. For five or six hours there were no road signs or other land markings to indicate a route on the dry, cracked soil. Each vehicle was equipped with a radio and the drivers talked to each other now and then. The vehicles drove quite a distance from each other because of the dust they raised as they moved across the desert.

When we arrived at the doctor's village, at least thirty patients were waiting on the ground outside his little house and infirmary. He was happy to see us, stopping his work immediately and inviting us all in. I sat quietly, watching him talk and serve tea, finding him unaccountably intriguing and appealing. He was about 50 years old and had a delightful, soft smile. His eyes were blue and very bright and alive. He appeared wonderfully serene as he moved around the room and served us. He carried himself with grace and dignity and a touch of deference, but it was clear he also had a deep reserve of inner strength. After we left, I asked my boss a little more about him and learned that this man was not only a doctor, he was a missionary as well. Much later in life I would become more familiar with the peace and serenity that devoted and spiritual people possess.

On this trip I finally met the "blue" people I had heard so much about. These nomads were dressed in long, pale and dark blue jelebas, and over years of wearing these clothes the dye had rubbed off into their skin. Atop their camels, with their deeply burnished faces and the wind blowing into their colourful garments, they looked absolutely stunning.

Some of the villages we passed through were partially covered by sand from the windstorms. At one point we encountered a few families in tents in the middle of nowhere. The men had gone to the market several days away by camel. The women and children, left behind, stayed hidden from us until they saw the few women in our group. Our presence made them feel safe enough to reveal themselves. The children were very interested in me, pinching me a little with ill-concealed curiosity. One of our guides told me that the kids wondered if I was real, with my blonde hair and blue eyes.

What struck me most was the cheerful, friendly nature of these impoverished people. Though they lived in worn-out cloth tents and were so poor they had scarcely any clothes, they still wore broad smiles across their faces. We were offered tea with large pieces of brown sugar everywhere we went.

In several of the villages we passed, men would approach my boss and offer to buy the three women in our group. Apparently any women who were kidnapped in Europe and brought to Morocco's desert villages would have no chance of ever getting found, and I truly believed that.

After five days in the desert, our Land Rover broke down in the middle of the day. The heat was unbearable and the only spot we could find to escape from the intensity of the sun was under the jeep. We waited there until the other Land Rover showed up to fix our vehicle. I had no idea how they found us—the drivers did not use a map or compass.

There was nowhere to go to fill up the gas tanks or buy more drinking water. There were no villages or amenities in sight—only sand: sand so fine that we had to filter it from our lungs by covering our heads and faces with cloth until only our sunglasses were visible. In the dry heat, I swore I could see lakes ahead in the distance on the parched landscape, but they were only mirages—heat vibrations hitting the ground. During these trying moments, I wondered how long we would last if we were not found after our coolers had no more water. I promised God that I would never again take drinking water for granted—and I never have. It is interesting that many of us turn to God, or a "higher power," for help when other options seem exhausted and we feel utterly vulnerable.

We finally found the villages the film crew was searching for; after that, the actual filming took only a few days. During that time we stayed in a very simple hotel which had "cold" showers— what a treat! The heat was so intense that I would get up several times during the night for another cold shower, then hop into bed again naked, soaked, and temporarily refreshed.

It was difficult for me to remain in Morocco until the end of my contract, but I stuck it out. I'd had enough of being surrounded by so many people, both guests and staff, who were interested only in partying and laughing when there was nothing to laugh about, and pretending to have fun. Most of them seemed to be seeking something they could not find. Even though they were surrounded by some of the most beautiful scenery in the world, treated to the most scrumptious food in first-class accommodations, and had every whim attended to by the resort's staff, they still seemed dissatisfied. I was eager for a simpler life again: to rejoin Martine, live in our own place, shop for groceries together, prepare our own meals, and enjoy each other's company.

* * *

So it was that after my stint in Morocco, I decided to leave my employment with the club and settle in Paris with Martine.

Again, we had kept in contact with each other through the company's mail exchange. Every week before each tour's departure and arrival, Martine had visited the club's headquarters in Paris to drop off and pick up our letters. We had missed each other terribly. I promised her I would not sign up for another season with the club, but would try to find a job in Paris.

For some time we lived with Martine's parents while I looked for a job. It was extremely difficult to find a job in Paris, as a Catch-22 in the law specified that I needed a work permit to get a job, but I needed a job to get a work permit. I went job-hunting each day from early morning until late afternoon while Martine was at work. Her parents were very supportive of me, saying they had never seen anyone seek a job so assiduously.

One afternoon, before I gave up and headed home for the day, I decided to give my search one more try. I applied as a multi-lingual hostess at the 1968 Olympic Games in Grenoble. The address for the interviews proved to be a distinguished-looking old building on the Champs Élysées. I entered a room full of very well-dressed upper-class women. I knew I was no competition for them and sat down just to have a rest before I left again. Suddenly a numbered application was put into my hands. "What the heck," I thought, "I may as well fill this out while I'm here."

To my surprise, my number was called. I walked into a large, thickly carpeted room with one massive desk, behind which sat a fashionably dressed middle-aged man. A woman stood quietly next to him. He looked me over several times and said nothing. I could see him thinking. After he had seen so many poised and beautifully groomed women all day, here was one who looked tired, without makeup, and wore out-of-date clothes. I looked him straight in the eyes and said bluntly, "I am here for the job," and he nodded. He asked me if I had a working permit. I did not. He asked what country I was from, and switched from French to English and then to German. He left out Dutch. I could see him thinking, and imagined his reaction to me: "She has guts to apply for this job." But he surprised me—he finally turned toward the woman beside him and said, "Please take her measurements for the uniform." He looked back at me and smiled. "You are hired."

Thus I attended the 1968 Olympic Games as a translator and hostess. I spent time with the Dutch speed-skaters and the Princess (now Queen) of Holland, Beatrice, and her late husband, Prince Claus. Together we celebrated the gold medals won by our speed skaters. Our royal family spoke French fluently and didn't really need my help, but I had a lot of fun.

During the many years I lived in Paris after the Games, I worked as a tour guide on one of the sightseeing boats on the Seine, close to the Eiffel Tower. Martine would wave to me from the quays on the weekends. I also worked as a multilingual secretary for a large corporation that imported photocopiers from Japan.

Martine and I moved into our own apartment. We had both come from dysfunctional families and were not a "normal" couple either, but we loved each other and found that our relationship gave us enormous stability. We didn't know any other female couples and decided that we would later on marry men and have children like everyone else. Years went by as we lived like most people do, busy with work, friends, and family. Then I met Rodriguez.

Thirteen

After attending a job interview at the Paris airport, I walked onto what I thought was the airport bus for a lift back into the city. After I had seated myself it crossed my mind that the bus was surprisingly comfortable. But my thoughts were still focused on the interview, and I did not notice the people who were boarding. A man approached me and asked in English if I was heading into town. I replied, "Yes," and attempted to hand him the money for the fare; by this time I was so easily fluent that I did not even notice whether people were speaking in English or French. He smiled and sat down next to me, explaining that this bus was reserved for the group he was with. I apologized and got up to leave, but he assured me they would be happy to drop me off in town since they were going there anyway. We began to talk and introduced ourselves. Before I got off the bus, Rodriguez invited me to join him for dinner. I declined. He invited me to have lunch with him the next day, and I agreed to that. I was in between jobs and had time on my hands. We met and explored Paris.

Rodriguez was a Venezuelan engineer whose specialty was transportation. When, several days after we had met, he invited me to join him on a business trip to Germany to meet the CEO of Mercedes Benz, I declined. Upon his return he invited me to a fun party at the house of the Venezuelan consul. During the course of the evening, I heard Rodriguez tell the consul that he wanted to take some time off to stay with me in Paris. The consul responded that he would take care of it. I wondered briefly why a consul would do that for him, but then put the thought out of my mind.

Rodriguez stayed in Paris for several weeks and when he finally had to leave, we promised to stay in contact. After that, we often talked to each other on the phone and exchanged long letters. The day arrived that Rodriguez mailed me an open airline ticket in a letter that stated, "without any obligations." Martine encouraged me to go, so off I went to South America.

I stopped for a few weeks in Guadeloupe in the Caribbean islands to visit Martine's sister before heading to Caracas. Upon my arrival, Rodriguez met me inside the plane, which I found odd. I had no idea about any of the customs in Venezuela. As we disembarked, I noticed soldiers saluting someone, and I looked behind me to see if it was anyone important. No one was there, and the puzzle remained. Rodriguez handed my passport to customs officers and I was escorted through very quickly. Rodriguez's brother was waiting outside, standing next to a limousine. We got in and drove away, but soon we were caught in a snarl of traffic. After a time Rodriguez talked to the driver and a siren was placed on top of the car. It started wailing and as the cars ahead of us moved to one side we passed them.

Suddenly everything I had ignored flashed into my mind: the consul being so agreeable, Rodriguez greeting me inside the plane, the saluting soldiers, passing through customs so quickly. I questioned Rodriguez about this special attention, and he said he would explain everything as soon as we got home. When I stepped out of the limousine at his home, I noticed the government emblem on the number plate of the car and at once I realized his job was more important than he had let on.

Rodriguez's mother, sister, and brothers all welcomed me with open arms. His family all lived together with the exception of his eldest brother, who was married.

The following day, Rodriguez and I talked about his government job and why he had been reluctant to tell me about it. He had not wished me to know he was so important; he wanted me to care about him as a person. I assured him that everything was fine as long as he was able to respect me for who I was.

After several days Rodriguez took me to his workplace. During the entire outing we were accompanied by bodyguards; I knew by then that Rodriguez also carried a gun in his pocket. Access to his office was strictly limited. The door would not open until everyone and everything entering was thoroughly checked.

So far the unusual turn of events had not bothered me very much. Rodriguez did not have a chip on his shoulder. He was jovial to everyone and had an easy smile, not to mention the fact that he was a brilliant man. I loved his family. I had no worries about money; all my expenses were discreetly covered. Each day I was picked up for a hairdresser's appointment; people bowed and smiled and no one argued with me. It was fun to attend lavish dinner functions and get to know the wives of ambassadors. We had dinner at the palace a few times and I met the president of Venezuela. To get away from the busy city, we spent weekends with his family, friends, and business acquaintances at luxuriously appointed ranches in out-of-the way places.

I spent many afternoons at the government swimming pool, which was surrounded by tables with sun umbrellas where people were served their meals. When the ministers were in town, government limousines would come by and drop them off so they could lunch with their wives and children before returning to work. After lunch the nannies would take the children back to school and the women would linger on. The pool was used mostly by the children and their fathers; I didn't see any women other than myself enter the water.

Of course, as time went on, the big question loomed: when were Rodriguez and I going to get married? It came up more and more frequently, although he hadn't asked me directly yet. Rodriguez showed me areas where he wanted to live in the future and we even visited some houses that were for sale. But I was feeling more and more claustrophobic. It began to irritate me that we were followed everywhere we went. We couldn't even go to a movie by ourselves. Everyone always knew what I was doing and where I was going. Rodriguez arranged when I was to be picked up for dinner outings and business trips. He seldom came home directly from work as there were always meetings or parties to attend.

I eventually asked Rodriguez for a car so I could go out by myself a little. He agreed only reluctantly, but got me a driver's licence and gave me his mother's car. I finally took off to explore.

I had a wonderful afternoon getting lost in Caracas. People were friendly; I went for coffee and visited some galleries. I arrived home several hours later than the prescribed time. Rodriguez was furious, saying many people were already searching for me. He should have given me a gun. I should have called him on his mobile phone. I should have at least had a driver with me. So many "shoulds." I told him that this kind of lifestyle might not work for me—it felt too restrictive. He replied, "After we get married you will be busy with the house and our children anyway." It was the first word I had heard directly from him about us getting married. He suddenly realized that by mentioning his marriage plans he had gone too far, and he backed off.

The subject was not mentioned again, and we left on a business trip several days later. For safety reasons, government officials did not travel with their wives or children or any other family members, so we always flew on different planes. While Rodriguez was busy in meetings I remained in our suites or at the swimming pools of the opulent hotels where we stayed. I felt lonely and without purpose, and I seriously pondered, "Is this really the life I want to live?" I shared my feelings with Rodriguez. To his credit, he tried to resolve the issue quickly by saying, "We will bring Martine over too, and she can marry one of my brothers." That really made me laugh!

The incident that helped clarify my decision of what to do occurred at lunch one day. As we were all eating, Rodriguez's mother complained about the young woman who did the cooking. Rodriguez became angry. He slipped off his belt and headed toward the kitchen, and before I realized what he was doing, he began striking the young woman. Yelling at him to stop, I jumped up and tried to pull him away from her. He was stunned and dropped his arm. "How dare you hit a woman!" I said, outraged. He told me that in his country it was perfectly normal for a man to hit a woman if she did not listen or behave. "I have no wish to live in a country that condones such behaviour," I said. I had seen enough abuse at home and would not tolerate it anywhere around me, especially from him.

He apologized only when he saw me preparing to leave, and asked me to take a few days for reflection. His grandmother, whom I had come to love dearly, came to his aid. She pleaded with me to stay, but I told her that although I had forgiven Rodriguez, I could not see a future for myself living this kind of lifestyle. We cried together.

I returned to Guadeloupe to take some time to process what had happened over the past four months. Rodriguez called several times and begged me to come back. Although it broke my heart to do so, I refused.

Fourteen

I was happy to return to our apartment and rejoin Martine. It might sound strange that we lived together and apart for long periods of time and went out with men whenever we met someone interesting; our male partners did not know about our intimate relationship. We did have the occasional jealous outburst, but we each still intended to get married later on. The arrangement, on the whole, worked well for us.

On one of our many trips to Holland, when I finally told my mother about Martine's and my relationship, she wasn't that surprised, as my youngest brother Cor had announced some time ago that he was gay. At that time Mother admitted she didn't know much about homosexuality, so she turned to our family doctor to ask him about it. My brother took her to some of the bars he frequented in Amsterdam and introduced her to some of his friends. It was not a daily event that a parent of a gay man would visit those bars, and she was spoiled lavishly. She ended up having a wonderful time. To me, she said, "I wish I had fallen in love with a woman, but then I would not have had you." My father said nothing. Although Martine's father loved me dearly he had difficulty in accepting our lifestyle. Martine's stepmother simply loved us the way we were—I will always admire her for that.

I returned to Paris to find a job and once again fell into the grind and frenetic pace of the big city. It is not possible to walk slowly in Paris—people automatically start moving with the crowd, and if they don't, they get forced along anyway. One day in the metro with a friend, I was so squashed that I lifted my feet off the ground and hung between the people on either side of me without touching the ground. I said to my friend, "Guess what I'm doing?" "What are you doing?" she asked, and I said, "I'm not doing anything. I'm hanging." We laughed so hard that we had to get off the metro for a while.

My job as an executive multilingual secretary at a large corporation was going well and Martine and I were having fun, but my health was slowly deteriorating. I was often very tired and I was inexplicably losing great quantities of hair. The doctor I visited several times could not find anything wrong with me. He finally referred me to a specialist. There, I was examined thoroughly, blood tests were taken, and many questions were asked about my life: where was I born, what had I been doing all these years, and what about my current lifestyle? When I met with the doctor again one week later, he informed me that there was no cure or medication for what I had. I was simply not fit to live and work in a large city. The pollution and the hectic pace of life had a bad effect on my health and depleted my normal energy. The doctor thus recommended that I move to the countryside and begin living at a slower pace.

Fifteen

I was now 30 years old. Martine and I decided to immigrate to Canada to join my youngest brother Cor, who had emigrated to be with his German partner in Vancouver, British Columbia. I had visited him a few years earlier with my mother. During that holiday I had fallen in love with British Columbia and its gorgeous snow-capped mountains, sprawling lakes, and forests. I had immediately felt at ease in this country. Even my mother was impressed with Canada and easily understood why her children wanted to live there.

I went back to Holland to file my Canadian immigration papers, while Martine applied for hers in Paris. With my language skills, a relative already living in the country, and the excellent political relationship between Canada and Holland, I passed the tests easily. Martine and I decided that I would move before she did in order to find a job and a place for us to live while she waited for her immigration papers.

It took several months before she received a negative response. We were both devastated. Martine did not speak English and it surely did not help that France was not getting along politically with Canada at that time. On a visit to Canada, the French president, Charles de Gaulle, had enraged the English community by telling the French people in Quebec, "Vive le Quebec libre" (Long live free Quebec).

Martine reapplied and many months later her immigration request was turned down again. By this time, I was settled into a new job taking flight reservations for an airline company in Vancouver. About a year passed with no prospect of Martine moving to Canada. She began a new relationship and moved to the south of France. Soon she started to undergo major shifts in her life, becoming interested in spiritual pursuits and taking courses in meditation and Shiatsu. Later on, she joined the Bhagavan Rashnese movement and spent most of her time in India. Twenty-seven years later, Martine's spiritual path would lead me to Amma in India and, ultimately, to my own spiritual path.

Upon my arrival in Canada, I moved in with my brother and his partner until I found a job and my own apartment. For the first time, I was able to really connect with my youngest brother as an adult. We enjoyed each other's company thoroughly and regularly went out for dinner, walks, and concerts. We often drove to Seattle for the day, went to the opera at night, and then drove all the way back to Vancouver again. We laughed about our dysfunctional upbringing and became close friends.

I was promoted to reservation supervisor at work and was in a position to hire people for the first time. I took some pleasure in hiring the people about whom I had a good intuition, rather than just going by their résumés. Having only made it to Grade 7 myself, I was naturally drawn to people who were also handicapped by a limited education. When I could see a willingness to learn and a spark of passion in a person, I hired them. It worked. The people I hired worked hard and were committed to their jobs. When a plane was late or cancelled they would stay until their work was done. I was promoted again and became the Western Canada coordinator for all the Hawaiian flights and hotel packages.

I enjoyed my job and my life. Canada became my home. I felt as though I had always lived there. I loved the mixture of people and the space, and spent all my time off hiking and climbing mountains. I learned to play tennis and my health thrived with all the activity and clean air.

Several years later, my car was rear-ended. My subsequent whiplash injury was so bad that I lost my ability to balance. I could not walk by myself and had to hold on to the walls or crawl around my apartment. It was a very humbling experience. Finally, a Polish massage therapist was recommended to me who worked daily on my head with her thumbs. She told me that my recovery could be credited to my good health at the time of the accident!

Altogether, it took me nine months to heal sufficiently and return to work. On the day I was finally able to return to my job, I was informed that my position had been eliminated. I knew very well that this was not the case, but I had no way to fight the decision and was still too fragile to undertake a battle. I knew that the real reason for the termination of my position was that the director had been harassing one of my staff and I had told him to keep his hands off her or I would report him. He had also made several major errors in his work that he tried to blame on me. When his boss didn't believe him, he deemed that the place was better off without me. I was chagrined but just as glad to leave. Why work for a company with such ethics? A month after I was laid off, the director was fired. Poetic justice?

After my accident and illness, I became acutely aware that my health and my life were very precious. I did not want to find work in a large faceless corporation again, try to climb up the ladder, and then be let go without a "thank you."

Sixteen

Although I had no experience in the area, I was hired as the outdoor recreation director at the Vancouver YWCA. One of my responsibilities was to run an outdoor centre in the middle of a forest owned by the large logging company, MacMillan Bloedel, on Saltspring Island in B.C.'s Gulf Islands. Built on 10 acres of land, the centre had cabins that lodged about 88 children and 10 counsellors, a long dining hall with a large kitchen, and a barn with pottery wheels and space for other arts and crafts. The site was surrounded by many acres of unlogged wilderness that provided hiking trails all the way to a wonderful beach on the waters of the Strait of Georgia.

The YWCA's Yawaca summer camp for girls was known to welcome a great mixture of children from different ethnic and socio-economic backgrounds. Many children from families on social assistance were referred by social workers and had their stay at camp paid for by government agencies. I found it very rewarding to work with these children, and to be able to give them extra attention and expose them to some of the many positive things life has to offer. Many children would come back year after year, often taking on extra responsibilities in different areas and becoming counsellors as they grew older.

Groups on their way to camp met in Vancouver. With packs and sleeping bags in hand, we all boarded the ferry to Vancouver Island, where we switched to the Saltspring Island ferry. When we reached Saltspring Island, we walked together up the long hill to the centre. As soon as we arrived, the children always ran to see the animals that lived at the camp. We had sheep, goats, pigs, chickens, and cats and dogs to look after. The centre offered many different activities including hiking, camping, arts and crafts, swimming, and canoeing on the lake nearby. We played volleyball, baseball, and tennis and we offered horseback riding on horses from a neighbouring farm.

It was like nothing I had done before, but somehow the job suited me very well. My director, the executives, and the board of directors at the YWCA gave me some freedom to create programs for different minority groups and I could come and go as I pleased. Because they gave me so much freedom and responsibility, I worked much harder and put in many more hours of work (often unpaid) than were expected of me. I relished it.

I loved working with the children. I was good at raising money for special programs, and also gathered a large collection of clothes and sleeping bags for the kids who needed them. I kept my budget in line, initiated new programs, and got the buildings into perfect shape.

I faced some interesting challenges along the way. One day we had a serious lice problem at the centre. We scrubbed everything down—the cabins, the beds, and the kids—and then occupied all the laundries on the island to wash the campers' clothes and sleeping bags. I took a quick trip to Vancouver to get bottles of special lice shampoo, after which there was some serious hair-washing going on for a few days. When some of the kids panicked and wanted to go home, I initiated a spaghetti fight at the dinner table to cut the tension. There was spaghetti on the walls and the ceiling—it was everywhere. An incredible soap fight followed and soon not a spot of spaghetti was to be seen anywhere in the dining hall. One of the kids enthusiastically told her parents about this event and I was called into the executive director's office to explain the situation. She wasn't amused, to say the least.

Seventeen

I initiated the centre's first two-week program for single mothers with children as well as weekend retreats for women only and a two-week-long program for mentally challenged adults.

I had never worked with mentally challenged people before. This particular program came about when I was approached by the director of the Easter Seal Camp, who literally begged me to offer a program for these individuals because their camp was always overcrowded. Their parents and caregivers also badly needed a break. I promised to visit them and have a look at their program. While there, I had the most wonderful time and thought that this "minority group" would fit very well within the guidelines of the YWCA. However, my boss told me there were no funds available to sponsor the program and that offering a co-ed program might not be such a good idea. I promised to go out into the community and get the money somehow. My research indicated that mixing men and women was a good motivational tool in these programs. I successfully applied to the Vancouver Foundation and, funding in hand, went ahead with the creation of the program.

I began by visiting the homes and institutions that housed mentally challenged people. It was clear that there was a great need for a recreational venue for them. However, how would I handle their various levels of disability? Which persons could I accept into the program and which ones would have to stay home? How would they interact with one another? I decided to hire two nurses and have them decide. The question of liability also entered the picture. I was warned about accidents and injuries—what if someone got hurt? This attitude bothered me; after all, kids and adults could get hurt anywhere, at any given time. Different organizations promised to stand behind me just in case something did happen.

We prepared the camp counsellors as best as we could, but it was still a shock for them when they saw the first 40 "special" campers arrive at the departure parking lot in Vancouver. We had planned to assign one counsellor to four people. Our first challenge was how to keep everyone together on the ferry. As I had no experience in this area either, I was obliged to improvise and create guidelines as problems arose. I suggested to the counsellors that each camper could walk around the ferry freely, and that they should just be monitored from a distance. I advised the staff in the ferry's cafeteria about our group and requested that they simply serve them as they would anyone else. If one of our campers bought too much food and didn't have enough money to pay, I would come and settle it later or some of the food could be returned.

It was fascinating to observe the group and other people's reactions when they mingled with strangers. Mentally challenged people are very friendly. Thus, although some people were taken a little by surprise at first, many helped our campers with their trays, watched over them at the cashier, and even assisted them at their tables. Our special campers had no trouble talking to people and I overheard many conversations about going to camp and being on the ferry. Food was a big topic too.

Because we did not have any experience working with mentally challenged adults, we treated them just like any other campers. They had to set the tables and clean up after meals. It always took a very long time, but they got things done. Sometimes their shower time proved interesting, as the showers in the cabins had two knobs—one for cold water and one for hot. We couldn't have known that in the institutions, showers had only one knob and the water was delivered at a preset temperature. The campers would come to me and say, "Nurse, the water is too hot." I instructed them to use the other knob too. Two minutes later they would return, saying, "Nurse, the water is cold." Sometimes I would go to have a look only to find the cabin full of steam and the shower overflowing, but after a while they got it right. Many times campers would show up in the mornings or after a swim, dressed in clothes that belonged to their cabin-mates, but their achievement was in dressing themselves, and their roommates didn't mind about the "sharing." They would just laugh and say, "Hey, you have my clothes on!" and that would be the end of it.

The handicapped campers participated in all the regular camp activities. It often took hours for them to set up a tent or to prepare for a one-hour canoe outing. Of course, people fell in the water, but they had good life jackets on and just floated around until we rescued them. We had so much fun! They loved to feed the animals and during their stay at our camp our goats, pigs, and chickens were well overfed. If anyone was "lost," we would invariably find them sitting with the animals. Freddy, for example, was a man of about 50 who would do nothing but sit on his bed in his cabin after he arrived. It was hard to coax him out; being at camp was just too great a change for him and he was frightened. One day a goat escaped from its pen and made its way to Freddy's cabin, where it stopped to eat the flowers that grew in front. That piqued Freddy's interest. I asked him to come out, and together we coaxed the goat back to its pen. From then on, if we couldn't find him in his cabin, we all knew that Freddy was with the goats. I have a beautiful series of slides showing Freddy, a huge smile on his face, caressing and feeding the goats.

The mentally challenged campers also loved the horses, and if some were too afraid to ride them, they would just walk next to them holding the reins. We went bowling with the whole crowd in the small town of Ganges for the day. They loved it and were quite adept at it.

Some of the campers could not talk. David had never spoken before, but, almost miraculously, we got him to say a few words while he was at camp. Each time he would say something right the whole group would applaud him, and we would dance around the tables and on the chairs while he jumped up and down with joy. Nothing and everything was a big deal.

Staff from the institutions came to observe our programs and were astonished to see how our "special campers" had progressed in such a short time. I think they learned so much because we expected them to and did not take things out of their hands. When unfamiliar situations arose, we simply adjusted the program and ourselves.

We had a wonderful time, we did not lose anyone, and no one had to be flown home early. I have such fond memories of this period in my job at the YWCA—they still make me smile. Normally I consider myself an impatient person; however, with the children and the special needs people who attended camp, I found I had endless time, energy, and patience. Together we had lots of creative ideas and lots of fun. Every single person signed up again for the following year as soon as they arrived home.

* * *

My office-mate at the YWCA, Mary, was a single mother with two young boys, and she expressed an interest in coming to camp with her children. We explored the possibility of inviting other single mothers and dreamed up a special camp for single mothers and their children. Remember, this was the 1970s and single parents were not yet very common. We decided to give it a try.

What stood out most about the single mothers' program was that the children had an opportunity to learn new skills both with and without their mothers, and to appreciate that even if they did not have a father living with them, they were still a family. I had learned from my own childhood that my family functioned much

Single mothers' camp at Yawaca on Salt Spring Island.

better when my father was absent—there was much less tension in the house, even though we had to manage without his salary.

At the centre, the children were able to meet many other families like their own, and thus they became better able to accept their own situations. I took the programs with the mothers while the counsellors took the children, and we would mix the groups at different times during the day.

Most of the mothers were out of shape, so we began each day with a walk through the woods, adding on a little extra distance every day. We also taught them yoga and meditation. They learned how to canoe and set up a tent. We organized an overnight camping trip under the stars without the kids. Like the kids, they got to work with clay and paints. There were mixed teams to play softball or volleyball. In the evenings, the mothers performed for their kids and the kids for their mothers.

The program was such an overwhelming success that afterward, the mothers met with each other in town regularly to continue hiking and camping with each other and their children. Since the inception of this program, the YWCA in Vancouver has initiated and still runs many different programs for single mothers and their children.

Eighteen

Although my formal education was limited and I had never attended high school, college, or university, I often signed up for the evening classes offered by the Vancouver School Board, even while I worked full-time. I took language courses as well as classes in computers, small business, communication, leisure counselling, and first aid, and later in carving, sculpting, carpentry, and even welding.

Since I was so thoroughly enjoying my outdoor recreation job with the YWCA, I applied for admittance to a two-year full-time outdoor recreation program at Capilano College. I did not have enough formal education to join the program, but because of my current job and work experience they were happy to have me, and the education requirements were waived. I was older than the other students. Everyone in my classes knew I had a full-time job, so getting information from other students when I missed any classes was easy. During the course of the program, we went on some spectacular backpacking and kayaking field trips throughout the province.

On these field trips, I gradually became friends with my classmate, Penny, and we often shared a tent or canoe. We were both quiet types who preferred to read at the end of the day instead of joining our more raucous peers.

On one occasion my classmates and I decided to head out to Mt. Washington on Vancouver Island to join a cross-country ski marathon, although I intended only to cheer the others on and ski for a few hours by myself. When my classmates taunted me for being too old to take on the challenge of the marathon, I suddenly changed my mind and entered the race at the last minute. At the starting line they joked and wished me well before they took off.

Well, I might not have been fast in anything I did, but I had completed a ski marathon before in 100 Mile House, B.C. Until my car accident, I had been in the mountains every weekend since my arrival in Canada, and as soon as I mended I was out running and hiking again. I would see just how far I could get in this marathon and I would enjoy the exercise.

The first few miles of the course were flat and then it wound slightly uphill. The real challenge came as the course took us steadily uphill for 13 kilometres. That is where I slowly started to pass people. They were breathing heavily, and I knew they had started out too fast and now had to slow down. One by one I passed most of my classmates and finished seventh in my category. That evening at dinnertime, those good sports gave me a standing ovation.

Ultimately, however, I learned more on the job than I did at college. While at work, I was exposed to real challenges every day. I pushed to get decisions made and was therefore able to see the immediate results, but I also received many new ideas and much support from the students and teachers. To this day, I still have some good connections with some of the people I met at the college.

Nineteen

I began offering many different weekend retreats at the centre—one of them for women only. They were wildly successful. We offered many different workshops in outdoor recreation, fitness, health, politics, assertiveness training and social issues. There were long waiting lists to attend the retreats.

It was during one of these women's retreats that I met my next partner, Karen. It was time, as I had been living alone for more than three years. Having a male and then a female partner was just too complicated, and although I enjoyed the companionship of men, on an intimate level I preferred sharing my life with a woman. Interestingly, many of my female friends had male partners before choosing a female partner, and some of them were married and had children. Karen and I moved in together and went on a holiday to my birth country, where I introduced her to my family. In Vancouver, she joined the outdoor club and we had many adventurous outings. I was happy in my new country and happy with my new life and the people who were part of it.

* * *

Another first in Canada was the creation of the Vancouver Outdoor Club for Women. Initially, as part of my volunteer time, the YWCA asked me to administer the co-ed outdoor club that met in their building. I went to one of the group's meetings and was invited to make the sandwiches while the men set up the slide projector. The slide show demonstrated that, on their hikes, the men strode along at the front of the group while the women trailed along at the back. The men set up the tents and the campfires while the women were in charge of the cooking.

I told my boss I was not interested in volunteering my time at this club—they seemed to be doing very well on their own.

I suggested creating an outdoor club for women only, so that women could learn on their own to camp, climb mountains, cross-country ski, kayak, canoe, and enjoy other outdoor activities in a non-competitive environment and free of the sometimes intimidating presence of men. She answered, "It will never work."

These four words can be either an excellent motivator or an impediment to the exploration of people's full potential. For me, they became challenges; when I heard them, something inside me stirred and motivated me to prove it could be done despite the odds. Conquering each challenge in turn gave me more confidence to face the next one.

After a while, the co-ed club folded. Once again I extended my offer to open an outdoor club for women only, saying, "This organization is focused on the welfare of women, and that should include giving women a chance to become more familiar with healthy outdoor pursuits in a non-competitive atmosphere." This time in addition to "It will never work," my boss added, "Don't count on any funding."

I had just read a National Geographic magazine article about an all-women group, led by Arlene Blum, that had climbed Annapurna I in 1978. Two women had died on the expedition. After some searching, I was able to contact one of the women from the expedition. I invited Mrs. Joan Firey, of Seattle, to come and give a presentation to the Vancouver YWCA about the expedition. At first she declined my request, but when I explained my interest in creating the first outdoor club for women in Canada, she asked what other kinds of programs I had created. After I mailed her some of the brochures from my other programs, she accepted my invitation. Our second guest of honour was Mrs. Mundy, a famous climber from Vancouver who'd had a mountain in British Columbia named after her.

To promote the event, I had large posters made of the team climbing Annapurna I and distributed them all over the city. The tickets were sold in a matter of days and the evening was a huge success.

Although she had not climbed to the top of Annapurna I herself, Mrs. Firey spoke at length about her role on the expedition. What I didn't know then was that she was seriously ill with a rare bone disease when she came to give her presentation to us. She died several months later from the illness.

Having these two famous women climbers come to talk to us was inspiring to everyone who managed to obtain a ticket to the event. At the end of the evening, I declared the Outdoor Club for Women officially launched.

In the beginning we chose to limit the club's membership to 50 as we did not have enough experienced leaders for the trips. I was out every weekend leading trips for the next three years. We soon had enough money from membership fees and donations to start buying outdoor equipment, including tents, sleeping bags, backpacks, and climbing gear, in order to ensure that everyone had the best possible equipment on the outings.

My intuition had been correct—the women were far more motivated to take risks and learn when men were not present. We didn't care if we couldn't make it to the top of the mountain because it was pouring rain. We were perfectly willing to turn around and head back for coffee and cookies in a warm tent or hut and try for the summit again the next day. We cross-country skied up

On a hike with The Vancouver Outdoor Club for women 1979.

mountains and went to bed in our snow huts at four in the afternoon. We fell out of canoes and kayaks and scraped our knees on the rocks of the local mountains. On one occasion, after a day's hike we found our tents drifting in the lake because they hadn't been pinned down! We created friendships that are still strong nearly three decades later.

Many women who joined these outdoor pursuits were capable of doing much more than they had initially thought. Over the years that I led these trips, I saw many women weep with excitement and happiness after they challenged their own limits and reached mountaintops and other goals they had never dreamed of.

My nickname in the club was "Just around the corner." When someone asked me on the trail how far we still had to go, knowing they were getting tired and wanting to keep them motivated, I often answered, "Just around the corner." By the time we got to the next bend that person had hopefully forgotten what she'd asked. My nickname fit me well. I was always curious about what my next challenge would be. If I did not like the view, I would continue on and see if I liked better what lay around the next corner.

Twenty

I "came out" to my boss after she praised my work performance during a job evaluation. She awkwardly reassured me that it made no difference to her if I shared my life with a male or female partner.

That year, when the YWCA staff Christmas party was organized at her house and partners were invited to attend, I made it known that I wanted to bring my partner so my colleagues could finally put a face to the woman I was living with. While same-sex marriages are now legal in Canada, it was still a very touchy subject 25 years ago. In any case, I was ready to tackle the issue. Only one of my colleagues took issue with my partner's inclusion and made it clear to everyone that she would not attend the party if my partner did. Other colleagues came by my office and offered their full support. They complimented me on my courage. Karen did attend the party and it made things much more comfortable for me at work.

Many women had begun to ask the YWCA for a gay women's retreat. Still in charge of the programming at the outdoor centre on Saltspring Island, I decided to explore the possibility of creating workshops for gay women. One thing I was certain of: once created, I wanted the existence and content of these programs to be made public. The executive director and my direct supervisor were not at all happy that I brought this subject to the table, especially because I was determined not to let go of it.

First, I was told that it simply could not be done, but I did not buy that. Next, they tried to cajole me into dropping the idea, but that did not work. Then the executive director called me into her office and threatened that if I refused to back down, this matter would have to be presented to the board. I stood my ground. By then something had touched me to the core and I felt the need to stand up for my gay sisters and brothers. This was my chance—it lay right in front of me. For the most part, being gay is of little importance to me; it is just part of my life. But it is very important that all of us have equal rights and a place in society.

The executive director and my supervisor did not know what to do with me or my ideas, and an emergency meeting of the board was organized. The issue on the agenda read: "The director of the Outdoor Recreation Department wants to offer gay-oriented programs at the Yawaca Outdoor Centre." There was an undercurrent of excitement at the office—this was the first time this issue had been addressed at a YWCA anywhere in the country. What would the reaction be on a national level? Some people wished me luck and a few shunned me.

Some of my lesbian colleagues felt they could not support me, saying they wanted to remain anonymous. I assured them that I would not reveal any names. This was my own little battle and I was ready to lose my job if necessary.

The director of social services, Arlene, approached me and offered to prepare me for this historic meeting. She would ask me the questions the members of the board were likely to pose, and together we would prepare the answers. We decided that I should dress very conservatively and put on a skirt even though I had not worn one for years. I thought, "Well, whatever it takes!"

When the board convened, the president explained the meeting's agenda. Every member of the board was quiet. Then one of them said, "You mean lesbian women?" and the answer was, "Yes." Minutes passed and the room remained silent and the atmosphere palpably tense and cold. It seemed that no one wanted to begin. Perspiration dripped down my back. Finally, a woman spoke. She said, "I have been a board member for many years and I've never heard anyone discuss this subject. It's about time we do." The tension in the room eased.

When I was invited to speak, I referred to the YWCA's mandate and stated objective—to take care of minority groups. With a membership of over 5,000 women in Vancouver, we could estimate that 10 percent, or over 500 YWCA members, were lesbian women.

The board wanted to know more about lesbianism and the implications of becoming involved in gay issues. They decided to form a committee to look into what was available in the community for this specific minority group. Guest speakers were invited to address the subject, and at one of these meetings Dr. P., a very well-known Vancouver psychiatrist, spoke. I had heard her speak before and recalled being very impressed, thinking that if I ever wanted a therapist, I would choose her.

Dr. P. was seated right next to me at the table. She whispered to me, "So you are the trouble-maker." I confirmed it. At the end of the meeting, as Dr. P. walked toward the elevator, I ran after her and asked if she could come into my office for a moment. I wanted therapy, and I wanted this doctor. I explained that I had never undergone therapy in my life and asked her if she would be willing to see me. She asked me a few questions about my childhood and what I thought my issues were, and promised to call me the next day. She did, and soon I started therapy at her office.

The YWCA finally did offer workshops for lesbian women. Our committee had made preparations to provide answers to the press in case they published anything about the workshops. They did, but due in part to our willingness to discuss the issue, everything went smoothly and there was no outcry or backlash. Soon all of the workshops for lesbian women at the centre were fully booked and had long waiting lists.

At the National YWCA Conference in Victoria, B.C., this matter was put on the emergency agenda. Although it was very difficult for some of the rural YWCAs in the country to come to grips with the subject, it was now out in the open and people were trying to deal with it as best as they could.

On my 38th birthday I was laid off from my job with the YWCA. My position was eliminated and the $90,000 I had raised during a capital campaign to renovate the outdoor centre was used instead for other special projects. Hoping that the YWCA would continue the outdoor programs at a later date, I asked to work without pay for several weeks so I could organize the centre and my files and slides in such a way that anyone could restart it again quickly. The management team agreed, but the Yawaca Outdoor Centre never reopened.

For some time I had been feeling it was time to move on, so I was not resentful about losing my job. However, it was a real shame to let the programs disappear—their benefits were so apparent. The centre had been running at full occupancy; the rentals to school groups in the off-season were doing well; we had received grants for special programs and were running no deficits. The cabins at the centre were old but in good condition, as they were cleaned and painted by the kids, counsellors, and volunteers at the end of each summer season. There were new mattresses on all the beds, new curtains in all the windows, the arts and crafts barn was a joy to work in, and fundraising efforts had brought in sufficient money to build a new hall. To this day, I think that the directors and the board of the YWCA had no idea how important these programs were. Closing the centre was an unfortunate mistake on their part.

I was also informed that the Vancouver Outdoor Club for Women had to fold. I had poured over three years of volunteer time into this club, and I told the YWCA management that I was unwilling to let it collapse. The club now had enough leaders, members, and assets to continue without the YWCA. We would find another location and carry on. There was some bickering, and it was strongly suggested that the club's assets ($3,500 plus equipment) belonged to the YWCA, but I stood my ground and insisted that they belonged to the members of the club.

The Outdoor Club for Women created its own volunteer board and continued its meetings and many activities from a co-operative housing building in East Vancouver. The club celebrated its 25th anniversary in October 2004. This shows again that when something with real meaning and tangible value is created, it will last.

Twenty-One

During my tenure at the YWCA, Martine sent me a letter from the South of France announcing her impending visit to North America. She had been following a guru by the name of Osho, or Bhagavan Rashnese, and planned to attend a retreat at his ashram in Antelope, Oregon. She thought it would be a wonderful opportunity for us to reconnect, and asked if I would be willing to drive to the ashram for a visit. Her parents had already warned me about her joining a "cult." They were unhappy about it, but had reached the conclusion that there was nothing they could do about it.

I called the Rashnese Organization in Vancouver and asked if visiting my friend at the Antelope ashram would be all right. I was assured that there would be no problem and that I was sure to enjoy my visit. I had no idea who this guru was and got some books from the library to familiarize myself with his teachings. While reading the books, I concluded that I did not understand much of what this was all about, but if Martine was happy, I was happy for her. Who was I to judge? I certainly did not appreciate it when people told me how to live my life. When I told my friends in the outdoor club that I was heading to visit the ashram, they taunted me mercilessly about disappearing and joining a cult, joking that I would surely be brainwashed. Despite the light-hearted jibes, my friends expressed honest concern for me, and wondered what to do in the event that I did not return in several weeks. I gave them my itinerary and assured them they could come to the ashram and forcibly bring me back if I did not return on my own within two weeks.

Martine had informed me that Bhagavan devotees all wore a type of orange outfit in the ashram. I happened to have a burgundy T-shirt and pants that I planned to wear in order to show my support, even if I didn't understand what she was doing.

Because my car was an old clunker, it took me two full days to get to the small village of Antelope. My first personal exposure to the devotees occurred when I met several of them running the gas station in the village. They gave me directions to the ashram. I was told to follow a dirt road for about 13 miles, but after driving for some time I could see nothing resembling an ashram. I saw no buildings, only desert. A few times I wondered if I should return to Antelope and check to make sure that I was on the correct road. Then, suddenly, I saw buildings, an airstrip with two planes, thousands of blue tents on wooden platforms, a large entrance, and lots of buses. Thousands of people were walking about. Everything looked very new, polished, and organized. It was like watching a movie, jumping right from the stark desert into a compact, well-functioning, autonomous little town. I parked my car near a huge tent with a sign announcing "Information," and went inside to find out how to locate Martine.

The woman who received me told me in a friendly voice that I needed to pay $660 US to enter the compound. I told her I was not there to attend a retreat; I simply wanted to find my friend from France and have coffee with her. The devotee told me that it was not possible to get in without paying. I asked her if someone could go and get Martine for me, or perhaps leave her a message to let her know I was at the entrance of the ashram. She informed me that was not possible either. Then I told her I had been assured by their Vancouver branch that visiting my friend would not be a problem, and that I had just spent two days driving to get there. She was not sympathetic; neither was she willing to see if Martine was even at the ashram. In fact, she was not receptive to anything I proposed. I stayed where I was and tried to think of any idea that might persuade this devotee to help me find Martine. I certainly was not going to pay the money she demanded. However, she made it clear that she was finished with me and focused her attention on someone else.

Suddenly, there was a commotion outside and everyone ran from the tent to the main road. I followed. A line of white Rolls Royces without any passengers drove past. Apparently Bhagavan was sitting in one of them, but I did not wait to see him. I decided to seize this opportunity to go and look for Martine myself before I headed back home. I turned and walked through the entrance to the compound while everyone around me strained to catch a glimpse of the guru.

I ventured into the campsite area and asked around for Martine. I visited the restaurants, the retreat areas, and the stores, all without any luck. I had no trouble boarding the brand new buses and touring around the compound. Everything seemed newly built. My set of burgundy clothes came in handy and helped to camouflage me, and my long shirtsleeves disguised the fact that I lacked one of the coloured wristbands everyone else was wearing. Although I was getting hungry, I was not willing to buy any food as I was afraid of being discovered as a trespasser. And frankly, the behaviour of the people around me seemed so overly excited and lovey-dovey that I wondered if they were putting something in the food.

It was now several hours since I'd slipped in and no one seemed to be taking any notice of me. I became a little bolder and decided to return to my car through the dried-out ditch—a pathway I'd noticed when I parked. Once there I ate some leftover peanut butter sandwiches. My energy renewed, I decided to go back into the ashram through the ditch and look for Martine one last time before heading home.

Back inside, I looked around until dark, watching people dance and sing and overhearing conversations I did not really understand, while I continued searching for my friend. When I got back to the car, I was too tired to drive and fell asleep on the back seat.

The following morning, I was awake very early. I walked back into the compound through the main entrance as no one was in the information office. Again, no one paid any attention to me. I saw that many people were already up and walking in one direction and I joined the crowd. We finally arrived at a large hall. It had thick pillars supporting a roof with a small open platform constructed beneath it. There were no walls, but it had a large wooden floor. Suddenly, everyone flashed their wristbands and removed their shoes; these were deposited in open sheds, where bags and other personal belongings were also being secured. For-tunately, there were too many people hovering around for me to be noticed. I quickly took off my own shoes, pushed them into a bush nearby, and followed the crowd into the hall, thus avoiding the checkpoint.

Hundreds of people were sitting on the floor and swaying to loud, unfamiliar music that poured from speakers set up at each corner of the stage. All of the devotees faced the stage and the large, empty guru's chair at its centre.

Still frantic to locate my friend, I looked around the hall. Above us on the open platform men in uniform with machine guns paraded back and forth while they scrutinized the desert. This did not give me a safe feeling. What where these people afraid of? Why did they have to defend themselves?

I had just made up my mind to leave when Bhagavan came in and sat down on the stage. The music stopped and everything became still. People settled into their meditation posture and closed their eyes. Bhagavan looked like his pictures: tall, wear-ing a long beard and a woolen hat. I had never seen an Indian man like him. His eyes seemed unusually large and very dark and his gestures were slow. I felt tempted to be at ease but stayed on my guard. I was curious about what he was going to say.

After sitting there for about an hour without saying any-thing, Bhagavan arose and left the stage. Now everyone went berserk. Some people rolled around on the floor, while others danced and sang. I got up and walked out of the hall. I just didn't know what to make of these people's behaviour and wondered if it was perhaps for the best that I didn't find Martine after all. After I retrieved my shoes from the bushes, I bumped into the woman who had refused to let me in without paying. She recog-nized me and gave me a big smile. She said, "Ah, you signed up after all." I responded, "No, actually, I didn't." Her face went sour. She grabbed the portable radio she was wearing and called in the "Peace Police."

Within a minute a Jeep pulled up and four Peace Police of-ficers jumped out and grabbed me by the arm. I turned to them and said twice, "Don't you dare touch me," pulling myself free. I told them I could get into their Jeep without any help, thank you, and I would leave immediately of my own accord. They drove me to my car and proceeded to follow me all the way down the main road into the town of Antelope. I drove home and called my friends to inform them of my safe return. I still did not know what to make of this ordeal.

Several days after my return home, Martine called to ask me why I hadn't shown up. I gave her a quick overview of my visit, but we couldn't determine why I hadn't been able to find her. I asked her why the guru owned so many Rolls Royces that were driven around empty. Osho, she said, was trying to point out that money is not important to him. To me this seemed a contradiction—parading expensive cars seemed like flaunting wealth, not denying it. I told her I didn't get it and probably never would. I felt rather sorry for people who needed to go to such extremes while there was so much poverty in this world.

Martine was sorry that I hadn't found her and suggested that I drive to Portland to meet her there, but I told her that if she really wanted to see me, she would have to come to Vancouver.

Twenty-Two

When I began my therapy work with Dr. P., I explained to her that I often felt troubled by my quick temper and impatience, and that I didn't feel right in my skin. I wanted to understand the parts of my behaviour I didn't like. I desperately wanted to get over these hurdles and get on with my life. I felt that Dr. P. was the right therapist for me. Together we explored my childhood traumas. I enjoyed her directness and how hard she made me work. After every session I walked away with new insight and between sessions I pondered the things we talked about. I started to put her suggestions into practice, trying to place distance between myself and things that made me upset. I began to listen more before reacting. I bought an answering machine and waited before returning calls from my mother and other family members. Contact with them made me more upset than I had realized, and that feeling was carried into my daily life and work.

After working with Dr. P. for several months, I was beginning to understand the things that troubled me much better, but my understanding didn't bring out any feelings. I didn't cry or fall apart. My new insight was all coming from my head and not from my heart. It was difficult for me to express and to feel my feelings at the same time; it was as if a huge wall existed between my logical thinking and my emotions. I was experienced in going into survival mode by hiding my hurt and emotions, and I could not remember when I had cried last. My whole body felt uneasy and tense. I wanted to change this; I wanted my heart to become involved and to soften my total being.

Then I heard about Day House—a special seven-week-long group therapy program. Run by Dr. Knobloch, a well-known psychiatrist, Day House was part of the University of British Columbia psychiatry program. Although the thought of group therapy scared me, I wanted to give it a try, and asked Dr. P. to refer me to the therapy group. Dr. P. supported my request and made me promise to complete the program, give it all I had, and return to see her afterward.

It took a great deal of effort to get into Day House. To be accepted, I was provided with a long list of questions, the answers to which were carefully examined by the therapists at Day House. I had to explain what I thought my problems were, what effect they had on me and the people around me, and what I hoped to accomplish in the therapy. I was asked many details about my family history.

As I sat on the beach working on one of these questions, I started thinking and writing about my sister. My tears began to flow. I simply could not stop them. It was clear to me after all these years how much I still missed Willie.

Writing about my father and mother provoked a lot of anger that only served to strengthen my determination to join this program. If I passed the first stage of approval after mailing in my questionnaire, I would talk to one of the therapists, who would examine my file in my presence. If all went well, I would be invited to present myself to the group of 24 participants taking part in the program already underway.

It was not easy to stand in front of a group of 24 participants and six therapists and answer their questions. They wanted to be certain I was ready to do the necessary work, that I could be trusted, that I would be supportive of the others, and also that I was willing to follow the program rules, some of which were difficult to understand at the time.

I agreed that I would not look for a job until after I had completed the program. I was asked how much I had saved in order to attend the program and take care of my other expenses, and what I planned to do until a space became available, as there was a waiting list. I told the group that I had plans to undertake an extended kayaking trip until there was space available in the group.

The entire group voted to approve me for the program. If certain participants had not voted for me, they would have had to stand up and voice their concerns. At this point the therapists had no votes in this process; it was entirely up to the group participants to vote me in or out.

Once I was accepted, I had to read a binder full of suggestions and stories from people who had completed the program and were willing to share their experiences with the newcomers. One thing I knew for sure: this program was not going to be easy. We were not allowed to meditate, nor to take any painkillers. Socializing was forbidden. We could not work, take drugs, or drink alcohol. We had to commit to total honesty, and to immerse ourselves completely in the program, attending every day for seven weeks from early morning until late afternoon or into the evening. All the meals would be prepared by our group and eaten at Day House. There were four "family groups" of six people and a group therapist. Off and on we would work in our family or in the large group, which was normally led by Dr. Knobloch himself. One suggestion in the binder left behind by a previous graduate stood out for me: it said whenever something made you feel uncomfortable, to have a good look at it, maybe it was a sign that work was needed on that issue. I would follow this advice several times when I was in the Day House program.

Twenty-Three

I loved ocean kayaking and decided to go touring for some time before I began the Day House program. For many years I had been busy with my job and unable to take time off during the summer months. My recent five-year-long relationship with Karen had ended, and for this reason, as well, it was time for some soul-searching away from everything. I wanted to kayak to all the places I could think of on B.C.'s coast, including the hidden spots my kayaking friends had been talking about for years.

I counted on being away during the spring, summer, and fall, and mapped out the areas I would attempt to cover. Friends expressed interest in joining me at various stages but otherwise I would be alone. Safety wise, it was perhaps not the best idea to take off ocean kayaking by myself, but I wanted to. On numerous occasions I had gone on hiking and kayaking trips by myself and had enjoyed the solitude. Even as a very young child, I would wander off into the polders, where I climbed the fruit trees and hid until my parents became angry as they tried to find me. I also enjoyed taking calculated risks and being dependent on no one but myself.

To strike out on my own on this adventure would take much preparation. I had to be confident of my kayaking skills, and every piece of equipment I carried would be extremely important to my survival. I had an older, 17-foot, Sea Otter kayak. Slow but sturdy, it could carry about 200 pounds of gear in addition to its passenger. I had a full wetsuit for bad weather and the long crossings between islands. My belongings were stored in three long, watertight olive barrels that I'd found at a grocery store for $1.50 each. One contained my sleeping bag, one held my clothes, and one stored all my food. The hatch behind my seat held an emergency kit, cooking pots, a stove, tent, water bag, and daily meals and snacks. On top of the kayak I carried fishing gear, my water bottle, some food, and a map and compass.

I departed, pretending to carry all I owned and leaving nothing behind. My first visit was to some of the San Juan Islands on the Washington coast in the USA; I then paddled back into Canada toward the Strait of Georgia and the Gulf Islands, territory with which I was quite familiar.

By the time I re-entered Canadian waters I was confident that all my gear was in good working order and I had all the basic provisions I needed. I journeyed north toward Nanaimo on the east coast of Vancouver Island, protected by the Gulf Islands to the east. The Strait of Georgia can be rough and hazardous past Gabriola Island, so I opted to drive from Nanaimo west across Vancouver Island to Port Alberni, there to paddle the Broken Islands.

I would be paddling the islands with Penny, my classmate from Capilano College. She was hoping to join me on my journey for a few weeks here and there depending on her work schedule. She was working as a kayak instructor and was an experienced outdoorswoman. Although she was much younger than me, that didn't bother either of us. Our temperaments suited each other. We talked very little, yet worked well together because we knew each other's strengths and weaknesses. We each liked to go to bed as soon as darkness set in, and we were both very early risers. Each day we arose while it was still dark and were well on our way when daylight broke. In the early morning the ocean was often very smooth and still, providing us with excellent opportunities to undertake long crossings on open water. I loved this peaceful time at the break of dawn.

The Broken Islands, called the Mecca for sea kayakers, are located on the west coast of Vancouver Island in Barkley Sound. Most of the small islands lie in sheltered waters with the open ocean nearby. Some of the outer islands are more exposed—we planned to paddle around them to watch the sea lions. We encountered some pretty rough water and lots of rain. We were drenched when we finally found a little cabin for shelter on Clarke Island, where we rested for a few days and dried our gear. We left the

Broken Islands with a plan to meet up again several weeks later, farther up the coast.

In the meantime, I headed to Hornby Island and then to Denman Island, where I visited some friends and explored the area with my little boat. The currents can be tricky here, so it took a bit of planning to catch a current that would help push me in the direction I wanted. I had paddled the waters around Hornby several times before and enjoyed being back. This small beautiful island with its lovely sandy beaches has a large artist community and a wonderful bakery. So before I left, I loaded up with several loaves of delicious breads—a real treat on this adventure.

Penny met up with me again and we headed north to Clayoquot Sound to see Hot Springs Cove and the grey whales. While I was walking along the beach one day, a whale suddenly came up for air so close to me that I was really frightened for a moment. I thought it might land right on the shore! We camped on empty white beaches and observed lots of sea lions and birds in the area.

We were disappointed to see the amount of garbage that had washed up on shore, and left behind by the many people who visited Hot Spring Cove in their motorboats. We spent several days cleaning and burning their picnic leftovers. We hoped that when people saw the clean beach they would keep it that way, at least for a little while. Why boaters left behind such pollution in the very places they enjoyed visiting for their pristine beauty was a real mystery to us.

Our food was packed in such a way that we generated very little garbage. Everything was stored in reusable plastic bags and containers. Most of our food was dried, and we either caught fresh fish ourselves or bought it from the fishermen on the water, who often refused to take our money. If they stayed around long enough we offered to cook for them, but they sometimes cooked for us too, just to have some company.

A surprising number of fishermen did not know how to read their charts with a compass; most of them relied on their computerized equipment. When we asked them what they would do if their gadgets failed, they just laughed. When we offered to teach them to navigate, they laughed even harder. Sometimes we hitched a ride with them when the weather was too rough for our small boats. We helped them clean the fish they caught and watched them drink beer. Some had a habit of throwing their empty beer cans overboard and we begged them not to do so. When we offered to carry the cans with us, they appeared to listen, but we never knew if they threw them in the ocean again after we had left.

Because we had both already been farther north up the coast to Nootka Sound, we headed for Telegraph Cove and took several weeks to paddle the area. When a pod of six orcas came to feed on salmon at Robson Bight in the Johnstone Strait, we heard them coming from a long distance. We stopped paddling to watch quietly, hoping they would head toward the shore where we knew they liked to rub on the rocks and stones. And they did. They rolled over and around, massaging their enormous bodies on the rough, craggy stones. There were no other boats in sight and the orcas stayed, playing and feeding, for quite some time. When they eventually swam off, we left as well, as the favouring currents were strong. We landed on one of the nearby islands to camp for the night.

We passed many islands, visited some abandoned Indian fishing villages and discovered some beautiful old totem poles. The fishing was spectacular. We caught many salmon and rock cod while trolling behind the kayaks, and trapped some crab as well. We saw lots of oysters but wouldn't eat them because we had forgotten to check the warning bulletins and weren't sure whether they were edible. On one small island we counted 21 bald eagles perched in the trees. We paddled Knight Inlet and then Kingcome Inlet in Queen Charlotte Strait.

On Penny's last trip of the summer, we headed for Kyuquot Sound on the west coast of Vancouver Island to visit the Bunsby Islands. We planned to paddle 5.5 miles of exposed, open water along the rugged coastline. By then we were pretty good at estimating the weather conditions for the day, and often checked with the fishermen to get the forecasts. That day, we were confident we had anticipated the weather correctly.

Unfortunately, we badly misjudged the conditions. In no time, the wind was howling, whipping the ocean waves into a frenzy. The rain fell so heavily we had little visibility, and the tide was against us. There were no fishing boats in sight. We spent several hours trying to land but it was just too dangerous. We had to keep far enough away from shore to stay out of the biggest waves and their dangerous backwash. We needed to attack each wave exactly the right way to keep from capsizing, and then redirect our kayaks—stroking, redirecting, and stroking, over and over.

The waves were huge and unpredictable. Ahead of me, I caught glimpses of Penny as she courageously paddled between them. She signaled now and then that it was impossible to land. She then gave me a signal to turn around, which was extremely difficult to do in such rough water; adding to the difficulty, my kayak didn't have a rudder. I saw her succeed, but I was having serious trouble myself. Over and over the waves were hitting me hard. Which was the right one to turn into? I was singularly focused on approaching each wave the correct way. I had no time to think of anything else, scarcely even to be afraid. When a wave hit, it was impossible to stay above water, and it took all my strength to pull myself through the crashing crests. Each wave completely immersed me in the icy water, leaving little time to recover and get my bearings before the next wave made its onslaught. At times some waves seemed to come at me from every direction at once. But each time I gasped for another breath of air and pulled myself through. And each time I pulled through, I was surprised that I hadn't dumped. My boat felt like a cork bobbing violently to and fro. My full wetsuit was my saviour; in addition to warmth it gave me a small measure of extra confidence.

By the time I finally succeeded in turning my boat I was utterly exhausted. I had been on my kayak trip for over three months now, and I was not only strong, I knew how to save my strength for endurance. On this day, though, my boat was tossed so wildly by the turbulent waves, wind, and tide that I made almost no headway even though I paddled furiously. It took every ounce of my strength just to keep afloat.

Penny was no longer visible and I had no idea whether she had capsized. My energy was depleted and I knew I couldn't hold out much longer. I was now in pure survival mode; I could sense the presence of death. Finally, I could no longer go on, and accepted my fate graciously. I let go. My body relaxed and I felt a strange peace.

Then, at that precise moment of my acceptance and letting go, I watched my arms move as they continued to paddle—I knew they were mine but somehow they moved by a different energy. I was there and not there, but I was at peace. I felt that a presence—a force or power—had taken over the situation, taken over my life. I wasn't aware how long this went on—time had ceased to exist.

Suddenly, I noticed Penny's hat appear above a wave. That could only mean that she was still in her boat, too. I also saw a small plane flying above us; it circled around a few times and left. A little later, the same plane returned and I knew the pilot was keeping an eye on us.

Finally, Penny and I were slowly able to paddle back into the small harbour of Kyuquot. A fisherman felt sorry for us, drenched to our bones and too exhausted to pitch our tent, and offered us a stay in a little house he owned near the entrance of the harbour. We prepared ourselves some hot soup and fell asleep without saying much. We were safe and that was all that mattered.

The next day I was unable to explain to Penny what had happened at that critical moment on the ocean. How could I explain something I did not understand myself? I did, however, remember a time when this had happened before, when my father had nearly beaten me to death. I could still remember that moment of accepting death's inevitability, the moment all the fighting and resistance ended, leaving nothing but acceptance and a total peace. In each case I completely lost any awareness of my body. I could see it but not feel it. It would take me many years to find an explanation.

The storm raged for several days. We were cozy and warm and used the time to rest and eat and repair our gear. Then, suddenly, the skies cleared and the winds calmed, as though nothing had happened.

The fisherman who had offered us the little house invited us to join him and his brother fishing near the Bunsby Islands, the spot where we were heading a few days earlier, and we accepted. We saw many sea lions and caught lots of fish. We celebrated our catch with a salmon dinner with their families, who barbecued the fish in aluminum foil with brown sugar and cognac. It was delicious.

On the long paddle back through quiet, safe waters from the small village of Kyuquot toward Fair Harbour where our car was parked, we saw a herd of deer swimming crossing the inlet. It was a peculiar sight to watch their little heads bobbing along, almost unidentifiable until we got closer. For a time we wondered if we had stumbled on some mysterious unknown sea creatures.

When Penny left to go back to work, I journeyed on, paddling for a few more weeks by myself and trying to absorb what had happened during my very close call. Perhaps, after all, I would die when I was supposed to, and this was not my time. But I knew there was something more to my experience, something that my brain was just not able to comprehend.

Twenty-Four

Next, I met with my friend Joy from Vancouver and together we went to Victoria to meet two more women kayakers. We had heard they also wanted to kayak the Queen Charlotte Islands and hoped the four of us could travel together. They were fun women and experienced kayakers. Gail was a single mother who needed a break from her two children; Alex, also from Vancouver, was an avid outdoorswoman. We studied the navigation chart and planned our gear and food for a one-month trip. Within an hour we were organized. Gail decided to paddle a double kayak for safety reasons, in case one of us became ill and we needed to pair up. We could then tow the empty kayak. The double boat also allowed us to take more fresh food and a few bottles of wine. We would paddle together for a few days around Quadra Island to get to know each other a little, and if everything went well we would meet up again at the ferry terminal in Port Hardy. From there we would go together to the Queen Charlotte Islands.

Our time on Quadra was very pleasant and we all felt compatible. We were all quite excited when we met at the Port Hardy ferry terminal. At that time very few people were undertaking this kind of adventure, and we were the only women moving boats onto the ferry. As soon as the ferry disembarked and our gear was stowed, we headed for the bar to talk more about what each one of us expected from the trip. We shared some of our habits, likes, and dislikes and exchanged life stories so that we would have an idea of whom we were travelling with. It was very important for us to know the others' strengths and weaknesses because we would depend on one another day and night.

Looking back, I now realize it was our long conversation on the ferry that cemented the success of our trip. Gail was dreaming about not having to get up and make breakfast every morning, because she did that every day for her children. Alex, like Joy and I, was an early riser and the three of us had no trouble getting breakfast and doing early weather checks. We agreed that Gail would be exempt from preparing breakfast during the whole trip.

My request of the other women was for time alone on shore to meditate and get away from everyone without having them think I was upset. I explained to them that I was preparing to join a seven-week-long therapy program upon my return to deal with some of my childhood issues, and I needed to reflect and prepare for that. I also shared that I had just broken up with my partner of five years and might shed some tears at times. Alex and Joy had no special requests; they were just looking forward to an adventurous trip.

When we arrived at the Queen Charlottes, we rented a truck to take us, our boats, and gear to our departure point at the end of the inlet at Moresby Camp.

About a century ago, there were numerous Haida villages on this route, and we saw many beautiful unpainted Haida totem poles at the land's edge. Most of them were located on North Moresby Island at Skedans Point, on Louise Island, and on Anthony Island on South Moresby. Some were still standing,

Kayaking the Queen Charlotte Islands 1983

but many lay half-rotten on the ground, covered with soft moss. Under the trees we saw hundreds of old graves and noticed a few moss-covered skulls scattered about.

The area had a large sea lion population and so much bull kelp that we were able to stabilize the kayaks and take snack breaks while holding onto it. While we slowly made our way down the coast, we came across more human skulls and totem poles so old they were falling apart and slowly becoming part of the soil.

Close to Reef Island, I felt something happening inside of me. By now, I had been on the water for more than five months, tuned in with nature, the space around me, and the weather. Being so vulnerable to the environment had demanded intense focus and attention at all times—in fact, my life had depended on it. I had spent many hours a day meditating while I paddled my small boat, but now, somehow, something had changed. I noticed that it was becoming increasingly easier for me to predict the weather during the day. It was as if I could feel the atmospheric pressure changes in the air. As we left the island, I suddenly realized that I could feel the energy of the trees, as though I had become one with them. I felt as though I was living on a different level of energy, one that corresponded with the life force of the trees. Although I was aware of what was happening to me, I was unwilling to share it with my friends—I worried they might suggest it was time for me to go home. During our long days of silent paddling, I pondered about this profound experience.

On our way to Hot Spring Island the waves were massive and powerful, and we were pushed through the channel at a very high speed. It was difficult to keep a straight course. Immediately after we passed a very small island, Gail's kayak was suddenly thrust into one of the bays and then spun around by the currents. The rest of us were moving so fast that it was impossible to stop or go after her. As soon as Alex, Joy, and I were out of danger, we hugged the island's shoreline and waited. It was impossible to turn around. We discussed Gail's options and fervently hoped she would be able to get back into the current that had pushed the rest of us away from her. At last we saw her racing around the corner. Upon inspection of her kayak, we discovered that the bow, including the front seat area, was too light. Extra weight was put into her bow to stabilize the craft for surfing in the future. We all sighed with relief and headed for Hot Spring Island, the spot from which many kayakers make their way back up north through Darwin Sound.

Hot Spring Island had an area where hot water flowed into two man-made bathtubs inside a shed that provided some privacy, as well as several smaller outdoor pools and one large pool next to the ocean. Each had a different temperature; the indoor bathtubs were the closest to the spring and were the hottest. All the hot water from the tubs and smaller pools eventually flowed into the large pool before it slowly seeped into the ocean. The large hot pool had spectacular ocean and mountain views, and was separated from the ocean by a cement wall on which candles were lit at night. It was the area where kayakers, fishermen, and natives gathered to socialize at any time of the day or night. If you wanted company, this was where you went. If you didn't feel like cooking, you just took something from your stash and joined someone making a meal on the fire that always burned there. Breakfasts always included salal berry pancakes. The island was full of salal bushes ripe with the most delicious, large, sweet, dark blue berries. By midday, fishermen would come by and drop off some of their morning catch so we could prepare it for our communal meal that night.

While we rested on Hot Spring Island, I left the camp one day for some solitude. The day was warm, and after several hours of exploring I fell asleep on the beach. When I woke up a wonderful lunch of sandwiches made from freshly baked bread had been placed right next to me. My friends had quietly followed me and surprised me. You cannot imagine how wonderful fresh bread tastes after you have been on the ocean for several weeks. I can still taste them—the bread and the memory.

The day arrived that we had to cross Juan Perez Channel to get to Section Cove on Burnaby Island. We got up at four in the morning and, a little nervous, moved fast to break camp and get into our boats. We had received a forecast of good weather from a fishing boat the night before and had prepared as much as possible before going to bed. This area, especially, was known for its strong and sudden winds.

It was still somewhat dark when we left; I recall with clarity how beautiful the early morning sunrise was. After paddling for about five hours, we started to feel safer under an ever-brightening sky. We arrived at Newberry Point for lunch, but we still had hours of paddling ahead of us. Then the weather changed. It began to rain, but the wind dropped and the tide was with us. We were so tired that everything began to seem silly. Joy kept saying, "We're nearly there. You see that tree there in the distance? That's where we're going," as we looked at a million trees in the forest ahead of us. We thought it was very funny and laughed hysterically for a long time. We were more than ready to get out of our kayaks for the day.

We finally landed, set up camp, and got a fire going with the dry kindling we had brought along from Hot Spring Island.

The tides in the Queen Charlotte Islands flow north and ebb south. We had to be acutely aware of the tides—they could easily ruin our day if we left at the wrong time. There was no use paddling when the tide was against us. Navigating through the narrows was a little tricky because the tide was so low. But hitting a high tide could be catastrophic—they could reach up to 12 knots or stronger, far too swift for a small kayak. So there were times that we simply had to get out of the boats and stay put for hours while we waited for the tide to change. We would usually take off at a slack tide during the times the tides were changing and going in the direction of our course. We knew we had to go through Burnaby Strait at low tide.

The scenery was absolutely spectacular. The majestic profile of Yatza Mountain dominated the sky as we were slowly pushed through the narrows without much paddling. We picked up a few crabs on the way; there were so many that we chose only very large ones, and had a feast on our arrival at Dolomite Narrows.

We spent a few nights in a cabin at Smithe Point, while during the day we explored the Swan and Bolkus Islands. These are a range of very beautiful, small islands with rocky beaches and breeding grounds for many different species of birds. The Queen Charlotte Islands are the native home of many bald eagles, falcons, ravens, oystercatchers, puffins, cormorants, pigeon guillemots, ancient murrelets, cassins auklets, and albatrosses, just to name a few.

We knew that we had some very serious paddling to do in the upcoming days. We would be exposed to some open ocean and areas known for strong winds. I had been keeping track of the information that other kayakers and fishermen had shared with us, and my chart had many important notes written all over it indicating weather patterns, good spots to land and camp if necessary, where to find fresh water, good fishing spots, bear spotting, sites of abandoned Indian villages, and many other points of interest.

We decided to cross to the Copper Islands, stay the night, cross over Skincuttle Inlet and head to Deluge Point. At once the weather changed rapidly, tossing us into gigantic, unpredictable waves. It was very difficult to land and we all capsized, one after the other, near East Copper Island. At least our gear had been stored well and nothing floated away or got lost. Trying to get back into the boats after capsizing wasn't practical among the huge waves; we were too close to shore anyway. We just held on to the boats; luckily we were being pushed toward the shore. I stayed in the water and watched my friends as they were thrown up onto a rocky beach covered with tree debris. It was not easy to get out of the water and onto shore, but we had no option other than to attempt to climb out. None of us panicked. We had each been able to hold on to our paddles, boats and gear, and with my wetsuit on I was able to help the others without getting too chilled.

Nothing was more comforting than a hot cup of tea or soup after such an experience. Our campsite was very uncomfortable, but we were too tired to notice, and in any case, we had no alternatives.

The next morning was calm and we moved on immediately after breakfast. We discussed what we could have done differently to prevent capsizing, but concluded it had been inevitable. Having our paddles attached to the boats had been a good idea. My companions were now wishing they all had wetsuits. Now, more than 20 years later, there are very few kayakers who do not wear wetsuits on long trips.

We began to see a good number of bears and had to be careful where we camped. Ideally, we preferred to pitch our tents close to the rivers and fresh drinking water, but now we had to stay farther away from their banks because too many bears lingered at the river mouths, where the fresh river water met the ocean, to catch salmon. We spent the night in the bay near Gona Point. Here we risked losing our food and clothes simply by leaving our containers too close to the ocean. We were tired and certain that our gear was safe. However, as I tucked into my sleeping bag, something did not feel right. I got up again and moved everything higher up behind a large fallen tree. Several days earlier, my kayaking buddies had teased me a little for being overcautious.

The next morning, an extra-high tide had moved in and our boats were floating around loosely, held only by their ropes. The ocean had moved in very close to our tents; storage containers and the spot where we had left everything the previous evening before I moved them were covered with water. It made us a little more humble. During these extreme tides, especially under a full moon, we often had to carry our gear and kayaks a good distance inland from the beaches and ocean. One of us would have to stay behind to watch everything in case it all floated off while we retrieved more gear. It took a great deal of time to carry everything back and forth, but after sitting in our boats most of the day, this task gave us some walking exercise and an opportunity to use a different set of muscles.

Twenty-Five

We had learned of a French woman who lived in Rose Harbour near an old whaling station. With a name like Rose Harbour, we thought there might be a few houses and, perhaps even a small store. It was rumoured that the woman was a doctor, a hermit, who had lived there for eight years after giving up on the world and its material pleasures. Other people thought she had left an unhappy relationship.

Interestingly, many of the people we met who lived in these remote areas had Ph.D. degrees. Why on earth would anyone do all that studying and then disappear from civilization? Most often it was because they craved a simpler lifestyle away from the hustle of big cities. They enjoyed being dependent on themselves as much as possible, living mainly on the fish they caught and produce from their beautiful, extensive vegetable gardens. Everyone possessed a gun to shoot deer and keep the bears away.

When we disembarked in Rose Harbour, we found the French woman in the only cabin there. She was bathing outside in the garden, in a tub heated by a wood fire that burned beneath it. She was not very talkative, but softened up when I addressed her in French and she saw that we were all women. She invited us to come back in the early evening, and she pointed to a safe spot across the channel for us to camp.

We returned later with some food and were invited for tea in her cabin, which was small but comfortable, with lots of books lining the shelves and herbs growing in pots everywhere. She had a small vegetable garden. In her late forties, she was friendly, and at one point she shyly asked if we could leave her some of our books. As much as I love solitude, however, I couldn't imagine being in a place so remote during the winter months. We talked about the history of Rose Harbour and she showed us what was

119

left of the old whaling station. Before we left, she invited us to go fishing the next day. When we joined her the following morning, she caught a large salmon before I even had my hook in the water! Thereupon she informed us that the fishing was over because we had enough for an entire army. That evening we feasted.

Within the next few days a fishing boat came by to pay her a visit and drop off food. The owner of the boat invited us to join him on his trip to Anthony Island. We accepted the invitation and explored the area for several days, especially enjoying Rose Inlet, where we could hike and observe the bears.

It was time to head north again. Half of our trip was over. We had no choice but to take the same route back and endure exposure on the open ocean until we hit Smithe Pt. on Burnaby Island. This time, however, we knew what to expect. We all expressed a sigh of relief when we arrived safely back at Smithe Pt. A few days of rest was in order. It was so much fun being pushed through the Dolomite Narrows into Burnaby Straight. We picked up lots of crab again, returned to soak in the hot pools, then headed into Darwin Sound. Now we were protected from the open ocean but encountered several days of thick fog and drizzly weather. Here and there we came upon a few cabins, some inhabited and some deserted.

After a very long day of paddling into Darwin Sound, we were exhausted and our tempers were short; we had not talked for hours while we endured the work of paddling. We had departed early and, with no real opportunity to leave the boats during the day, were all desperate to relieve ourselves. The fishing had been terrible and we'd caught nothing. By now, the sky was dark and it was still drizzling. The shore was just too soft and wet to set up camp, and it did not feel safe—many bears still roamed around.

Finally we saw a small cove and moved in, hoping we had found a spot that might be suitable for our camp. I was the only one still in a kayak when I noticed what I thought was a large fishing boat anchored in the distance. I told my friends that I would paddle over to get some fish. They discouraged me, saying, "Who cares about fish?" The last thing I really wanted to do was stay one more minute in my kayak. I'd had enough, but somehow I needed to go and have a look at that boat. As I neared, I realized that it did not resemble a fishing boat. Thinking I would just paddle around it and leave again, suddenly I caught a whiff of freshly baked bread. A man came out onto the deck of the boat and waved me closer. I greeted him, we chatted a little, and I mentioned I'd mistaken his boat for a fishing boat and that I wanted to buy some fish. His wife came on deck and greeted me. "Well, we don't have any fish," he said amiably, "but we have some fresh bread and cakes if you're interested, so why don't you come aboard and join us for a few minutes?" If I was interested? I hadn't seen or tasted any fresh bread for weeks.

After I climbed on board, they warned me that the spot we had chosen to stay the night was not a good one because of all the bears that gathered there in the evening. We needed to be extremely careful because a mother and her cubs were roaming around the area. They told me they were missionaries from Nanaimo, and for years they had been visiting workers in the logging camps in the area. They loaded me up with several loaves of fresh bread, some muffins, a pie, a container of homemade jam, and a jar of peaches. I could hardly believe their generosity and burst out in an astonished laugh. They asked if they could join us for a campfire that night and said they would bring more pies.

When I was ready to leave, this kindly couple helped me into my kayak and put the huge paper grocery bag full of goodies on my lap. I laughed all the way back to shore. I was laughing so hard that I could not even talk to my friends when I arrived at the campsite. Still sitting in the kayak, I asked them to guess what was in the bag. When I told them what I'd brought back, they erupted with giggles too, and soon we were all howling.

We made tea and ate almost everything right away. We just could not stop eating. During the feast, I described our benefactors, explaining they would be joining us at our campfire that night. "Ah," they said, "bet they're going to bring their Bibles!" We talked about moving camp because of the bears, but decided instead to keep the fire going all night to ward them off. There wasn't another suitable spot, and we had neither the interest nor the energy to break up camp and get into the kayaks again.

Our missionary friends appeared in their zodiac with two more pies and we had a lovely evening. There was no mention of religion until later when they made a move to leave and asked if they could pray for our safety for that night. We all prayed in thanks for the good food and for our safety.

Bears surrounded the tent throughout the night but none of them bothered us. When I went to relieve myself early the next morning, I encountered a large black bear. The surprise was so sudden and so close to me that I didn't have time to be afraid. I'd forgotten all about them. We broke up camp early and went by the missionaries' boat to thank them before leaving. They invited us all aboard for breakfast and we feasted again on coffee and freshly baked breads. We even had a wonderful fruit salad for desert. I kept contact with this lovely couple for several years later.

After saying our goodbyes, we disappeared into the morning fog, silently paddling on the still, calm water. The fog lifted and some blue sky was beginning to show when suddenly, directly ahead of us, a magnificent orca leaped straight up out of the water and fell back down into the ocean with a huge splash. What a sight! What an enormous body, and with such amazing strength. We left Darwin Sound with wonderful memories.

When we finally returned to Vancouver Island, we agreed that it had been the trip of a lifetime for us. It was time to separate and we were teary-eyed when we said our farewells.

Since I had no idea whether I would ever have a chance to take a long kayaking trip again, I decided to paddle toward Desolation Sound on my own. When I had to break the ice in the rivers to get fresh drinking water, I knew it was time to return home to Vancouver.

Twenty-Six

My kayak trip had prepared me well for the intense group therapy program I was about to undertake. I had taken time to ponder life and examine my priorities. I was now certain that I always needed to be close to nature to find my centre. I had also learned that maintaining a positive attitude worked well for me. My belief was and still is that positive energy is far more powerful than negative energy. That was what kept me going and gave me the courage to try new things and take new risks over and over again. Some failures had to be accepted; they were just a part of life, right? So far, many of my efforts had paid off.

The people taking part in the Day House program came from all walks of life. They included accountants, lawyers, secretaries, students, sales clerks, business people, and a prostitute.

Dr. Knobloch often invited psychologists and psychiatrists to attend the large group sessions he led. However, each one of the guest professionals had to be accepted by our smaller groups before sitting in on those sessions. In the event that they were invited to attend our smaller group sessions, they had to participate in our role-playing, and if at any time one of us felt uncomfortable with one of them, that therapist would be asked to leave. This was our program; we were spilling our guts and we did not want anyone with whom we were uneasy to interfere with our process. Dr. Knobloch explained to these specialists that the participants in this difficult program had the courage to admit that something was not going well in our lives and that we wanted a better quality of life. To us he then added, "Do not think you will float out of this building after graduation and be healed, but you will be able to deal effectively with the normal daily ups and downs of life again."

Each participant in the group was required to do a presentation in front of the large group at some time and to start preparing for it as soon as possible. We had to gather an object from the outside and select a person from the group to play the role of a family member, a lover, a friend, or other person who was involved in our life in a significant way. We were also told to choose an object to represent ourselves. We were to present the items and explain how they related to us.

When it was my turn to go into the "arena," as I came to call it, I chose a small cactus plant to represent myself. The spines meant, "Be careful. Do not come too close and do not hurt me," while the soft inside represented my tender heart, meaning, "I want to trust and love, but I am bruised. Where do I go from here?" For the person who would represent my sister, I brought the same flowers that had been placed in Willie's coffin. Interestingly, I chose the same group participant to represent both my sister and my ex-partner.

Dr. Knobloch had me repeat several times the significance of the small cactus plant I had brought. I could sense he was trying to either have me say something else or provoke my anger, but neither happened. However, when the person representing my father goaded me in many different ways and I remained unresponsive, I knew I had to try to move back in time for it to work. I was given a cloth buffer with which to hit my "father," as long as I did not hit his head. The group members could see that I needed help and encouraged me by yelling, "hit him, hit him hard," until I finally let him have it. While hitting him, something interesting happened. Unconsciously I began shouting at him in Dutch and my voice changed into that of a child's. In the distance, I could hear someone translate—it turned out there was a Dutch-speaking therapist present. I kept striking this man until I was worn out and unable to stand up.

My most elucidating discoveries took place with the person who represented both my sister and my ex-partner. When Dr. Knobloch asked me to close my eyes to meet and talk to my sister again, I broke down and sobbed for a long time. I finally felt the doctor's hand on my shoulder, and he said, "You are still looking for her, aren't you, even with your partners?" I learned that as long as I compared my partner with my sister, our relationship could not survive, since no one could ever live up to my sister. When I was able to look around the room, there was not a dry eye to be seen; everyone else in the group had been grieving their own losses.

Tuesday evenings were "parent" nights. These evenings were very difficult for all the parties involved. If a group member had not spoken to their parent for years and was told to invite that parent, it had to be done no matter where the parent was living. The rest of the group members were to do whatever we could to help the participant extend the invitation. Letters were written and read in front of the group, suggestions were made, and responses were discussed. The parent meetings were heartbreaking, but many breakthroughs occurred. Contact was renewed between estranged family members and participants made a lot of progress. But it also happened that hurtful things were said and bitter arguments erupted. We were well prepared for that and ready to protect one another. Some people could not handle the confrontations and walked out.

I invited my boss from the YWCA to attend a session and she graciously accepted. During our session, she stated her admiration for my integrity and loyalty as an employee, and also my courage and tenacity in standing up for what I believed in. However, she also noted that I had high personal expectations and could be very hard on myself and others, with excessive demands of excellence and standards that were, in some cases, impossible to meet. On several occasions the YWCA secretaries had gone into her office crying after I had been too harsh on them about getting my typing work done. Projecting my high expectations for myself onto others had made many of my relationships difficult.

Because neither of my parents would come from Holland to attend parents' night, I had to commit to visit them after my graduation and ask each of them why they had mistreated me as a child.

One day, I confronted a female participant who had been irritating me for some time, telling her to buzz off for a while. She turned around and said, "Ah. You always want to be in control."

I tried to ignore her. The therapist on duty said, "Who also thinks that Clasina always wants to be in control?" Thirteen people raised their hands, even people I thought liked me. This was a humiliating experience, to say the least.

When something like this came up, the group was required to sit in a circle. Then, whomever was singled out had to walk around the outside of the circle and listen to comments from the people who had raised their hands. I had to listen without speaking or interrupting. It took a long time, and what they said about me was right. The therapist invited me to talk about why I thought I needed to be in control all the time. Instead of thinking silently, I was encouraged to talk out loud as I walked around the circle. In my childhood I'd had so little control over anything in my narrow existence. Not over whether my mother would arrive home on time, not over having enough food in the house, not over what would set my father into a rage, not over losing my sister. Thus, when I was able to wield any type of control, I would cling to it for dear life. I needed to learn that I was no longer a child and did not need to hang on to those external forms of control any longer.

Actually, many people in the group struggled with similar control issues, and each was trying to let go in their own way. When the time was appropriate, group members were encouraged to let go of their control completely. Several members of the group would hold a person down on a mattress and let him or her scream, cry, and fight until they were totally exhausted. These were heart-wrenching times for all of us. Working in this setting and being exposed to the suffering of each individual made our group very close. Some people were not able to handle the pain or the effort, and would either leave the group of their own accord or break one of the rules several times so they were expelled. I had terrible migraines and nightmares, causing me to become afraid to sleep alone in the house. My friend Joy, who had been on my kayaking trip to the Queen Charlotte Islands, moved in for a while and that helped.

Each evening we had to write about our experiences in a journal that we handed in the following day. The therapist would read each night's entries and return them just before we left again.

This allowed the staff to keep track of where we were in our progress. One day I went home with a raging migraine. I could hardly drive on the way home and took two painkillers. The next day I realized that I had to confess to taking the pills. One of the rules was that we were not to mask our pain with medication—we were to face it. I was given 2,000 demerit points and had to write several pages in my journal about my control issues. I was told that it would not take many more "mistakes" before I was kicked out of the program. They were dead serious.

About five weeks into the program, my stomach began acting up. I felt like I was carrying a large piece of heavy steel somewhere in my stomach and it just would not go away. I even had a metal taste in my mouth. When she read about it in my journal, the therapist told me it was a good sign. I was assigned a buddy. I knew what that meant; something was brewing. As I entered a critical time in my healing process the buddy would keep a close eye on me, even follow me to the washroom and sit in front of the door until I came out. After several days my breakthrough came. My "family" therapist asked me to lie down on a mattress and my fellow group members sat next to me on the floor. My therapist asked me to go back to the time my father had nearly beaten me to death. She talked about the kitchen, where it had happened, and what was in the kitchen. She reminded me that my mother had not shown up on time again because she had been with another man and that it was not my fault if the dinner preparations were not quite right. I felt nauseated and began to vomit; I vomited for a long time. It brought me to total exhaustion. I cried for all the times I had not been able to cry in the past. Later on I was told that during this process I had spoken like a seven–year-old; I hadn't even been aware of it. After this session all I wanted to do was sleep. Instead, I was told to clean the windows, inside and out, of every car in the parking lot. Physical work would enable me to process what had just happened. Often we had to wash all the cars, work in the garden, or cook meals after some intense therapy. Once I was absorbed in my task I began to feel more grounded. I was feeling utterly exhausted, but at the same time there was a feeling of lightness and calmness in my body and mind.

At graduation, the rest of the group surrounded each of us one at a time while we let ourselves fall in different directions, trusting that we would be caught and held. Then, as music played, they sang and carried us, swaying, above their heads. We were thrown up into the air three times and then let go. Later on that day, each of us sat in front of the group at a podium and talked about what we had learned and what we would do next in our lives. Each person commented on what was said and then gave their good-bye.

With a great wellspring of new courage, I shared that I was no longer going to seek a job working for someone else. Instead, I was going to start my own business in tourism. I would buy my own minibus and offer tours in Vancouver and the surrounding area. The group assured me that I could do it well, asked me to think about them in hard times and to remember what they had said. They wished me luck. Neither they nor I could know that I would think about them on many occasions when times were rough in the years to come.

Twenty-Seven

Next, I joined a special group called "after-care." Led by a wonderful therapist, this group invited each participant to return for as long as they wished to deal with any setbacks or ongoing problems. I made arrangements to travel to Holland to face my parents, and the after-care therapist helped me to prepare for this visit. It would not be necessary to tell my parents about the program. I was not to confront them in a hostile way, but to focus on getting as much information from them as possible. If they became angry or felt threatened, they might close down and not reveal anything. If I felt anger or resentment rising, I was to take a break and go for a long walk. After my trip, in my after-care group, I would have the opportunity to deal with any residual feelings. I did a lot of role-playing in the group before I got on the plane and headed home to Holland.

Some time passed before I had an opportunity to approach my father alone. One day, as he was reading the newspaper in his favourite armchair, I summoned all my courage and asked him, calmly, why he had mistreated me so badly when I was a child. Without putting the paper down, he responded, "You must have deserved it." I asked, "Was I four years old when you started?" He answered, "No, three, after your brother was born." And I thought, "Ah-ha. I was right all along—my youngest brother is not his son." I said, "Was it because he is not your son?" No answer. I tried again. "The way you beat us up was not normal. Your anger was far out of bounds—more than once you nearly killed me." "So what," he responded dully, hardly flinching and never glancing my way. It was a very short answer, but it was enough for me. His demeanour made it clear that the conversation was over.

My mother did not want to hear any of my questions. "Why take old cows out of the ditch?" she replied. This was an old, well-known Dutch saying, meaning, "Why talk about things that happened so long ago? Leave them in the past where they belong and forget about them." She was not willing to talk and soon it would be time for me to leave. I finally had to push her, telling her that if we could not talk about it now, we would have nothing more to talk about and I would not return home again. When she saw that I was really serious she invited me out for lunch. There, I asked her to tell me about her life as a child, her young adulthood, and what it had been like for her to live with my father while we were growing up.

My mother began to open up. She talked of being abused as a child, her lack of education, of having been sent to live and work at a stranger's farm at the age of eleven, and of the brutal farmer who would not keep his hands off of her. She spoke of not being able to tell anyone because there was no other place for her to go. She could not even go home because the house was already too crowded with her 12 brothers and sisters. She told me about falling in love with my father, how he had been such a good-looking man, and that everyone at the gym club where they met was envious of her good "catch." She revealed that she had become pregnant and they were compelled to get married. She told me about my father sexually abusing her younger sister, who had moved into our house when their mother died at the age of 46. But people just did not talk about things like that in those days.

My mother described what it was like during the war, having to watch as several of her brothers were shot and killed before her eyes. To save his own life, her father was forced to join the SS and provide information to the Germans. He was later deported, but he did survive. I remembered my grandfather very well. I had never liked him. Once, at a family gathering, he handed out five-cent coins to all of my cousins, but he gave me a German coin. Because I didn't know the difference, I headed to the candy store with my money along with everyone else. However, once there, of course I could not buy anything. When I returned home crying, he laughed so hard that I lost all my desire for any candies. I never truly forgave him.

My mother continued, laying bare her feelings about losing two of her children. Afterward life was never the same for her, and because she had no emotional support from my father, she turned to other men for a little attention. After a long time, she looked at me and asked for my forgiveness. She acknowledged that as bad as it was for my father to abuse her, it was even worse that he abused us so badly and that she was unable to protect us. She expressed a wish to be able to turn the clock back.

As I listened, I knew she was not withholding anything, and more importantly, that during my childhood she had not been capable of giving any more than she had given. No, it had not been enough, but what could I do? I began to feel sorry for her inability to leave my father, not even at this stage in her life. I thought about all the good things that had happened in my life. I was pleased that I'd had the good fortune to leave home at the age of 16 and happy that I was on my way to a different and interesting life, especially now that I had graduated from Day House. Yes, I was proud to have come through the Day House program. I had given it all I had and it had been one of the most difficult things I had done in my life, but now I felt strong and was looking forward to life and to starting my own business. I thanked my mother for telling me about her life.

When it was time to leave for Canada, I said goodbye to my father in the kitchen and shook hands with him saying, "What you did to that little child at that time was a terrible thing." They were the last words I spoke to him. He died about a year later.

I returned to Canada and attended a few more sessions at the Day House after–care program. During one of the sessions, some of the group members pushed me to admit that I might have some buried love left for my father. But I could not do it, and finally the therapist explained that it is possible that all love for a parent can be slowly beaten out of a child. It is not that I wanted any harm done to my father; I simply knew that I didn't love him. But I didn't hate him either. I just felt that he was a human being I never knew.

As promised, I returned to see Dr. P. again for several sessions. During one of these sessions, it came out that I had placed a picture of myself at about age nine on the mantelpiece in my living room. The picture was taken in front of the cemetery gate next to the elementary school where I always stood to speak to my sister Willie, and it showed me shyly smiling at the photographer, my face full of so much hope. This picture now evoked so many feelings in me that I would stare at it and cry for long periods, feeling so much compassion for that child. I wanted to protect her, to cover her with the love she so deserved. I cried for the child that was me. My therapist smiled and answered that it was very healthy to cry for that child, because in this way I was re-nurturing myself.

Soon, I also said my goodbyes to Dr. P. She hugged me and said, "You are my success story. Just do not expect from others what you expect from yourself; each person has his or her own potential. You can come back any time you want."

Part II

Twenty-Eight

I started my business on April 1, 1984. I was forty years old. Although it was April Fool's day, this certainly was no joke; I was never more serious. There would be no more looking for a job with my seventh-grade education holding me back, no more chance of being laid off, no more being ordered around. It was something I had dreamed about on my long kayaking trip. I would finally do something I really liked and was very good at, and I was not afraid of putting in long hours.

Energized and motivated from getting through Day House and in possession of a little money left over from my car accident settlement, I was ready. I had never run a business before and had to rely solely on a few school board classes in business, my past experience, and my intuition. I had no office, no typewriter, no fax machine, no photocopier, nor a secretary, but my dear friend Chris had some occasional spare time, and she offered to help me out. I knew vaguely how to form a business plan and had some experience in preparing budgets from my work at the YWCA. The mortgage on my house was too high for the bank to loan me money, so I had to rely on being creative and frugal, and start off small.

Having worked most of my adult life in tourism and outdoor recreation, I decided to mix these skills and offer nature tours in a small, comfortable minibus. No other company in Vancouver was offering anything like it. The work had an element of fun and I needed the money. I was not planning to take any days off and would offer different tours every few days, seven days a week. My thinking was that once customers were interested in these types of tours, they would want to come on more than one while they were in town.

I called the company "Circle Nature Adventures." The word circle implied "to return to where we started from." The logo was a picture of a blue heron taking flight. I loved blue herons and could approach within a few feet of them in my kayak, something no other kayaker I knew could do. A Native Indian once told me it was because in one of my previous lives, I had been a blue heron. Printed on all of my brochures was my motto: "I feel that to enjoy travelling, it's the quality of the experience that's important. It's not just where you go, but how you get there and what you do along the way."

Vancouver is one of the most beautiful cities in the world. I had been exploring the areas in and around the city since my arrival in Canada nine years earlier and had no difficulty finding many options for tour destinations. Part of my research consisted of visiting hotels in town and asking the concierges what they thought of my idea. They were enthusiastic, especially at some of the very large hotels, because I was able to offer tours in English, French, German, and Dutch. It seemed that multilingual guides were available in town, but they were only "step-on guides" on the large buses. The concierges were looking forward to having someone drive as well as guide people. I thought, "Well, if I'm going to gear my business to the large and fancy hotels, I'd better get a first-class minibus." But where would I get the money?

I visited all of the minibus dealers in town and finally took a test drive in a beautiful, cream and burgundy 11-passenger vehicle with luggage space. The seats were burgundy as well. It was so beautiful that I was nervous driving it. I returned to test drive it a few times but I was afraid to ask the price. Finally I could wait no longer. Because I kept returning to test drive that special minibus, the salesman had prepared a sales form and was eager to make the deal. Thinking about my mother made me decide to buy it. She would have said, "If you do it, then do your best and get the best." Finally, I sat down to sign the papers. When I got to the down-payment box, I put down my little Ford Fiesta sitting out in the parking lot. The salesman looked at me and said, "I'm sorry, lady, but I can't do that. It's just not enough." I calmly answered, "Yes, you can, and I want lease payments on the balance." We went in circles for a minute or two, each repeating the same words, and he finally left to look for his boss. He was gone for a very long time. But I knew that dealers do that no matter what you intended to buy. It just gave the impression they were busy calculating, trying to get you the best deal. Sales must not have been good for them lately because he returned smiling with the lease forms.

The cash money I had was spent on designing and printing 15,000 brochures. I could only afford a two-colour brochure, the same colours as my little bus. It had no photographs, but I inserted interesting drawings and used the same lettering I used on the minibus. Everything looked professional and polished. I was well prepared and ready to go.

At that time, I focussed on about 60 hotels in the downtown area. It took me some time to talk to all their front desk people and persuade them to let me display my brochures on their lobby racks. Most racks belonged to a brochure distribution company in town, but I could not afford their monthly payments. However, some hotels had reserved a few spots in those racks for their choice of brochures, and they made a pocket available for mine. Many hotels also carried tour brochures behind the counter at the front desk.

City and Nature Sightseeing, my first mini-bus.

I was about to experience my first major setback. I was not aware that a long and hard battle was forthcoming; one that would require all my accumulated survival skills and perseverance to overcome. It is true that when getting involved in a venture like this, it is often better not to know every detail that lies ahead. Had I known what lay in store, I probably would have gone out seeking a nine-to-five job again.

Very few people signed up for my tours, and my brochures were nowhere to be found when I returned to the hotels two weeks later. I could not understand why people would take all the brochures, yet so few would sign up. All kinds of questions came to mind: perhaps people were not interested in these kinds of tours and preferred doing other things, or perhaps the brochure was not appealing enough or didn't attract as much attention as the flashier ones in the racks. I decided to go by the hotels once a week. The same thing happened: my brochures were gone, but I had no clients.

Out of curiosity—and desperation—I called and left messages for the managers of the hotels where I had left the brochures, but none of them returned my calls. I soon had to reorder brochures, and it put me in a financial bind. Several months went by and making the lease payments on the minibus became difficult. I decided to rent out the top floor of my house and move into the unfinished basement, a space that had no proper walls, insulation, or heat. There was one little room for my bed and a small kitchen. At all times of the day and night I could hear the renters upstairs treading on the hardwood floors, their noisy children, and the sounds of their music and television. Surrounded by constant noise, it was hard to focus and get any sleep. For grocery money, I resorted to tutoring French to schoolchildren.

In addition to resolving my financial hardship, I was determined to discover the reason my business had no clients. Something did not feel right. I started asking questions at the tourist office and the hotels, but was rebuffed with such comments as, "Well, you're just starting off and it takes a while to get known." I understood that very well, but going through thousands of brochures every week did not seem normal, even if my tours did not appeal to visitors.

Then I received a letter from the Motor Carrier Commission telling me to stop offering tours immediately because I had no proper licences. I didn't know licenses were needed. This government agency took care of all the commercial licences for trucks and buses in our area. I went to their offices, asking how to go about getting the proper licences. Instead of an answer, I was told that I needed to be in possession of these licences before I could continue to offer my tours. That meant I was to cease business immediately. I surprised myself by gently saying that I could not afford to stop now and was not willing to do so. I thought, "What can they do anyway?" At the worst they would take my minibus.

It was clear that the Commission agents were not used to hearing objections or disagreement, and they looked at me incredulously, wondering if I was serious. Then one of the younger agents winked at me as he nodded his head toward the door. He looked friendly, so I walked out. We met in the hallway, where he motioned for me to come into his office. There, he pulled out some files, offering to copy a few samples to show me how to apply properly. He also advised me to apply for an interim licence immediately so I could continue working while my application was processed. A little later, I returned to the main desk and did exactly as he had instructed. Now there was some action, papers got filled out and signed, and soon I was on my way out with an interim licence. Over the years I have learned that, unfortunately, most government employees are bureaucrats and not business people, and they rarely seem to understand that their salaries are being paid by the tax dollars that businesses and ordinary people pay.

A breakthrough occurred when I attended a friend's party in late June. There, I met a sports reporter for The Sun, Vancouver's daily newspaper and the largest newspaper in town. After exchanging pleasantries, our talk turned to our careers, and gradually the story of my new business unfolded. I told her about my confusion over the brochures disappearing by the thousands, adding that something did not feel right because all of them were always gone when I went back to check on them after one or two weeks. I said I wished I could monitor the brochure racks day and night to see who was taking them. Before she left, she promised to talk to the newspaper's editor to see if there might be a story there.

To my surprise, about a week later I received a phone call about the issue from Sarah Cox, a Sun reporter. The newspaper had just hired her, she said, and she wanted to meet with me. At that point, I was desperate for anything that could shed a little light on this mystery. My debts were piling up and it would not be long before I had to bow out. I had already half-joked to my mother in Holland that if my phone was disconnected I was probably out of business and off to Costa Rica or South America, hiding from my debts. She had laughed and agreed she would do the same if it were her.

When we met, Sarah suggested we go downtown and distribute the brochures together at a selection of the largest hotels in town. We took off together and I distributed my brochures the way I normally did as she followed behind me, observing. After about an hour or so and visits to seven large hotels, we went for coffee.

Next, Sarah suggested that we return to the first hotel to check on the brochures. I would wait while she went inside. When she returned, she said, "They're gone, all of them." At the second hotel the result was the same. At the third hotel she was getting agitated. By now we were both certain something fishy was going on. All my brochures had disappeared within one hour. "I'm going to get to the bottom of this," she said as we parted. "I'll call you soon." And indeed, several days later she called, saying excitedly, "You have no idea how big this story is."

It began with a small, pink, telephone message found in her newspaper's archives from a downtown bed and breakfast. The owner had called the paper to complain that her brochures were disappearing after she had started offering small city tours to her bed and breakfast clients. Next, the journalist astounded me when she said that this assignment was now too big for her, and she was working on it with another well-known reporter. Apparently, several of the newspapers' lawyers were looking at the legal implications of an exposé in the newspaper, but she was not able to reveal what they had so far uncovered. I would have to wait.

In the meantime, Sarah asked me to park my minibus in front of the Four Seasons Hotel, directly ahead of a double-decker bus belonging to Gray Line of Vancouver, the largest tour operator in town. The newspaper's photographer would come by for a picture. That made me really curious. Why would Gray Line of Vancouver, a company that owned at least 30 large buses and was a franchise of a New York-based association of at least 200 bus companies, be involved in taking brochures from a single 11-passenger minibus company? But I was hyped up now and did as I was asked. Then the waiting game began. Sarah had promised that as soon as the Sun's story went to press she would call. About two weeks later she called me in the middle of the night and said, "Your story is on the presses right now, so pick up the first paper you can get." Of course, I wasn't able to get back to sleep. Within a few hours, I had a copy of the newspaper's early edition of July 09, 1984 in my hands. The front page announced:

CHARGES FLY IN BUS TOUR COMPANY FEUD
By Sarah Cox and Moira Farrow

A feud between some of the city's sightseeing companies has erupted into verbal warfare with the filing of a formal complaint against Gray Line of Vancouver. Gray Line, meanwhile has counter-claimed in interviews with The Sun that other companies have tried to take away its business. The complaint about Gray Line to the federal department of consumer and corporate affairs, is the most serious development in the long-simmering dispute. Various allegations about the business methods used by Gray Line have also been made to The Sun by former company employees, several city business people, and representatives of competing tour companies. Their major charge is that Gray Line, the city's largest sightseeing company, is attempting to monopolize Vancouver's tour business before Expo opens in 1986.

Dahlia Cassel, president of Scenic Line Tours, said last week her company has filed a complaint about Gray

Line's business practices with the department in Ottawa. In her letter of complaint Cassel wrote: "Gray Line has more or less a monopoly of the market in this city and are attempting to seal off any competition which may have existed until now."

A spokesman for the department declined to confirm or deny whether Gray Line is under investigation. However, Cassel said the department has been in contact with her since the complaint was filed.

Allegations made to The Sun include statements that:

• Gray Line employees were told to remove the brochures of competing companies.

• Gray Line has attempted to stop other companies from entering the tour business.

• The brochures of competing companies vanish from the Vancouver hotels.

• Gray Line has contracts with hotels to recommend the company exclusively to tourists.

Gray Line co-owner Peter Armstrong denied allegations made by various people to The Sun and said in an interview he's just trying to be an "effective marketer" in a competitive business. However, he said he's aware a complaint has been filed against the company.

The article is too long to copy entirely but here are a few other quotes:

One former Gray Line bus driver, Roger Rioux, commented "If we found brochures (of other companies) we were supposed to remove them."

Another former driver, Les Ennis, who worked four years for Gray Line, said bus drivers from other companies became angry when their brochures kept disappearing. "It's common knowledge that it was being done," Ennis said.

The following was reported about Gray Line's contracts with the hotels:

The Sun has obtained a copy of a contract form drawn up by Gray Line for use with Vancouver Hotels.

142

The contract says the hotel accepts Gray Line as its "exclusive sightseeing and tour company" and will "not allow any other sightseeing or tour company to promote competing services in the hotel."

Armstrong refused to name the hotels with which Gray Line has contracts or discuss the nature of the agreements saying only that "some are verbal and some are written."

The article went on to report:

In another interview, a former employee of a major Vancouver hotel said she was ordered by hotel management to distribute only Gray Line's brochures. "There was a time when hotel management ordered us not to give out other pamphlets," said the woman, who requested anonymity. She said she kept other brochures under the counter and sometimes gave them to tourists because she was unhappy with the hotel's contract with Gray Line.

Dahlia Cassel who operated Scenic Line Tours a mini-bus company was quoted:

She believes Scenic Line Tours would have grown by 100 percent this year, its fifth year of operation, if it were not for the constant disappearance of company brochures from hotels. "Every week we realized our brochures were disappearing like water. There were no reservations to back up the interest shown by taking our brochures."

A large picture of me was printed in front of my little bus, holding a brochure, in the background stood Gray Line's double-decker bus. I started reading:

TOUR COMPANY NIPPED IN THE BUD
By Sarah Cox
When Clasina Van Bemmel used her life savings to create the nature tour company she had always dreamed of, she didn't anticipate somebody would try and put her one-bus operation out of business.

143

She bought a maroon and grey van, 12 matching knapsacks and rain ponchos, and printed 15,000 brochures in April to advertise her guided tours through local forests, canyons, and alpine plateaus.

The brochures were quickly snatched up from downtown hotels and Van Bemmel waited for the phone to ring at her east Vancouver house and office. But no one called to inquire about the scenic hikes and Van Bemmel began to wonder why Circle Nature Adventure brochures disappeared so quickly. So on the evening of June 4, she dropped off 50 more pamphlets at each hotel and returned again to the Hyatt Regency a few hours later. "All of the pamphlets were gone," said Van Bemmel. "I couldn't believe it." The only visible bus tour pamphlets belonged to Gray Line, Vancouver's largest bus tour company, and hotel workers told her they didn't know what had happened to her leaflets.

"I was flabbergasted," said Van Bemmel, who acts as a driver, interpreter, and tour guide for her company.

She quickly returned to the other hotels. The wire racks she had stuffed with brochures were empty and hotel employees were reluctant to talk.

"I was so angry. I've put all my energy and thoughts and everything into this. I know that business is hard, but this just hit me in the stomach."

Armed with the determination which caused her to leave her job as outdoor recreation director at the Vancouver YWCA and start her own business, Van Bemmel contacted other tour companies and complained to the Greater Vancouver Visitors and Convention Bureau.

She discovered her brochures were not the only ones to go missing and the convention bureau told her they couldn't help.

Van Bemmel estimates 9,000 of her brochures have disappeared—a serious blow to her struggling business.

The articles made me so angry that I had 1,000 copies made. Early the next morning, I jumped into my minibus and parked it in front of the Hotel Vancouver, where Gray Line had its main office. Each day the Gray Line tour buses assembled there with the tourists they had picked up from all of the city's hotels, and then dispatched them to the appropriate tours. Gray Line had taken my visibility away; I was determined to get it back here.

I parked my little bus precisely in front of the main door where the tourists were gathering, well before any Gray Line staff were to be seen. When Gray Line's first large bus arrived, many people in the line-up were already reading copies of the articles I had handed out. The bus driver wanted my spot and honked, trying to make me move. He was surprised when I remained put, and he honked again, making angry gestures with his hands and sending me a clear message to move. I shook my head. Frustrated, he parked in front of me. A second bus arrived and did the same. Then a third and fourth came; soon there was a long line of Gray Line buses in front of and behind my little bus. Ah, my pretty little minibus looked so tiny, but so strong, sandwiched in between those big buses. The Gray Line drivers got out of their buses and assembled together, discussing what to do with me. By now the sidewalk was full of their customers reading the articles. Some people approached me apologetically. They shook their heads in dismay, clearly not understanding how such a large operator could do such things. They had already paid for their tour and it was departure time, but they promised to tour with me the next time they visited Vancouver.

Another large bus arrived, resorting to parking in front of the nearby city library as there was no more space at the hotel. As I walked toward this bus to hand out more copies, a large driver pushed me to the side and whispered close to my face, "If you hand out one more copy, I will smash your face." I had known that this might happen and was prepared. "Try it," I replied. But he realized that he was surrounded by many people and furiously stomped off.

The Gray Line drivers and their guides were talking into hand radios and mobile phones, but none came near me again.

145

Instead, The Gray Line staff swiftly boarded their passengers and left. When I got home, one of the local television stations called to ask if I would be willing to do it again. I declined; as far as I was concerned I had made my point.

Many people had read the newspaper articles. Cars honked when they saw my little bus on the road. Some drivers opened their windows at the stoplights and yelled things like, "Clasina, go and get those bastards." But what could I do next—sue them? I had no money to hire a lawyer. Now that this was all in the open, I was more determined than ever to continue with my little business, even though my close friends saw the toll it was taking on me. They expressed concern about my health and worried that I wasn't returning phone messages. They hadn't seen me for months. I could clearly see that they were worried as I often found little pots of food in front of my basement door when I arrived home in the middle of the night.

No, I decided that I lived in a free country, I was very good at what I was doing, and I was not going to give up. I was not going to let this large company get away with their bullying either. I hadn't planned on becoming competition for them, as my tours were totally different from theirs, but I decided in light of my recent experience, I was now going to become their competition. I changed the name of my company to City and Nature Sightseeing and started offering Vancouver city tours as well, exactly like Gray Line of Vancouver.

Then I called the suppliers to whom I owed money and made appointments to see them. Most had read The Sun articles, and, realizing that I had no money, were already planning to write off my debt. But I told them that I was not going to give up and that it was my intention to pay off every cent I owed them on a weekly basis. I promised each of them that I would come by personally every Friday afternoon and give them what I could afford. What could they say? The owner of Benwell Atkins, Don, printer of my brochures, came to greet me personally and offered to print the next batch for the cost price only, so I could get going again. I will never forget his kindness. Another break: I received a sympathetic phone call from the manager of the railway station. He had also read the articles, and he offered a spot for me and my leaflets at the travel desk in the station for the arrival of the 7 a.m. train from across Canada. It got me going again.

Business picked up and I faithfully visited my suppliers every week to hand in my payments, which might be anything from $10 to $50 per week; sometimes it was nothing. But even if I had nothing to give them I went in to tell them so. As time went on, I was able to make payments of $100 and sometimes $200. During the first few weeks, the employees at my suppliers' businesses were polite, but when they saw that I faithfully showed up each week, they became animated, as though they took a certain pride in me for keeping my promise. When I walked in, they would smile and say, "Hey Clasina, how much do you have this week?" Eventually, as soon as they saw me, they would happily report the shrinking balance.

The setup at the railway station was working well. Passengers arrived early, well before they could move into their hotels. I suggested that they have a leisurely breakfast and then take my morning city tour. I carried their luggage in the back of the minibus and dropped them off at their hotels after the tour. It worked perfectly.

A competitor who shared the brochure desk also had a small tour company, but no luggage compartment in his minibus. He was not happy that he now had to share customers. Soon, however, my brochures were disappearing from the desk in suspicious quantities, and one morning I caught him stealing them when he thought I was gone. Actually, I had hidden and was watching him from the second floor of the station. I left a message on his answering machine to the effect that I had seen him and I expected an apology from him, plus the return of my brochures by 6 p.m. Otherwise, I explained, I would charge him. He turned up, red faced, and apologized. He did not say another word to me for the next six years, at which time he sold his business.

Aware that my priority was the survival of my little business, I focused on driving and distributing my brochures to the hotels. I was up at 5 a.m. washing my little bus inside and out, no matter whether or not it rained. I made sure I was at the railway station at 7 a.m. and drove all day and some evenings before I visited the hotels at night. I often walked back into my bedroom around midnight, too tired to eat or even get undressed. Sometimes I would lie down for a few minutes only to wake up several hours later, cold because I was still on top of my bed covers, totally dressed.

I made sure my customers knew what was going on with the tour industry in town. I didn't bother them too much, but I kept copies of the newspaper articles in the bus. If they wanted, they were free to take one. My spot at the railway station also brought me customers who stayed at Vancouver hotels that would not carry my brochures. If, after the tour, they commented favourably on my service, I encouraged them to leave a little note to the hotel's manager, describing what kind of tour I offered and asking why my brochures were not at their concierge desk. Slowly I began to receive bookings from hotels that had not booked before. My strategy was working.

Then one day, I got a phone call from the president of the Vancouver Hotel Association. He requested that I attend an emergency meeting being held at the Holiday Inn. I had a vested interest in getting along with them, so I accepted, not knowing that the hotels were receiving visits from federal inspectors. When I arrived for the meeting I was escorted into a boardroom already filled with people. To my surprise, the president seated me at the head of the table, and as he introduced me to the others in attendance, one by one I realized that although I didn't recognize their faces I knew all of their names. These were the managers of each of the hotels I had phoned when my brochures were disappearing. Until now, they had never responded. But now I had them all in one room! They asked me why I was doing this to them! I was stunned by the stupidity of the question!

Taking a deep breath, I responded, "What would you do if you had a dream of having your own company and had invested all your money in your dream, even going into great financial debt for it? What if you had done your research and worked hard to make it work and then someone tried to take everything away? What would you do?" I added," True, I will never make you rich with commissions because I only have an 11-passenger bus. However, I can assure you that your clients will be happy customers coming back from my tours." I stopped there and let my words sink in. For some time I looked at their faces, one by one. I was not in a hurry and I felt strong. Then one of the managers spoke. He said, "You're right. My wife went on your tour and was delighted. You do give excellent service." I then told them it was unhealthy for a city like Vancouver to have one large tour operator calling all the shots. The hotels should be happy to offer a variety of tour operators and let their customers make their own choices. If they thought that the brochures, services, or transportation I offered to their clients were inadequate they were welcome not to recommend them. They promised to discuss the matter further without me and thanked me for coming in to talk to them. The next day I read in the paper that they had unanimously voted to open the doors to a variety of tour operators.

Next, the Department of Consumer and Corporate Affairs officers contacted me. They were in town looking into the exclusive contract issue with Gray Line and the hotels and asked me to work with them to take Gray Line of Vancouver to court. They also told me that their investigation revealed that the Gray Line Company in New York had settled a court case 20 years earlier for an undisclosed amount for stealing competitors' brochures from hotels, and that Gray Line in other large cities in Canada and USA were trying to monopolize the tour industry using the same tactics.

As the scheduled court case approached, I began to get strange phone calls. At first, there was only silence. In subsequent calls threats were uttered, such as, "If you go to court we will come after you," or "Hey lady, don't be stupid. You'd better get out of this mess." I was advised to take these threats seriously and suggested that I put my bus into a locked garage and go on a holiday for a while.

I called my mother in Holland, but when she answered the phone my throat was blocked and I could not say a word. She said, "Is that you, Clasina?" I could not answer. Then she said, "It must feel like you are swimming in a big ocean and you do not know what to do—to keep swimming or to stop." Again there was silence, then she said, "Keep swimming, my child," and hung up.

After filling my kayak with camping gear, I paddled into nearby Howe Sound. While I was camping at Douglas Bay I became sick and vomited. Of course, my mind was constantly preoccupied with the threats I had received. It was an inauspicious way to start a business.

One day I paddled out to see the seals on Pam Rocks, a little island close by. The wind came up strongly and the tide pushed against me. The waves were getting angrier and my kayak kept getting pushed back no matter how hard I paddled. This was exactly what was happening with my business, I thought, one step forward and two back. I could have taken a different direction or headed for shore, but as I thought about what had happened since I'd started my business and how now I even needed to hide, I suddenly became really angry. I don't know if the final straw was battling with the ocean, but I abruptly made a decision not to hide anymore. I felt a vast amount of power flow into my body and it gave me enough strength to get back to my campsite. I packed up camp and fought against the strong elements of nature as I paddled back to Porteau Cove.

When I arrived home I went to visit my doctor, who told me that it was a normal reaction of a body under extreme stress to vomit. He suggested I should reconsider carrying on with my business. Was it all worth it? Some of my friends agreed. Why bother? You can't fight the big guys.

When I am at the point of total exhaustion or desperation and I really do not know what to do anymore I let go and allow an inner voice take over. I call it the voice of my sister Willie's spirit. At these moments her voice is clear and calm and she tells me step by step what I should do.

This time I heard her telling me to let go for a little while and have a rest. And that is what I did. I gave all of my troubles over to her. I slept well because it seemed that she was carrying my load. Then she told me not give up, but to let things happen on their own for a little while, to go back to work and keep focusing on my clients. I took a rest. I stopped being the doer, and slowly things began to fall into place.

The court eventually ruled that the Department of Consumer and Corporate Affairs must closely watch Gray Line of Vancouver's business practices during the next seven years.

Now the legal battle was over. I wasn't totally happy with the outcome, but I knew that it was time to focus on my business, which was starting to blossom. It was also becoming more fun. The concierges and customers were responding well to my tours. I was especially creative when it was raining, and it rains a lot on the West Coast!

In my small group we could do things that were impossible on large coaches. During rainy periods my clients and I would have a powwow and throw the itinerary for the whole day into the air, coming up with a variety of ideas to please each passenger. I carried all sorts of things in my small bus: a small library with bird books and information about our local artists, binoculars, blankets to sit on while we enjoyed the scenery, some extra umbrellas, rain jackets and a few fleece jackets in case someone got cold. I often bought local cherries, strawberries, or blueberries and we would sit in the local parks, mountains, or near the ocean to eat them. When we were thirsty or hungry, we would stop at my favourite special haunts or a local deli. We toured the best dessert places in town, visited local painters in their studios, stopped at small galleries and often visited my friend, Dominique, to watch her work on a large stone sculpture on a piece of land near Granville Island.

I looked after the customers who needed help with their plane tickets or I would drop them off at the airline company. If someone had broken their glasses or camera, I took them in for repair. If someone wanted to play golf I would take their gear on the bus and drop them off at the golf course at the end of the tour. One day a customer asked about our lottery ticket system and we all went into the store and bought tickets, promising each other that we would share if one of us won.

People from different countries who hardly understood each other created friendships on the tours and some even changed hotels to be with their new friends. They often showed up together for my next tour. Many people spent their whole holiday with me. Returning clients promoted my other tours to their fellow passengers on my bus. Slowly, my reputation was growing: the concierges got positive feedback from my clients and became eager to please their next customers by sending them on my tours.

Vancouver hosted a very successful World Exposition in 1986, but it was not so for the larger tour operators and restaurants. The expected visitors arrived, but they mostly stayed on the Expo site where there was plenty to see and many good, reasonably priced restaurants. The companies that had invested in extra buses were out of luck and they complained loudly. I'd had no money to buy anything extra and was happy to load up my little bus every morning, afternoon and evening. I still have no idea how I made it through those months working so relentlessly. All I knew was that I had to hold on until October 31st, the end of the tourist season, when I could take a holiday.

When I woke up on the morning of November 1, my voice was totally gone, but my business had gained an excellent reputation. I paid off the last cent of my debts and none of the suppliers charged me a penny of interest. Each of them complimented me for my integrity in honouring my debts, and they offered their support in case I needed recommendations for future bank loans. I gave notice to my renters and moved back upstairs. What a luxury to get my house back again! I felt like I was starting all over with a clean slate.

Twenty-Nine

Soon after that, I heard about a long-haired German Shepherd puppy that was going to be put down if a home was not quickly found for her. Being the sucker for animals that I am, I could not imagine this dog being killed. I went to have a look at "Broom" and fell in love with her immediately. Since childhood I had wanted my own dog. I asked her owner, who had rescued her from the pound, if he could keep her until I had a fence installed so she could use the backyard. He agreed, and soon Broom was living with me. It was clear that she had been abused and needed patience and a little training. Ah, when we give love and patience, most animals are so willing to forgive and start loving again. They surely do that much better than many humans. Broom dug holes in the garden, ripped out the vegetables, and still came to sit right in front of me and look like the picture of innocence. We got along splendidly.

On one of my free Sundays, I called a friend to join me to see a movie. Instead, she invited me over for dinner and there I met my new partner. Toni had grown up with dogs and instantly fell in love with Broom. She was completing her master's degree at the University of British Columbia and taught nursing at a local college. She was not really a businesswoman, but possessed all the qualities I did not, and many more. She had the most beautiful smile I had ever seen; her whole face radiated when she smiled. People were quickly attracted to her. Toni was easily approachable, intelligent, good-hearted, and a great skier! She came from an upper middle-class family in Winnipeg, and many of our friends thought we were a most unlikely couple. Some made a little fun of us, which we took in stride.

We both worked hard and long hours. After several months, Toni moved into my house. She was wonderful with the business phone. Calls came in at all times during the night and because at that time answering services did not operate 24 hours a day, she often answered those calls. Life was wonderful; we kayaked and hiked, with Broom at our heels, swam and worked. Now that I had created a little more free time for myself, I was reconnecting with my friends.

In the winter of 1987 we removed the seats from the minibus, loaded it up with our kayaks and camping gear, and headed to Baja, Mexico to go kayaking. On our way south we visited a few small tour operators in San Francisco to see how they ran their businesses. Over the years, I had found that most professionals in the sightseeing business in other areas were helpful in providing me with information. I found it easy to ask questions. I knew men sometimes did not take me seriously, but that did not concern me. I learned while they were talking. I could not ask questions of my Vancouver competitors as they would not give me a true picture of what was going on. What competitor wanted to admit to the challenges of business or reveal ideas that were working?

In San Francisco I met a Swiss tour operator who owned about a dozen minibuses. He was interesting to talk with and willing to relate stories about some of his hurdles, as well as tips about how he overcame them. I learned about his problems with his staff and the competition in his area. He told me to keep the company small so I could keep an eye on the whole operation myself. Becoming big would not automatically mean more profit or more spare time for me. I remembered and held to his advice. At the San Francisco airport, I discovered some intriguing-looking minibuses and for future reference took note of the companies that built them.

We returned home to the end of a particularly cold winter. The ice was melting. One day, Broom and I headed to the lake in a nearby park for a walk. Broom jumped onto the frozen surface and before I knew it she had disappeared through the only hole in the ice, just off the wharf. I saw her panic and swim in the wrong direction and then she disappeared farther under the ice. I became frantic—there was no way I could jump in. She was too far away and the ice was just too dangerous. I yelled and screamed. Some men playing soccer on the snow ran over to help. They took sticks and hammered on the ice to no avail. I was sobbing uncontrollably. Finally, one of the soccer players gently took me to his car and let me sit for a while before he took me home. Toni was shocked and tried her best to calm me. We both returned to the lake several times that day; I'm not sure what we were hoping for. Friends joined us later, and they also went back to the lake to search for Broom. We were all devastated. Once again, a dog had been taken from me. For some time, I blamed myself for not keeping her on the leash, but she had always loved running free in this area, one of the only places in the city where dogs could run off-leash. For Broom, sadly, the trade-off for freedom was an early death.

We told the SPCA and the city dog pound about Broom. Every day Toni and I walked around the lake a few times, hoping we would find her body. One week later we received a phone call from the pound letting us know that Broom had been found. We asked to see her one last time before the cremation, but as we walked into the hallway I suddenly realized I couldn't bring myself to see her. We returned to the car and cried for a while. I asked Toni to take Broom's blanket in to cover her. We sat in the car for a while longer until it was finally the pound's closing time. I knew this was my last chance to see her and decided to go in. The staff took me to her. When they wheeled her out of the cooler, I saw that they had put Broom's blanket over her very neatly. I caressed her and said good-bye to her and told her that I was so sorry for her short life.

I vowed, "No more dogs," but several weeks later I read an ad in the newspaper offering a two-year-old, long-haired German Shepherd for $500. I called the number. A woman answered and asked me why I wanted a dog. I could not answer properly and burst into tears. She kindly waited until I composed myself; then I told her about Broom. I added that I did not believe in buying animals, especially dogs and cats. "So if no one wants your dog, I will be happy to take her." When she invited me over anyway, Toni and I went to meet her.

When the woman opened the door, the dog, Shasta, jumped on me so eagerly that she scratched my face. Her owner said, "She never does that to anyone." I played with Shasta and we bonded immediately. We learned that Shasta was well loved, but her owners each had two jobs and were no longer able to give her the attention she needed. They felt guilty about leaving her inside their home all day until late in the evening; the only exercise she got was at night when they would open the back door so she could go outside to relieve herself.

While I played with Shasta, the phone rang five or six times as people inquired about the dog. One person wanted a police dog. One wanted a guard dog. Toni and I finally decided to leave. When we got into the car, I hesitated; perhaps I should have offered the money Shasta's owner wanted. But we decided that if Shasta was going to become our dog, somehow it would just happen.

Two hours after we arrived home, Shasta's owner phoned to tell us that she thought Shasta would surely be happy with us and that she wasn't really interested in the money. She and her partner just wanted Shasta to find a loving home. She asked if she could visit Shasta sometimes, and we happily agreed.

It took some time for Shasta to get used to our home. She was a picky eater and very thin; the only way to get her to eat was to hand-feed her. I took her to the vet to have her examined, but was told that there was nothing wrong with her; she was just naturally skinny. After some time had passed with no signs of improvement in her weight or appetite, we took her to the vet again but again nothing was found. We took her in several more times but the veterinarians just could not figure out what was wrong with our dog. Then one day Shasta didn't come when I called her. That was very unusual, and this time we had to carry her to the clinic, where she was X-rayed and had blood samples taken. Once again the veterinarians could find nothing wrong with her, yet her condition was worsening. Finally, someone suggested that we request blood tests for Addison's disease (a disease caused by failure of the adrenal glands). By that time she was so weak that we carried her into the hospital, where she would stay for several weeks. The test results were positive.

Shasta, Toni, and I spent Christmas day in the dog pen at the hospital. With an intravenous drip line in both front paws, Shasta had been put into a small cage so that she could not move. We spent hours sitting by her cage talking to her. Shasta seemed to know the sound of my car; as soon as I parked, her tail would wag, even though I was still outside in the parking lot. The nurses commented that if this dog somehow survived, it would be due to pure love.

The vets finally determined the right dosage of medication and got Shasta up and going. We were told that she had a chronic disease and would have to be on pills her whole life. Every six months she would have her blood tested again and her medication readjusted if necessary. She could not tolerate much stress or many people around her.

We had Shasta, our precious gift, for 10 more years. She travelled with us everywhere in her large basket. She looked after us and guarded the house. Each night she slept at the end of the bed, unless one of us was not feeling well; then she would sleep by our sides. No matter how often I got up in the night to visit the bathroom, each time I would kneel down and have a little chat with her while she licked my hands and sighed. Shasta's unconditional love taught me how to forgive, have patience, and to be more gentle toward myself and others. I strongly believe that pets come into our lives for specific reasons.

I'd been told that dogs can tell you very clearly when it is time for them to die and I always wondered how that was possible. But when it was Shasta's time, at the age of 12, she made it very clear. She took to standing in corners with her nose toward the wall, then would come and stand in front of me, staring me in the eyes. She became restless, unable to sit or lie down comfortably anymore, and I knew that she was in pain and it was time to end her agony.

Since Shasta's death I have had no animals live with me; I travel too much. But I will always stop and take the time to talk to any animal that comes my way. I could not imagine life without some connection with them.

Shasta's illness had brought us into close contact with the SPCA, and when the business started to make some money, we became regular contributors to the charity by buying much needed surgical equipment for the animals.

Thirty

The year was 1988, and life was pretty good. I was making a decent living and having no trouble filling up my little bus. I was happy in my personal life. I intended to keep it that way, but the Universe had different plans for me.

By this time, I had applied for a few more licenses from the Motor Carrier Commission to allow me to offer tours to the surrounding areas of Vancouver, but they had been refused. Other tour operators had protested my application, crying that there was not enough business for all of us. But how many passengers could I take away from them in an 11-passenger minibus? I reapplied and reapplied. After I told the commission I was going to run those tours without the licenses if necessary, they eventually conceded and issued the permits. Perhaps they finally understood that there was no valid reason to keep refusing me.

That summer I was driving a tour to Shannon Falls near Squamish. We were stopped on the highway across from the falls waiting to turn left into the parking area, when a truck smashed into the rear end of the minibus. I checked to make sure that my passengers were all right. My own neck was seizing up and I felt nauseated. I called the police from my car phone, and the drunk driver of the truck that hit us was taken into custody. After filling out some papers, my group and I continued the tour, which I managed to complete, although I was not feeling well. The next day I was really sick, and I knew I had to take some time off. I decided to hire a guide to replace me for a few days.

I realized—not for the first time—that my one-person business was very vulnerable. If I became ill there was no backup. But my minibus would not provide enough income for two people, so I started thinking about expanding the business in such a way that it would be able to run on its own in case something serious happened to me. I did some calculations and decided that I needed two more minibuses.

During our San Francisco stopover the previous winter, I had noticed at the airport some luxurious-looking minibuses with very large windows.

At the end of the season, I returned to California to visit the dealer. I test-drove the bus and talked to a few people who had purchased them. After discussing the cost I realized a serious talk with my bank was in order, but first I needed to revisit the Motor Carrier Commission to apply for a permit to increase my carrying capacity to 21 passengers, and two extra permits for two new buses. I sensed that obtaining the permits would be a bigger hurdle than the bank. When I approached the agents after completing the applications, they stared at me incredulously. I assured them I had enough business to fill up the new buses. Of course, my competitors now cried even louder and opposed my applications again. But I simply was not going to take no for an answer, and called on the hotels, whose managers were now happy to sign letters of support for me.

The commission rejected my request again, finding that the proposed increase in passengers was too substantial. I applied once again with the same paperwork and added that if the commission rejected my application again, I would hire a lawyer and sue the Motor Carrier Commission. I knew that was a very bold statement, but after reading the conditions attached to the applications over and over, I knew their rejections were unfair. This time I didn't even have to go in front of the commission before I was awarded the permits. Now, I just had to persuade my bank.

After taking a close look at my business statements and prospects, and accepting all I owned, including my kayak, as collateral, the bank loaned me the money I needed. I was able to order the buses for the new tourist season, five months away.

Now my business had become a different ball game. I had to hire and train drivers, and order brochures with pictures of my new buses on them. Toni and I prepared a job description for my new employees and hired several men and women as driver/ guides. Each of them spoke at least one language in addition to

English. Toni came to my rescue again, offering to take on the tasks of preparing the payroll and staff schedules, in addition to answering the phone in the evenings and on weekends.

We awaited the new buses with great anticipation, as if they were newly adopted children. We finally got news that the buses had crossed the Canadian border and the drivers had stopped to rest for the night at the Delta Hotel just a few miles south of us in Richmond. I couldn't wait to see them, so Toni and I drove over in the middle of the night to have a peek. They were just beautiful. As I looked at them, I could not believe what I was doing. It felt pretty scary and entirely different from the purchase of my first minibus. I knew that there were new challenges ahead, but my calculations had made sense and Toni had said, "If anyone can do it, it surely is you."

As soon as they arrived in Vancouver, the two new buses were parked at the side of our house, and our neighbours got the first visiting rights. They were nearly as excited as Toni and I. Now, having three buses to wash in the morning instead of one, I had to get up an hour earlier. I knew that my neighbours could hear me at work at the crack of dawn, but they never complained.

Thirty-One

I quickly realized that dealing with and getting along with staff was very different from working as a tour guide on my own. With all of the changes I had implemented, my debts were so high that I could hardly see straight. Now I also had to pay drivers' salaries every two weeks. In addition, because the answering service was making too many mistakes on bookings, I decided to hire an office worker to take the reservation calls. The basement of my house became an office.

I cannot fathom how Toni put up with me during that period; I must have been no fun at all to live with. All I did was work, and if I was not working, I talked about work. I came home at the most unpredictable times. It was pointless for Toni to wait for me to share meals with her, and most of the time she was forced to socialize with our friends without me.

Getting up extra early, washing the buses, getting the other drivers on their way, driving tours all day myself, and going out again in the evenings to promote the business and distribute the brochures on Sundays was taking a heavy toll on my nerves. One day, I lost my temper when one of my drivers got back at the end of his tour with the bumper of the new bus ripped off. He had taken a corner too tightly and hit a pole. I was livid and yelled at him. He yelled back, until, as Toni later put it, we were yelling at each other like two four-year-olds. He stomped off. Toni gently told me that as an employer I had no right to yell at my staff like that. I would not motivate anyone to do a good job for me that way. I knew she was right and apologized to my driver the next day. He did the same, and the bumper got fixed.

I was learning and adapting as we went along. Toni was amazing with the staff, who just adored her. By now she had written a very valuable staff manual that we updated every season.

Although I made many mistakes when I became an employer, most of my staff understood I was doing my very best. I worked twice as hard as they did. I didn't spend time on business lunches or dinners—I found them to be a waste of time. I didn't want to owe anyone favours, nor was I interested in receiving any. I did not assume my clients were automatically right when they complained, and I always stood up for my staff when they deserved my support.

After some time the basement was renovated into a real office. The bank became accustomed to how the company operated and was now willing to finance more buses so I bought a few more locally, bringing the fleet to five. Years went by as the company flourished and I dealt with normal business ups and downs. Gray Line remained the biggest thorn in our daily routine. When we had customers waiting at hotels for our tours, Gray Line consistently approached them and pretended it was the tour company the tourists were waiting for.

One day when yet another call came over the radio telling me Gray Line had our customers, I got really angry. I was helping with the hotel pickups but had no passengers with me, so I decided to go after the Gray Line bus that I suspected had our party of six. My minibus was easy to manoeuvre and could move much faster than the large Gray Line bus. Because I knew the city so well, I caught up with it and cut the driver off. The large bus was obliged to stop. I got out of my minibus, knocked on the door of the larger bus and then boarded it, asking for a party of six by the name of Chan. There they were, seated at the back. I told them they were on the wrong bus and began to escort them out. The Gray Line driver was really annoyed. He said, "They've already paid." "Too bad," I said, "you'll have to refund their money." He said, "I can't do that," but I refused to move my minibus. By now we were causing a serious snarl in traffic. The Gray Line driver told me to get off his bus. Everyone on board was watching with interest. I told his passengers what was going on and soon they began to demand that the driver refund the Chans' money and get on with their tour. Finally, left with no other option, he gave me the money.

Later on, I called Gray Line's head office and threatened that every time they stole my clients, I would cut off their tour buses, one by one, until I found my customers. As a result, Gray Line left me alone for a while, and thus I learned that sometimes, in order to stand up to unethical business practices and bullying, I had no choice but to become obnoxious.

Thirty-Two

One afternoon, a passenger I picked up at the Pan Pacific Hotel hopped right into the front seat next to me. He was very quiet but seemed to enjoy the tour, and he signed up for several others over the following days. During his last day in town he invited me for dinner, saying, "I would like to talk to you about something important." When we sat down for dinner, he told me that he was from Switzerland and his company found new business ideas for clients. "I've been watching you for the past few days and think you're a very smart businesswoman," he continued. "I have an idea that might interest you. I think that you might be just the right person for what I have in mind." He went on to explain that he had just spent a few days in Boston, where he had ridden on one of the trackless trolleys that drove around town, letting people board and disembark every half hour. The trolley tour followed a circuit of interesting stops that allowed people to take a few hours or all day to see the city. He drew a trolley on his napkin to show me what they looked like, saying that he would mail me some pictures and a video he had taken. I never heard from him again, but I did call the Boston Visitors' Bureau, whose staff mailed me some brochures. I could not even imagine starting a company like that, but it was an interesting concept.

As I drove around day and night, I started to see that the trolleys would work perfectly in Vancouver, a port city that had cruise ship guests disembarking after clearing customs at 9 a.m. with a deadline of 3 p.m. to re-board their ship. All the local tour operators, including me, were missing many cruise ship passengers because our tours were set to leave at 9 a.m. and 2 p.m. The cruise ships only used chartered buses. The trolley service that had been described to me would give enormous flexibility to visitors, as they could then choose when to start their tour and when to call it quits, as well as how much time they wanted to spend at each attraction.

When Toni and I went south to Baja, Mexico, for another kayak trip, we investigated the trolleys in San Diego and boarded one to see what the tours were like. We checked out where they were built. During our holiday, my thoughts kept turning to how a trolley service might fit in Vancouver, until I could clearly envision how it would successfully work. I became very excited, wondering why the existing companies in Vancouver, some of them in business for 50 years or more, hadn't thought of this idea. Then I worked out the cost, which prevented me from putting the idea into action. For the next three years during tourist season, I was anxious to see if anyone else had clued in. In the meantime while my business grew, I kept working on the logistics of starting this new venture.

The company now had five buses and was incorporated and renamed West Coast City and Nature Sightseeing Ltd. We moved the office out of the house and into a building a five-minute drive from my home. It was time to hire a part-time mechanic. So far I had been driving the buses to the outskirts of town to have night mechanics work on them. After a full day of driving, I would spend all evening and often until the early morning in the shop, catching up on my paperwork and sleeping on the couch in the sales office, while I waited for the buses to have their maintenance work done.

I knew it was also time to hire a cleaning person to wash the buses. I will never forget how one person, during the interview process, began to argue with me about how long it took to clean a bus!

Part of our success was that I still drove clients myself and was very aware of what was going on both within my company and with other tour operators. By observing the number of passengers in their buses and talking to the hotel desk staff, I knew exactly where we stood compared with our competitors. By being "hands on," I was able to adapt and re-adapt quickly when necessary.

I became increasingly enamoured of the trolley idea, and I wondered how I could pull it off. I designed a two-hour tour circuit with a 30-minute departure schedule and 17 stops, and began experimenting by driving around the city pretending I was in a trolley. My stops included the most scenic areas of town and a nice variety of sightseeing attractions, such as parks, museums, and shopping areas. Because tourists were often afraid of getting lost, I decided on a circular system, so customers could start and finish their tour at any stop they chose, and the circuit would always bring them back to where they started. Cruise ship passengers would have plenty of time to take the tour and still get back to their ship in time for its afternoon departure.

I knew that the only way for me to start a company like this one was to find a partner with both knowledge about the sightseeing business, and money. My mind fixed on a woman whom I had accepted for a practicum in my company in the summer of 1988. Louise had been finishing a tourism course at Capilano College when she telephoned me one day to ask if she could complete her college practicum work with me. I had been in a hurry and had expressed little interest, but then she said, "I'll work for free. I really want to work for you." Certainly, having someone work for free sounded very good at that time.

We agreed to meet. A little older than me, Louise had run a business in the Caribbean Islands with her husband, and had employed over 400 people. After her husband died, she and her daughter moved to Canada. For an entire season she did the marketing for my company while I drove, and she had done an excellent job. She was a great asset to the company, but I could not afford to hire her after her practicum was completed. Now, I pondered how to go about building a partnership with her. For the past three years I had worked out all of the logistical and financial details. What percentage of the new company would I offer her? I wanted to be fair and decided on a fifty-fifty partnership. People advised me against this, recommending it was normal to keep 51 percent and offer 49 percent, but I wanted the two of us to start off on even ground.

I called Louise and invited her to go for a walk with me. As we walked around Stanley Park and discussed my idea, she listened carefully and sounded very interested. She had the money needed for her 50 percent share. We agreed to speak to each other again in a few days, and she promised to keep the idea secret. Two hours after I got home, she called me to say she was in. We made a five-year commitment to each other and the new business.

The Vancouver Trolley Company Ltd. was officially created in the spring of 1990. Our goal was to have the trolleys start to roll on the streets of Vancouver on May 1, 1991. Lots of work needed to be done.

The off-season was approaching, and Louise and I decided to visit San Francisco, another city where successful trackless trolley tours were offered. Once there, we rode the trolleys and Louise became more and more excited. We talked to the tour company owners and were invited to see their garage. They were interested in selling us the four trolleys we needed, but upon closer investigation, I noticed that their chassis were not new. They had built new bodies on old trucks' chassis. We learned that the trolleys were built in Oregon, and we left to visit the manufacturer. Although we would have preferred to buy the vehicles in Canada, no one was building them here.

The Oregon company was a family-run business with a shop that seemed quite small for the production of such large vehicles. The owner handed us a list of cities already using his trolleys and welcomed us to talk to the companies that operated them. Swallowing hard, we discussed the price and asked if he could build the vehicles to the specifications that were set forth by the Canadian Motor Carrier Commission. He assured us this would be no problem.

Louise and I headed home again, organized the contracts with the manufacturer and made arrangements to start applications for the necessary licences, knowing that as soon as we filed the paperwork, word about our plans would come out. By now I had enough experience dealing with the Motor Carrier Commission to know that they could not deny us the licences, because there was no service like this one being offered by anyone else in Vancouver. It would be a real coup in the tourism industry.

As word of our plans spread, colleagues in the industry had a hard time believing that Louise and I, "those two women," could pull off this new venture. Most of them didn't take us seriously. Skeptically, they said, "It will never work." Hadn't I heard those words before?

On July 20, 1990, The Vancouver Sun published an article by Alan Daniels, their tourism reporter, announcing our plans. It included a large picture of Louise and me holding a miniature wooden trolley in our hands. On December 29, the same reporter wrote another article in which he gave us The Vancouver Sun's vote for Tourism's Winner of the Year.

It took an entire year to acquire the business licenses, have the trolleys built, hire and train new staff, write new brochures, and look after other details. Louise had painstakingly developed an excellent business plan and the managers at the Royal Bank of Canada, where I had been banking since starting my own business in 1984, told me that they were on board. We visited them often to keep them up to date. I was putting absolutely everything I owned on the line as collateral, including my house and my minibus business, which I was still running full-time.

We decided that to save operating costs, my bus company, West Coast City and Nature Sightseeing Ltd., and The Vancouver Trolley Company Ltd. would operate out of the same building. There we had just enough space for the buses and the four trolleys.

After making the appropriate applications to operate the trolleys in the city, City Hall gave us trouble when we asked for signposts to be installed at each of the 17 stops. I showed them photos of how it was done in the USA, but they refused to discuss it. Their argument was, "We have never done this before and if we give you signposts other companies will want them." As far as I could see, only the city's public transit system had signs. But we also offered a scheduled service even if no passengers were on the trolley.

I kept going back to City Hall and they kept on refusing. This continued for a while until one day when the civic staff saw me coming again they told me that it was better not to push anymore. I laughed and told them that this time I had come in to ask for a designated parking spot because I now intended to show up every day. They laughed too.

Finally, they began talking among themselves and I overheard one of them say, "Perhaps we should just start the process and see what happens." It took a lot of time and effort, but finally we succeeded.

The next battle, fought over Stanley Park, was covered extensively in an article in the West Ender newspaper on August 30, 1990, under the headline "Stanley Park Trolley Plan Derailed." The park staff were in favour of our proposed trolley service right away, but during our presentation to the Parks Board, the commissioners balked. They had a hard time believing the trolleys would result in less tourist vehicle traffic in the park, a concept that seemed so obvious to us. We had also pointed out that our environmentally friendly trolleys, which would run on natural gas, would cut down on pollution levels. One commissioner wanted proposals from other companies, even though there were no other companies in town offering trolley tours, and another commissioner objected to our signposts. Then there were requests for a consultant's report and a planning committee. We attended many meetings before the trolleys were finally granted permission to enter the park. We were able to post our signs. These ongoing efforts were great lessons to me on how much time and repeated effort it takes for people to understand and accept new ideas.

Thirty-Three

Louise and I decided to apply for a loan through the Federal Western Diversification program, which provided interest-free loans to businesses that were starting something new on the market. The loans had to be paid back after a business had been in operation for three years. We read the requirements thoroughly and Louise did a great job of preparing our application. We presented it to the Western Diversification office in Vancouver.

We soon received the news that we did not qualify. We appealed and got the same answer. Finally, we appealed again and mailed our application directly to the main office in Ottawa, explaining that according to the written requirements for the loans, we certainly thought we qualified for the grant.

Subsequently we received an invitation to meet the Assistant Deputy Minister of Western Diversification in British Columbia, Mr. Robin Dodson, when he next visited Vancouver. We met and, after we had discussed several examples of projects in the tourism industry that had received the loans, yet did not appear to us to qualify, he said, "Who does and doesn't get the loans is up to my discretion." Then he closed our file and got up, signaling that he had finished with us. "Wait," I said. "How do we appeal?" He replied, "This is it. I am it." And I responded, "No sir, we have just started." He looked stunned, then replied, "I wish you all the best," and walked out.

As we entered the elevator, Louise asked, "What are we going to do?" I told her we would appeal directly to the minister responsible for the program and would state that if we were refused again, we would seek legal assistance. She laughed and said, "You can be so blunt." I knew it and did not enjoy it, but I constantly felt pushed to do business in this way. If I hadn't actually kept pushing, I would have gone broke long ago. Women were often not taken as serious contenders in the tourism industry, and to succeed, I often found my brashness and perseverance to be an asset.

We wrote to the federal minister in charge, John Crosbie, mentioned getting our lawyer involved, and were awarded an interest free loan of $175,383. Although this money was only a small portion of the total cost of this project, it made a big difference to us. It was a blessing not to have to worry about making payments on this loan for three years.

It was March 1991 when our first trolley arrived in Canada. Importing it had not been too difficult; the local Motor Vehicle Branch inspectors completed the proper inspections and the stamps on the front window proved we were legal. Ecstatic, we decided to celebrate by throwing a party at Science World on March 13, to which we invited about 500 people from the tourism industry. Because we had decided to convert all the trolleys to run on non-polluting natural gas, the BC Gas Company co-hosted the celebration with us. The Honourable Ms. Kim Campbell, MP for Vancouver Centre and federal justice minister, accepted our invitation to officially open the company by ringing the trolley bell.

In the late afternoon on the day before the party, Louise's face turned pale as she read a fax that had just come in. It was an announcement from the trolley manufacturer in the USA stating he would stop production on our remaining three trolleys if we did not pay him an extra US$40,000 per vehicle, a total of US$160,000. Needless to say, we were stunned. This could break us. We called him and made arrangements to visit him in Oregon. Until we could make our way south to speak with him, I was determined to remain focused on the one thing that I knew I could handle right now—the party. No one except me, Louise, and Toni had any idea what was happening with the manufacturer and we were determined to keep it that way; we had no choice but to pretend everything was on track.

The one trolley we had was parked in front of Science World for our guests to see. Many people attended, including representatives from city hall, the provincial government's deputy minister of tourism and our guest of honour, Kim Campbell. Pictures were taken and a photo of Louise and me hanging out of the trolley door made it into the newspaper. We had been getting a lot of press coverage lately. Little did we know that both the news coverage and our problems were just beginning!

As soon as the party was over we drove to the factory in Oregon. Arriving after a long, full day of driving, we asked the manufacturer, John, how far along he was with the trolley construction. He took us into his shop, where one main body was under final construction. He then took us to another location and showed us the other two units, which were far from complete. We were supposed to start our service about six weeks later on May 1st. Too tired for a discussion, we made arrangements to talk to him the next morning.

We met with John in the kitchen of his home. He had closed his factory, and he announced to us as he leaned back in his chair with his hands in his pockets, "No one can make me reopen unless I get more money." Our detailed contract specifically stated the cost of each trolley and the penalties that would be levied against his company if he did not deliver on time, but he did not seem to care. After some discussion amongst the three of us, I got an idea and asked Louise to take a walk with me. Once alone I suggested to her that we would "pretend" to give him the money he was asking for, but would do so in installments as the work progressed. We would also tell him that the bank would not give us the money otherwise. The last major payment would be made at the time of delivery. In the meantime, we would consult our lawyer, because as far as I was concerned we were being blackmailed. We went back to offer our solution. John was happy and promised to start work again the next day. Sure enough, he started building again.

Once Louise and I were back in Vancouver we met with our lawyer. We decided that when the trolleys arrived in Canada, we would deduct the payments we had made from the original cost stated in our contract and pay him what was left over. Until then, each time he completed more work we gave him more money. It was a very stressful time.

In the meantime, we continued our preparations for the trolley tours. We hired the drivers, trained them and bought their uniforms. Our brochures were printed. We were all excited when we heard that the three other trolleys were finally on their way.

When the vehicles arrived at the Canadian border on April 9, however, Canada Customs refused their entry into the country, stating that they did not comply with Canadian regulations. That seemed strange; we had already imported an identical trolley that had passed all the inspections. Canada Customs referred us to Transport Canada.

Transport Canada was not willing to tell us the specific reasons why the trolleys had been refused entry, and referred us to the regulations in their books. Yet nothing was written in their books about trackless trolleys, as they had never been imported into Canada before. The agency then informed us that we had imported our first trolley illegally. "What about all the tests they passed in Vancouver?" we asked. The stickers on the trolley window clearly indicated that it had passed the tests.

Our staff were stunned and decided to stage a protest at the Canadian border. Carrying large banners that read, "Trolley Supporter," we all drove to the border in our only trolley to protest. We not only wanted answers, we wanted the public to know about the unfairness of the situation. Both of my companies were on the verge of going bankrupt and over 40 people were about to lose their jobs. The media turned up—print journalists in addition to the television news crews and covered the story beautifully. The next morning's Province newspaper devoted the entire front page to our predicament and protest, and featured a picture of me driving the trolley. As a result, we received numerous phone calls from ordinary people asking how they could help. We directed them to Transport Canada and requested that they encourage them to tell us what to do. Several years later I learned that Transport Canada's phone lines were busy as people called about the trolleys; it seemed that the agency had never had anything like that happen before.

In the midst of these events, Louise was told by the manager of the Royal Bank that the bank was rethinking their decision to lend our company more money for the trolleys. We were stunned. Each hurdle felt like a mountain. I drove to the bank, walked into the manager's office and informed him that if the Royal Bank pulled out now I would get them their worst publicity ever. Not only that, the Vancouver Trolley Company would sue them. I walked out and slammed the door behind me. The following morning, I got a phone call from the Royal Bank head office apologizing and assuring us that they would keep their word and extend the loan. Again I had proved that although this was not the best way to work with people, it did get results.

After getting nowhere with Transport Canada for several days, we finally contacted our MP, Kim Campbell, for advice and support. After a meeting with Ms. Campbell in her Vancouver constituency office and numerous calls back and forth with her office staff at the Parliament buildings in Ottawa, we knew that strings had been pulled because Transport Canada finally gave us instructions to have the trolley windows and the sliding doors retested.

I found a testing laboratory in Seattle, met with the manufacturer, and then drove one trolley over. When we arrived, I asked if I could observe the testing, and they agreed. I watched the testers cover a wooden ball with chamois cloth and install a device to push it through the window. The ball represented the head of a person going through the window during a simulated accident. I thought the apparatus moved at an extremely slow speed and wondered how a person's head could possibly go through a window at that speed during a real accident. When I asked the engineer about it, he simply said, "That is what they want." He took lots of notes and pictures during the whole procedure. Then they removed the sliding door in the back of the trolley. The door had to be a certain weight so that in case of an accident someone could lift it out and escape. Since the trolley had sliding and emergency windows all around, it would have been very easy to escape in any case.

The preparation, testing and report writing took a full day at the cost of US$16,000. I rejoined the two drivers who were waiting at the storage facility with the other two trolleys and we headed to the border. The trolleys were finally admitted into Canada with the comment, "Don't count on importing any other trolleys." We would worry about that later.

When we got back to Vancouver, our staff was assembled to greet us, ready with welcome banners and a huge cake. They cheered as we pulled up. The trolleys immediately left again to be converted to burn natural gas. When they returned several days later, we began our tours. The brochures had already been distributed, our drivers were trained, and we were all impatient to get on with business.

In the meantime we were presented with the final invoice from the manufacturer. It included the extra US$160,000 he had decided to charge us and gave no deductions for going over the time limit specified in our contract. We consulted with our lawyers and paid what was legally due. We heard nothing for a few days but when one of the drivers returned at the end of his shift, he noticed a large tow truck idling close to our garage. We got the message. Our trolleys were now parked inside the garage surrounded by some of our buses, and we hired a security guard for the night watch. Then we discovered that tow trucks were following our drivers on their routes. We instructed our staff not to leave the vehicles out of sight for a single minute. Next we began to receive calls from Seattle companies requesting to charter all of our trolleys. Did they think we were stupid? There was no way our trolleys would cross the border into the USA again.

The Vancouver Trolley Company 1991.

Our company was served with legal papers by our U.S. manufacturer's bank, claiming that we owed them the extra money. We had neither the time nor the energy to fight them; we desperately needed to focus on making money. We left it to our lawyers to undertake this particular battle. Months of legal hassles went by, but eventually the U.S. bank recognized that our contract with the manufacturer left them with no legal claim against us.

Louise and I were totally exhausted and we still had a whole season of very hard work ahead of us. To this day I still do not know how we managed the sleepless nights, the relentless stress of having to resolve these huge barriers and uncertainty about the future events.

The trolleys were a novelty in town and received a lot of attention from the media and the hotels. The vehicles looked attractive and fun. Everyone, including the locals with their children and guests, wanted to ride in one. One day I drove behind one of the trolleys in my car to monitor the passengers getting on at our stops. When I passed the Vancouver Art Gallery, I noticed a large group of people who I assumed were waiting for the local bus, as the transit stop was right next to ours. However, when the trolley stopped everyone got on board. I burst into tears. They were tears of victory, of relief, and exhaustion. Here I saw with my own eyes living proof that what people had said "was never going to work," would actually become a great success. The only people who were not happy were my competitors. Our first summer in business, the Vancouver Trolley Company had taken a huge bite out of the tourism market pie.

Thirty-Four

My tour bus business was thriving as well. Between my two companies I now had 9 vehicles on the road. We had a secretary and several reservation staff in the office, two cleaners and a full-time mechanic in the garage. I no longer had the time to drive a tour unless it was absolutely necessary, but sometimes I would take over a shift in one of the buses or trolleys to gauge the reactions of the passengers. From 5 a.m. until after midnight, I was on the road or in the office, solving problems, supervising, and running errands. The business end of the operations, including creative problem solving to achieve better results - even competing with others - was, in a certain way, fun for me, but I found dealing with a large staff, large debts, court cases, government agencies and unfair competition very stressful.

Our office looked like a little United Nations. We had staff of all nationalities and, of course, very different personalities influenced by their cultural backgrounds and habits. I found that drivers were a special breed of people; they were different from office staff, who were, in turn, different from mechanics. Each required unique handling. Often I ran things by the seat of my pants. There were so many different problems to deal with every single day and quick decision – making was essential. An advantage of dealing with so much was that I could not dwell too long on the negative. Being able to have a good laugh about myself and the situation was always a good motivator for everyone.

One day, our operations manager and one of our reservationists were going at each other, bickering, again. Their conflict had been going on for months and by now it was having an unpleasant effect on the rest of the office staff. The two of them had been warned to stop their arguing to no avail. I didn't want to lose either one of them because each did a good job. I hadn't known what to do with them until suddenly on this day in the middle of their argument I sent them upstairs into my office, telling them to get over their mutual animosity once and for all. I told them that if they came out before they resolved everything, they would both lose their jobs and not be welcomed back. Shocked, into my office they went. For a while all that the rest of us could hear was a lot of screaming, but then it became quiet. After some time we heard laughter and about an hour later they came downstairs again. Their conflict was over. From that time on they worked well together.

On another occasion, one staff member who wasn't happy about being let go contacted the Labour Relations Board. I figured that the board was there for employers as well as employees, so I called them and asked to have an agent sent to my office to help me resolve the issue. They were somewhat surprised by my request but did send an agent, who suggested that I keep a book on my desk to note everything I communicated to my staff. From then on there were no more surprises. It was a handy little book.

Running a business with a partner was a great learning process for me. Louise and I were involved in very different aspects of the business. Louise was in charge of all the marketing and special projects, while I was focused on the management of the office, staff, and operations. The arrangement worked well. We respected and admired each other's different skills and both worked day and night. As the founder of the companies, I had a vision of how things would unfold. Sometimes I wondered if having a better educational background would have made things easier. But that was not my reality, and I just had to deal with things as they came.

Thirty-Five

The Gray Line Company must really have been hurt by the success of the trolleys because they announced that, beginning next tourist season, they would bring in four double-decker buses. Although they had used double-deckers before, they had stopped operating them a few years previously. Now, they decided to bring them back and copy our trolley tour. Louise read about it in the newspaper and was very upset. We had only one year under our belts, and to be faced with a large competitor so soon was devastating. It would have really upset me had they bought the same trolleys, but I was confident we could compete with their double-decker buses. However, Louise did not have the same confidence, and told me one month before the start of our second season that she wanted out of the partnership. But there was no way I could or wanted to stop now. In order to succeed, I had fought many battles over the years; I would tackle this problem as well. Our partnership agreement stated that I had six months to buy her out, so I had some time to ponder how I was going to do it. Eventually a deal was worked out with Louise and we parted company amicably.

Gray Line brought in their famous double-decker buses. At the Vancouver Trolley Company, we experienced a lot of nervous excitement and some fear about what might happen. We knew that the trolleys had some advantages over the double-deckers. We were now established and tourists sought us out. The trolleys could drive all the way around Stanley Park, while the double-deckers could not fit under an overpass on the park loop and had to make a short cut through the north end of the park, missing the totem poles and spectacular views of the North Shore. In addition, our vehicles were more maneuverable and we used natural gas. Our competitor brought in older, second-hand vehicles. The double-deckers seemed to break down frequently; the diesel exhaust they spewed out all over the city brought Gray Line no great publicity either.

While the double-deckers had trouble with punctuality, the trolleys continued to pick up our customers at the same stops at the scheduled times. Some visitors attempted to board our trolleys with their double-decker tickets, presuming the vehicles belonged to the same company. When our drivers told them that we were a different company and could not accept the Gray Line tickets, a few bought a trolley ticket if they had waited at the stop for too long for a double-decker, but most often we saw and left behind unhappy faces. We tried to be accommodating: when we saw that elderly customers of our famous competitor had been waiting too long, we would take them on the trolleys for free whenever we had enough space. Of course, these seniors talked to their hotels' staff at the end of the day. And they also enjoyed sharing their stories with other visitors. It did not take long before the hotels' concierges gave preference to our trolley tours.

Our second season was a tremendous success. Gray Line's competition had been a real motivator for everyone at the company. It had kept us on our toes and although we had worked incredibly hard we'd also had fun. Instead of going broke, all of the staff from both of my companies received special bonuses at the end of the season.

However, managing two companies was taking its toll on both my health and my relationship. Because we now had office staff, Toni was not involved in the businesses as she had been before, so I didn't see her often around the office. I was rarely home and when I was, I was usually asleep. After many years of long work hours I had learned to sleep at any time, anywhere—under my desk, in the car, even on a blanket in the aisle of a bus. One day, on my way home for a rest, I fell asleep behind the steering wheel and drove into a telephone pole. The car was demolished. Often I couldn't even remember if I had eaten. I was putting on weight because I gave myself no time to go for a run or a bike ride. Clearly, it was time for me to make some changes in my life, but I wasn't sure how to make the time.

Thirty-Six

In September 1992, I received a call from the Western Diversification program inviting the Vancouver Trolley Company ("VTC") to a product show at the Vancouver Trade and Convention Centre called "Success in the West!" The recipients of the program's loans could rent one or several booths in order to show the public and government officials how successful the Western Diversification program really was. Amazingly, they wanted us to rent a booth to highlight their program. I politely declined their offer, citing that I had no time and suggesting that their booth rates were too high. They were taken aback, and called again later asking what it would take to get the VTC there. After some thought, I offered to park one trolley in the Trade and Convention Centre during the show, at no cost to my company, so people could tour the vehicle. "That isn't possible," they said. However, two weeks later they called back to say it had become possible. They gave us a space equivalent to the size of four booths!

The next day the show began and our big, red trolley was quite a popular attraction in the hall. The Honourable John Crosbie, Federal Minister of Diversification, paid a visit and just behind him came some other government officials, including Mr. Robin Dodson, Assistant Deputy Minister of Western Diversification for British Columbia and the infamous "I am it" man who had refused both our applications and appeals for the Western Diversification loan. He approached me with a charming smile and introduced me to his colleague, saying, "This is the lady who wouldn't take no for an answer from the government."

"Why do things have to be done this way?" I thought. Why does everything have to be such a bureaucratic battle before things can get done? What about the people that do not have the courage or strength to go on and finally just give up after putting in years of hard work and all their resources?

That year, the Vancouver Trolley Company won the President's Award from the South Western Tourism Association. It was clear that an expansion would be necessary to keep ahead of my competitors. After all our misadventures building the trolleys in the U.S. and importing them into Canada, I knew there was no way we could ever buy another American vehicle. I also knew that no one built trolleys like ours in Canada. After pondering the problem, I concluded, "What is so difficult about building trolleys anyway? I've seen how they're built and if they can make them in the United States, surely we can make them here in Canada."

Over the winter months, I hired a technical engineer and told him to redesign the trolley and make all the changes I thought were necessary for Vancouver's temperate, wet climate. Our four existing trolleys were designed for California weather; here we needed something more robust.

Most of my business acquaintances, family, and friends thought I was a little crazy to begin with, but now they figured I was completely mad. Again I heard that now familiar saying: "It will never work," and this time they added, "You are risking everything you have worked for." Yes, I knew that. I also knew what it was like and how to live without much. If I were to lose everything, at least no one could take my experiences away.

In 1994, we celebrated the 10-year anniversary of West Coast City and Nature Sightseeing Ltd. with a wonderful party at the Vancouver Aquarium. Also that year, I became a finalist in the Canadian Female Entrepreneur of the Year competition. In addition, I won the British Columbia Female Entrepreneur of the Year Award with The Vancouver Trolley Company Ltd. in the "Starting New Business" category. For the occasion, my mother came over from Holland with her sister and my "step-parents" (Martine's parents) from France. The ceremony and celebration were held at The Hyatt Regency Hotel in Vancouver. When I was invited to speak, I included a special thank you to my mother, who had taught me dogged determination, perseverance, ethics, and the very basics of business. While I stood there with the award in my hands, Toni was the first to arrive at my side to congratulate me, whispering, "This is your Ph.D." For so many years, surrounded by friends who had master's degrees and Ph.D.s, I had felt I was lacking something. This award made up for it.

That was also the year I turned 50. On the morning of my birthday, I decided not to get dressed and instead lingered at the breakfast table in my nightgown. My mother and Toni kept urging me to get my clothes on. Because I so seldom got the chance to relax and read the newspaper at the breakfast table, I just ignored them. At about eight o'clock, I noticed a trolley drive by and wondered what it was doing in our neighbourhood. Soon I saw another one, then one tour bus followed by another. Before long, I saw that both my street and the neighbouring streets were crowded with parked buses and trolleys. The staff were assembled in the front garden and sang "Happy Birthday" while I stood at the front door in my nightgown. Then food was brought up from its hiding place in the basement for a party. It was a special time, a sharing of success and life's goodness with family, friends, neighbours, and colleagues.

The trolley designs were now finished and I created a new company called The Canadian Classic Trolley Manufacturing Company Ltd. I contracted a local company to build the vehicles and soon production was underway. But I made a critical error by starting vehicle production with this company without having the contracts finalized by our lawyers. The manufacturing company suddenly claimed the trolley designs as their own and as "public domain." This resulted in another court case, but the judge ruled in our favour and The Vancouver Trolley Company was able to expand its fleet to six trolleys.

After that court case, the Western Diversification Fund loan was repaid in full, the bank loans were very manageable and the companies' books showed a high rate of return. The companies were now fully established and were enjoying excellent reputations. It looked like this was the right time to let go. Interestingly, some men in the business thought I would be foolish to sell now. They said, "You can easily double the size of your companies," which I knew was true. The women in business said, "Get healthy again, go and enjoy yourself." I was very, very tired. I planned to join a week-long retreat on one of the Gulf Islands west of Vancouver to ponder what to do next. I needed to re-examine why I had gone into business in the first place, and think about the incredible things that had happened over the past 12 years. As far as I was concerned, I had accomplished what I wanted.

On my retreat, I suddenly became aware that I had never gone into business to become wealthy. For 12 years I had been in a kind of survival mode, just dealing with what was coming up day by day and often going at it on pure instinct. I had done the best I could. I could look at myself in the mirror and say that I ran very ethical and honest businesses. I had proved to myself that I could do whatever I set my mind to. One day, during an imaginary journey, I saw myself as a painter. I was painting on a massive canvas day and night, not knowing what time it was or whether I had eaten. I did not sleep; I was obsessed with, and focused on, painting and then, suddenly, when my painting was finished I walked away. This was the answer: I was done with doing business.

My financial advisor told me that I really didn't need to work anymore, that I was now financially secure. Selling the minibus company was fairly easy; tourism in Vancouver was thriving.

As soon as I decided to sell The Vancouver Trolley Company and the manufacturing company, I shared the news with my staff. They understood that I was tired and wanted to retire. Together we discussed at length the possibility of them purchasing the company. Going through this procedure, they ultimately decided it would not work. I then invited my senior staff to be part of the process of the sale to an outside buyer. It was an interesting experience to watch the staff's involvement in the sale. They were well prepared and asked a wide variety of questions of the potential buyers, recording their ethics, their lifestyles, their proposed working conditions, and so on.

Before the final decision had been made, however, my general manager began bringing me telephone messages from the owner of Gray Line of Vancouver, Tom MacDonald. At first I did not even glance at them, but my manager kept coming back, finally saying, "Why don't you just go and see what he has to say?"

Out of curiosity, I accepted a meeting, although I thought I knew what it was about. We met for breakfast and after exchanging a few niceties, Mr. MacDonald apologized for the hassles his company had caused me over the years. Then he came to the point. He had heard that I was retiring and interested in selling The Vancouver Trolley Company, and he said that the Gray Line Company would be happy to buy it. How much did I want?

It has been said that success is the sweetest revenge. I answered Mr. MacDonald gently, saying, "You do not have the money." He did not understand me, and said, "Just tell me how much you want, Clasina." Again, I told him that he did not have the money. Now he understood. He said, "Are you saying that because of all the troubles between us over the years?" I told him, "Yes, but not only that. The ethics of our companies do not fit together, and my staff would never be happy working for you." When we concluded our meeting on a polite note, he said, "Let me know if you change your mind."

Ultimately, I had several buyers, and I left the final decision to my senior staff. They felt honoured to be included in the selection process, and in the end, they chose a Canadian husband and wife team.

Thirty-Seven

I was 51 years old. My friends poked fun at me by betting bottles of wine that I would be back in business within the year. They could not imagine me being retired. When I went to see my doctor for a check-up, she was not happy and told me that my adrenal glands were not producing anymore and that my immune system was in trouble. For the next six months, I slept, read, walked, and sat on café terraces watching people. I was amazed to discover that when I let my body do its own thing, and it needed sleep, it did just that.

Toni was still working, so I spent a lot of time on my own and relished my turn to do the grocery shopping, cooking, and cleaning. After many months, I got my bike out and started cycling in a nearby park. I huffed and puffed going up small hills. Before going into business, I had been an avid runner, kayaker, cyclist, and skier. Now, 12 years later, I was a physical wreck.

Many times while I ran the business, I had reminded myself that I needed to balance work and self-care, but I wasn't able to do it. Whenever I had a moment, all I wanted to do was sleep. Had it all been worth it? Yes, it had, and I had done it the only way I was able. I had given it all I had and learned so much. I had no regrets because I couldn't have done it better—or differently.

Then a course in woodworking caught my eye. Offered by the local school board, it was just a beginner's class, carving African masks out of cedar wood. I bought the required tools and joined the class. There were a few other women, but most of the students were men. I enjoyed the smell and feel of working with the cedar. The teacher was a beautiful young African man. He sang and danced around the classroom while he helped us along.

After that, I joined a local wood-carving club and began to improvise with all kinds of native designs. I bought more tools and set up a workbench in the basement. Soon I started laminating slabs of wood into larger pieces. When I began to get up in the middle of the night just to have a look at the piece I was working on, and then remained to carve until daylight came through the windows, I knew that I was hooked.

After about one year, I was encouraged by other artists to start sculpting spontaneously and directly—with no preparation. They said that I was technically ready. My chance appeared suddenly while on a vacation in Arizona when I met Jennifer, a sculptor from California who worked with cement.

Cement as an artistic medium allowed only a few hours for the sculpting process. If the artist was not quick the cement hardened before the piece was finished. Jennifer offered to show me how her medium worked and immediately brought all the materials. We put wet cement into two empty cardboard boxes and went for breakfast while it hardened. When we returned, Jennifer peeled off the wet cardboard and put a tablespoon, a knife, and a fork into my hands. "Go for it," she said. I was completely intimidated and did not move.

In the meantime, Jennifer went to the second box, where she repeated the preparations and began to sculpt. All kinds of things were going through my head about what I could or should make. I was getting nervous and had a heavy feeling in my stomach. I did not know what to do. I would either walk away or start cutting. To my astonishment I said to Jennifer, "I feel like carving a prison, you know, one with thick walls and little towers." She did not interrupt her work, but again said, "Go for it."

Finally I began. During the process I could not believe I was making this silly thing. I was nearly finished and started carving the door. I did not like the way it looked and cut it open a little more and then a little more. When I cut the opening the third time, the parallel suddenly hit me—I was beginning to open the door of my own prison, giving myself the freedom to either stay in there or walk out. The realization was so powerful that I had trouble breathing. Jennifer knew all along what was going on and patiently waited for me to recuperate.

When the cement had hardened, I picked up my prison and

threw it into the Arizona desert. But I had become fascinated with direct sculpting. It seemed to connect me with something inside that I had not been aware of and it intrigued me so much that I wanted to find out more.

Back in Vancouver, I joined another school board sculpting course taught by a well-known Québécois artist, where we would learn to work with sahara foam. This is simply the brown foam used in flower shops to hold artificial flower bouquets. It was easy to cut with a pocket knife and we used a scrubby kitchen pad to sand the rough parts. We then used our fingers to smooth it out. Sahara foam was a very fragile medium, but it allowed for quick sculpting without too much thinking. The sculpted foam could be dipped in melted wax, which penetrated into the foam to give it more substance. After the wax was cleaned the sculpture could go directly to the foundry or be left as it was, as it looked like bronze already.

It was the middle of winter again; Toni and I returned to the dry climate of Arizona. I took large pieces of sahara foam with me to sculpt because the resort where we were staying had a large crafts room.

Later on, feeling a little more confident, I began exploring with wax, plaster, and stone. The forms and curves in my work were often simple, with rounded edges instead of sharp corners. I enjoyed this kind of elegance and simplicity in my work as well as in my daily life. Slowly, sculpting became more than an art form in which to express myself: the finished piece became an expression of myself.

Thirty-Eight

A biking buddy at the resort invited me to join a small group of women who met every Saturday morning for what they called satsang, a spiritual meeting, watching videos of a Californian spiritual teacher called Gangaji. Toni had joined the group a few times, but so far I hadn't been interested.

One Saturday morning I joined the group. I was told that Gangaji's teacher was an Indian guru named Sri Poonjaji and his teacher was the famous Sri Ramana Maharshi. Both these teachers had died. This didn't mean much to me, but during the video I found the questions from the audience intriguing. They were talking about the fear of death. Gangaji said we needed to look at fear and move into it instead of avoiding it, that the body will surely die, but that our True Self was indestructible. The message hit me; I recognized this Truth.

What is it that does not die? When the video was over, I asked if I could borrow the videotape as I wanted to see and hear again what Gangaji was saying. I watched and listened again. I borrowed a few more tapes and inquired about Gangaji's next weekend workshop. Soon I found myself driving from Apache Junction, Arizona, to San Diego for one of her retreats. I could not fathom why, but I was crying non-stop during the seven hours it took me to get there. Often, I could not see the road properly, but I did not care and somehow trusted that I would arrive safely.

There were about 350 participants at the retreat. Most people sat on the floor meditating until Gangaji came to the stage. When she arrived, Gangaji also meditated for a short while. After she opened her eyes, she calmly looked around at the participants. She smiled at a few people she recognized and then looked me straight in the eyes. I saw a few people with their hands up, indicating that they wanted to talk to her, but she didn't say anything.

Gangaji took her time looking around and stopped again, her eyes on me. I did not move. As far as I knew I had nothing to ask her, especially in front of 350 people. For the third time, she looked around. Again her gaze stopped on me, and now my hand went up automatically. She smiled and said, "Well, we have been eyeballing each other for some time. Please come up."

I got up and joined her on the stage. I told her that for some reason the words spirituality and God turned me off and most of what she was talking about I did not really understand, but some of what she said, I understood so well that it hit me hard. She took my hand and said, "What you say is true." She asked me some simple questions about my life and we talked about my artwork. We talked especially about the meaning of my pieces and how they were connected to the things that were happening in my life. After all my apprehension, Gangaji helped me feel quite at ease during our meeting in front of such a large group.

During the retreat, I bought some of Gangaji's videos and books, and some by her two Indian teachers. After my return to the resort, I devoured them all and slowly began to become familiar with the terms she used. I also began to see more clearly the real connections between my art and my new inward journey. I continued to learn more about Gangaji's teachings until I left for India a few years later.

Thirty-Nine

Back in Vancouver, I visited an open house art show of stone sculptures. The artist was present, and after I'd chatted with him for a while, he asked to see photographs of my work. He suggested that I join a 10-day stone-carving symposium in the U.S., where he was going to be one of the instructors. It took little convincing; after a brief look at all the information, I signed up, but a few days before it was time to leave, I got cold feet. I had never studied art and did not know how to draw. In my childhood years, I hadn't even possessed drawing paper or pencils. I'd never gone to kindergarten, and the word art was never mentioned at home. But then I thought, "Well, no one there will know me anyway, so I may as well go."

The International Stone Sculpting Symposium was held about an hour's drive south of the Canada/U.S. border at a summer camp in Mt. Vernon, Washington, where we slept in dorms and didn't have to cook. Outside, a large grassy field was dotted with small individual carving stations that had been set up by the sculptors. On one side, a big generator had been installed for people using electrical tools; farther away, the hand carvers had their stations. About 80 sculptors from all over the U.S. and Canada were present. Workshops were organized for beginner, intermediate, and advanced sculptors. The teachers were all well-known artists. Sculptors who had been coming to this event for years had brought their portfolios and we could refer to them at any time of the day for admiration or inspiration.

As soon as I arrived, I was put at ease by other women sculptors. There were no clues to tell me anyone else's level of expertise. We shared stories about our experiences and watched the large trucks full of stone arriving on the field from Alaska, California, Utah, and British Columbia. We were instructed on what qualities to look for and how to choose a good, solid piece. I picked a piece of soapstone, some Utah alabaster, and a piece of Indian pipestone, giving me three stones of different colour and hardness to work with.

I learned how to use and take care of hand tools as well as electrical tools and how to lift and move heavy pieces of stone without hurting myself. Between workshops I often walked around to see what other sculptors were doing. I was amazed at how easily people shared their knowledge; no matter what I was working on, they were genuinely interested. The evenings were filled with slide shows, discussion groups and drumming at the campfires. My soapstone piece made the front page of the stone sculpting magazine and is still a showpiece in Toni's living room. I had a remarkable time.

Before I left, I went a little wild buying all kinds of different stones to work with at home. My car was so heavily loaded that the border inspector wanted to see for himself what I was really bringing into the country.

While I was visiting some friends from Holland, well-known potters who now lived in Albuquerque, New Mexico, one of them got the idea to approach a local welding shop to ask if they would teach us how to weld and work with metal. She found a small shop whose owner was willing to teach us the basics for two days. We went out shopping for eye protectors and welding gloves for women, but discovering that they did not exist, had to make do with the smallest men's size. Once equipped, we got out the oldest clothes we owned and headed for the welding shop. The two of us had a great time and I was totally hooked; I really fell in love with metal work. I had been wondering what would ultimately be my favourite sculpting medium; other artists said, "One day you will just know." It was definitely metal. With the other mediums, I was mainly taking away from the material. Metal allowed me both to take away from the material and to add by welding other pieces onto the evolving shapes.

When the Vancouver School Board offered an adult education course in basic welding, I eagerly signed up. The course helped confirm that my focus would now be working with metal.

The workshop had the right equipment to cut and finish the sculptures and I was therefore able to finish about a dozen small and medium-sized pieces.

After leaving the course, I felt somewhat stalled and considered looking for a mentor or attending art school. My artist friends encouraged me to continue working "hands on." I approached Mr. George Rammell, a well-known artist, teacher, and head of the sculpting component of the Art Institute at Capilano College in the municipality of North Vancouver. After briefly looking at my work, he said, regretfully, that he could only accept 10 students per semester and he had no space. However, he put me on the wait list for the fall/winter semester of 2000 and recommended that I sign up for some art classes and continue my work. George's was a special course for those who had already graduated from an art program but needed direction to take the next step into composing and promoting their own art. I knew I was trying to skip two years of art school to get into his program, but I could not see myself attending two years of art school with teenagers and sitting behind a desk to study art. I wanted to work with my hands. I wanted to get into his third-year art program, which was for more accomplished artists who had pieces in a few galleries and some solo shows behind them.

During the winter, I approached George again with an extended portfolio. This time, having completed a course on how to present my work, I was better prepared. I had worked hard on my new presentation, which included photographs of my new pieces. He looked surprised when I walked into his studio, and again told me he had no space for the spring semester. I gave him my large envelope and said, "Here is my application with some new work. Keep it for the next semester, because I'll be coming back until you do accept me." He opened the envelope and held my slide sheet against the light, motioning to one of his students to get the slide projector. He put the slides in a tray and switched off the light. He began critiquing my pieces in front of the class, making references to sculptors I had never heard of.

Next, George invited me for a walk through the college garden, where he showed me some sculpture installations and asked what I thought of the pieces. Again, he threw out the names of sculptors I did not know, and this time I admitted it. He frowned and said, "You need to spend some time in the library and join some art history classes." I responded that, if he accepted me in this class, I would study extra hard. Again he reminded me that his class was full. But when we got back to his office, he opened his drawer and took out an acceptance form, signed it, and said, "You'll be number 11 then." I couldn't believe it! I thanked him and as I walked away, he called me back and said, "Clasina, you get an A for passion and an A for persistence. See you soon." These were the first A's I had ever received in school! I danced around my car before getting in, and then called Toni at her work. "You deserve it," she said. "You worked so hard to get in. Let's celebrate." She was not only my life partner, she was my friend, and had always been my biggest supporter.

I asked George for a list of artists to study. As promised, I started spending a good deal of time at the Capilano College and downtown libraries, studying well-known sculptors. One day my eyes fell on a book about a female sculptor named Inge King. She was an 83-year-old German woman now living in Australia. When I pulled out the book, my hands began to tremble so much that I had to sit down. As I leafed through the pages and looked at her work I felt as if I had seen it all before. I understood every line and form of her work on a level so profound that I could not explain it. Unaware of time, I suddenly heard the announcement that the library was closing. I was not allowed to check out the book; it was a reference work only. I would be back many times. After I had discovered their works, Inge King and British sculptor Barbara Hepworth became my inspirations.

Gradually, I became aware that I needed increasingly more space for my sculpting and myself. Weather permitting, I began to work outside in the courtyard at the Art Institute at Capilano College. Until then, most of my pieces had been, of necessity, smaller than I'd envisioned them, but here I finally had the opportunity to make pieces as large as I wanted. When sculpting my smaller pieces, still so large that I could hardly carry them myself, I envisioned them in very large form displayed in the middle of busy cities or in outdoor gardens.

Although I wasn't sure how to draw, I sketched my first large piece in a matter of seconds. It came spontaneously, and the moment it was done I knew it was right. It was designed for the seventh-floor roof-top garden of a new Vancouver social housing project for battered women. The women's communal sitting room looked out onto a large, empty wall in the garden, and there would hang my sculpture, called Flowing (see Appendix A).

My next large project was two metal chairs two-and-a-half metres high and one metre wide, placed side by side. This piece, called Looking at it and Looking from it (see Appendix A), again expressed the questions I was pondering now that I was retired.

When the piece was finished, it was installed in front of Capilano College's main building. Because I was there every day, I often watched what was happening around the sculpture. The college students climbed into the chairs at lunchtime. Several people could fit into one chair, so little groups often faced each other as they ate and socialized. The strongly coloured pieces stood out against the starkness of the college's cement structure and seemed to lift the building. And George was getting compliments from the dean of the college.

'Looking at it and Looking from it' at Capilano College.
Picture by George Rammell, see appendix A 2.

I was invited to show the piece in a sculpture garden in Oregon, but instead it was installed in Pyramid Hill Sculpture Park in Hamilton, Ohio, following an invitation from that facility. My fellow students could not believe it. This kind of luck happened very seldom; artists normally got a chance to show their pieces in such prestigious places only after years of hard work. It reinforced a lesson I already knew well, that even when something seems out of reach, at least we can try for it.

Currently, I have two more large pieces installed on the grounds of Capilano College. Spring is a large steel wave structure with different-sized metal balls rolling over the waves. It is a cheerful and playful piece, painted in my favourite colour, bright buttercup yellow. Chaos has large black curved steel pipes crossing over one another. Created immediately after September 11, it represents the World Trade Center towers coming down and the chaos that event created in so many different ways.

I graduated from the Capilano College Art Institute in May 2003. It was the first time I had ever graduated from anything and I wasn't sure I really wanted to attend the ceremony. But Toni encouraged me to attend, saying, "I'll show you how it's done." She took me out for lunch and showered me with gifts. That afternoon,

Graduating from The Art Institute. Sculpture "Chaos".

I wore a cap and gown and, with my fellow student peers, walked across the stage to receive my diploma. The ceremony marked a special moment in my life.

When I reflect back, I can clearly see that my childhood and my years in business had hardened me because I'd had to fight every step of the way. Sculpting allowed me to go back inside again, so I could quietly reconnect with my heart and let the fighter I'd become make more space for love and compassion for others and myself. Sculpting was my stepping-stone into spirituality.

Forty

Over the years my relationship with my mother was what I would call "push and pull." One moment we would get along, even have fun (she can make me laugh like no one else can), and in the next moment all hell would break loose. The arguments mainly focused on the troubled relationship she had with my father and the rivalry between my brothers. For example, I had just started work at the YWCA, when one day I received a phone call from my mother. She was calling from the airport in Vancouver! Apparently she'd had a fight with my father, slammed the door, got in the car, and driven to the Amsterdam airport, taking the first flight out to Canada—without any luggage. "That will teach him", she announced. But she was having trouble getting through customs and asked if I could talk to someone. The agent, who must have had trouble understanding her broken English, took over the phone and said, "Is this woman really your mother? She has come for a visit but has no luggage." It seems that when he'd questioned her, she had replied, "No clothes, nothing. Don't they have stores in Vancouver?" I eventually sorted things out with the agent and picked up my mother.

My eldest brother, Jan, had always felt that my mother favoured my two handicapped brothers, Dirk and Cor, at Jan's expense. In fact, he was right—she did that to extremes.

For years, my mother had run the snack bar and worked day and night with Dirk. Jan often asked, "Mother, when are you going to work for me?" My youngest brother, Cor, lived here in Vancouver, and was my mother's favourite. He had no trouble getting what he wanted from her. In the middle, I was considered to be the strong one, called in for whatever reason, when the others were not speaking to one another anymore. I am not sure if it was a Dutch idiosyncrasy, but when someone's feelings were even slightly hurt, my family members were capable of not talking to one another for years. When I asked each of them why they weren't talking, they usually would have forgotten, but they still found good reasons to maintain their silences. The main stumbling block became who was going to give in and speak to the other first. Instead of communicating between themselves, they would try to involve another family member. Typically, that meant me. The phone line to my home in Canada was usually very busy. It took me years to finally be able to say, "Just figure it out for yourselves."

Before I opened my business in 1984, Cor had been working as a waiter in one of the local Vancouver hotels. He decided that Vancouver was too dull and left for the U.S. to join his new partner in Los Angeles. His departure got off to a bad start right at the border when he lied about why he was entering the United States. His car was confiscated.

After he left Vancouver I only heard about Cor sporadically through my mother's phone calls. I knew that things were not going well for him. She complained that Cor constantly asked her to mail him money, which she did. The jobs he talked about did not materialize, and the money she sent always disappeared quickly. When I visited him a year after he moved, I understood immediately why he had never contacted me. I found him living in a rundown apartment in a derelict area of town. Actually, Cor was very ill, but he seemed intent on reassuring me that everything was fine. I suggested that he come and live in my house and work for the company, but he wouldn't hear of it. "I am not going to work for my sister," he declared. I tidied his apartment, stocked his fridge, and left feeling quite helpless.

Several months later I got a call informing me that Cor had been picked up off the street and was in the hospital. He had AIDS and double pneumonia, and little time left to live. My mother and Jan, who spoke very little English, flew in from Holland and together we visited Cor in the hospital. A terrible shock went through us when we saw him. He had been very sick for some time and had planned to die without telling us what was going on. His apartment had been emptied out by some stranger. He'd been robbed of everything, including his glasses and passport. Out of work for a long time, he was often so hungry that he would scratch the food pictures he found in magazines. He had no medical insurance and was now living in a small, dirty hospital room right next to the noisy boiler room. His eyes looked like those of a wild, frightened animal. After a while my mother and Jan left the room for some air and to get a handle on the situation. Cor whispered to me to come closer and then begged me to take him back to Holland, where he wanted to die with my mother. I promised him that if he could get well enough to be transported by airplane, I would arrange to get him home. The moment I said that, his expression became peaceful and he fell asleep.

While Cor slept, my mother and brother went for lunch, but I couldn't eat and remained at the hospital. While waiting to speak to the doctor, I looked into a large room where other male AIDS patients lay in beds. At that time, most people were still afraid to be in the same room as an AIDS patient, let alone touch him. Too many things remained unknown about the virus. As a result, there were no visitors in the room. I said a few words here and there, and sat at their bedsides for a few moments. They looked so lost and abandoned as they silently cried. There was so much pain and such loneliness. I left the room crying. I did not want my brother to die like that.

Cor's doctor was not hopeful for any recovery, and thus it became a wait and see situation. Finally, Cor pulled through and he was transported to Holland. In a way he was lucky, because he had kept his Dutch citizenship. When he arrived at the airport in Amsterdam, an ambulance and our family doctor were waiting for him and he was transported immediately to the hospital. In Holland, the new drug, AZT, had just begun to be dispensed to AIDS patients, and the new treatment made him well enough to go home. He had his own little apartment for a short while, but soon the drug's side effects caused him serious mental illness and, ultimately, blindness. It was heartbreaking to visit him in the psychiatric unit of the hospital, where he sat on the floor in a room with only a mattress, banging his head against the wall.

My mother grew very old during that period of time. It didn't matter to her that some relatives, fearful of AIDS, no longer came to visit our family home; she stood by her son. No matter what my mother had done wrong in her life, during Cor's illness I admired her greatly.

Cor died at the age of 41. It seemed very unreal to me. Thinking back to our childhood, I knew Cor had never been beaten, but this fragile and sensitive, young adolescent had been severely traumatized by witnessing the abuse in our family. I remembered him cowering and scared, watching it all, helpless to do anything. I did not know which was worse, being beaten or seeing the abuse.

My mother stopped working at the Snack Bar. She was now 72 and had lost all her vitality. The business was sold and Dirk and my mother moved into their own separate, small apartments in the village where all of us children had grown up.

Over the years since I moved to Canada, I returned to Holland about once a year to visit my mother and friends. Our relationship only became easier when I was finally able to visit her without any expectations and was able to fully accept her limitations as a mother and a human being. For too many years, I had clung to my desire for a mother who would give me approval, love, and affection. I finally accepted that she was simply unable to provide those things.

Toward the end of her life, my mother finally asked for her daughter, not her sons. I was with her for three days before she died. When I realized she was struggling with something, I asked her what was on her mind. Finally, she asked me if my father had ever sexually abused me. For a moment I wondered why she was asking me this now. Then I quickly realized there was no use at all in talking about this. I calmly told her that, no, he only beat us really badly.

When the end approached, she asked me to hold her hand, and I had to promise not to let it go before she breathed her last breath. When she was no longer responsive, the only sound was her intense, deep, loud breathing. The doctor said she was unconscious, but I continued to talk to her. I could see that she was struggling to let go. Her heavy breathing went on for several hours until finally I saw her eyes open as she took her last breath. As she looked at me, her eyes filled with tears, and it was then that I saw God. With reluctance, I use this word—God. Despite the things that were awakening inside of me, it did not fit into the lexicon of my reality. But I had no choice—there was no better word.

I had two weeks to organize her funeral and cremation. Before I returned to Canada, I called Martine's father and step-mother in Paris to let them know about my mother's death. Two days later, Martine called from Paris on her way home from India to give her condolences. I hadn't heard from her for at least 10 years. She told me a little about her guru, Amma, and the ashram in India where she and her partner had lived for several years. She encouraged me to come for a short visit with them in Switzerland before I headed back to Canada. Somehow, I found two days and flew over. After many years of silence and separation, we had a wonderful visit. Before I left, I promised to talk to Toni about visiting them in India.

On my last day in Holland, I put my mother's ashes in the grave next to my brother Cor's urn. As she had wished, a new stone with both of their names was installed. When my flight left Amsterdam, I felt a huge sense of relief. I was happy that I had been able to put my own feelings aside and be there, totally, for my mother. She was gone now, and I knew there was nothing more I could have done.

Part III

"I have no abode, I live in your heart"
Mata Amritanandamayi Ma or Amma

Forty-One

When I returned to Canada, Toni and I decided to plan a two-month trip to India and Thailand during the upcoming winter months. Our travels would include a one-week visit with Martine and her partner in the ashram in Amritapuri, India. As we exchanged mail with Martine, Toni and I began to get an idea about their lifestyle.

In the course of our correspondence, Martine had written to us about their guru, Amma, which means Mother. She had even mailed a few pictures, but none of it meant much to us. According to Martine, Amma spent every day hugging great numbers of people, often over 10 thousand each day, without getting up or eating. Martine also wrote that Amma did not sleep and actively ran many different charities. I could not imagine how anyone could physically and mentally do the things she described. I also had a great deal of trouble believing that the sheer number of people she claimed Amma hugged each day could be true. We asked our friends if there was a dress code in the ashram. They explained that most people wore white, but it was fine to wear whatever we wanted, except shorts and short-sleeved shirts.

When we arrived in India and stayed at a guesthouse in Trivandrum, the owner directed us to a well-known shop in town to buy fabric and then to a tailor, where we had some fine white cotton clothes made. Whether visiting an ashram or not, being dressed in soft, white cotton in such a warm climate felt very comfortable.

During our stay in this cozy guest house we met a few other Western travellers. When we told them we were on our way to visit the backwaters in Kerala and our friends in the ashram, they became enthusiastic about visiting the area. Together we decided to rent a traditional rice boat for the journey. The boat would go as far as the ashram and drop us off. The others would try to see Amma and get their famous hug, visit the ashram and the temple, and continue their trip.

While gliding silently through the backwaters for the next four hours, we passed many small villages with little activity; here and there some people in little boats were fishing or transporting people. It was a peaceful and beautiful ride. After a time I began to wonder where all of the Divine Mother's thousands of devotees were supposed to live. Finally in the distance we noticed some tall pink buildings, entirely out of place with the gentle scenery and small huts. It was our first glimpse of the ashram. The rice boat crew attached the ropes to the dock while taking nearly all of the landing space on the ashram's sandy property.

Amma, we were told, could be seen that evening when people would gather to sing bhajans (devotional chanting). The following day she would be receiving people for darshan (meeting with the Divine)—in Amma's ashram it refers to receiving her famous hug. Our travel companions decided to have a look around and leave.

Our friends were expecting us. Martine told us that we were really lucky—they had been able to book a tiny room with a window and an attached washroom, including a toilet and shower, for the two of us. Normally, the apartments were shared with at least two other people. Toni and I were installed in the little apartment after we handed in our passports and were provided with thin mattresses, sheets, and pillows. The cost of US$3.00 per day included our room and board, which consisted mainly of rice and curried vegetables.

The ashram provided Western food when Amma was not travelling. It also had a Western-style café that stayed open most of the day where we could get coffee, omelettes, porridge, yogurt, fruit juices, muffins, and cookies—all at very reasonable prices. Inside our room, everything was constructed out of cement, there was no wood. We discovered there was no need for blankets in January or February. The large, beautiful cotton scarves we had purchased from the street vendors served just fine for sheets and covers.

While we explored the ashram grounds, we noticed right away that, rather than hugging or shaking hands, Indians as well as Westerners were greeting each other by putting both hands together and bowing their heads slightly or putting their right hands on their hearts. I especially enjoyed the greeting, Namah Shivaya, which was a way of saying, "the spirit in me greets the spirit in you."

Our first glance of the guru was that night. We joined thousands—yes, thousands!—of Indians and Westerners dressed in white or soft colours gathered in the big hall and now sat quietly on the floor waiting for Amma to arrive. Finally, we watched as a small, dark-skinned woman in a white sari quickly walked up to the stage, followed by a few other women dressed in white, yellow, and orange. We learned that the people dressed in orange robes were the swamis and swaminis. They were the men and women who took the monastic vows of celibacy and renunciation and had dedicated their lives to serving Amma for many years.

Amma bowed to the people seated in the hall, then sat down, crossed her legs, and whispered a few words to her swamis. The chanting started. I had never heard this kind of chanting or music before. I had no idea what they were chanting, but it was soothing and after a while, I closed my eyes and let it all sink in. Slowly I began to distinguish a kind of primal voice. I focused on this sound and soon a vibration began to touch the core of my body. A little later I realized that this was the Mother singing. I had never heard a voice like it and I have never been able to describe it properly. I was told that Amma calls all the people she meets and hugs "her children;" here she was singing with her children. It was a new experience for me; my birth mother had never sung to me. That first evening and ever since, I've had the feeling that Amma is singing for me alone, whether she is in front of me on stage or on one of the many CDs I've since bought.

The next morning, we were told that Amma would teach the newcomers how to meditate and then give satsang, a gathering for spiritual discourse, for everyone in the temple. She would then bless and serve lunch. Our friends wanted to make sure we had a close view of Amma, so we were seated on the small balcony inside the temple. The men sat on one side of the temple and the women on the other. Normally during satsang, Amma answered questions from her devotees, but this time she asked a few questions and invited people to come to the microphone and speak. Her questions focused on the recent terrorist attacks of September 11, 2001 in the U.S. Why would people commit such atrocities? What was the suffering of this world all about? To say the least, it was an interesting debate. Some Western devotees were passionately outraged and unforgiving, still too hurt to even think about forgiving. Others were subdued and compassionate about the broader issues. Amma listened quietly and later explained that we bring suffering upon our own selves. We forget that we are ultimately One. It is our separateness from each other, taking care of our own selves instead of thinking of others and the universe first, that causes our suffering. We are always striving after more and more. It is this endless need to satisfy our five outer senses that creates so much accumulated greed and anger. This was a very simple comment but one so profound it made me ponder for quite some time.

Around noon, the doors of the temple opened and large tables, heavy pots and piles of plates were brought in. A table was installed in front of Amma, and the women devotees started filling up metal plates with rice, vegetables, and curry sauce. The men got up first and formed a line. I glanced over to Toni and rolled my eyes. We were in a land where men were served first no matter where you went. But we knew we would do as the Indians did. However, after some time, I noticed that the men, who had already picked up their food, were not touching it, but were quietly waiting. I was told that Amma would first serve everyone and then take her first bite, after which we would all eat together.

It had taken a while to get into the food line, but I was finally getting closer to the table where Amma was serving "her children". Although several thousand were to be fed, it was well organized and the plates, full of food, were moving fast. During the entire time I was in the lineup, I was fascinated and couldn't take my eyes off Amma. I watched her as she served food and smiled and said a word here and there. Everyone walked away with a plate full of food and a smile on their faces. When the woman in front of me walked away with her plate I moved forward. Finally it was my turn. Now I could see Amma in full view, close up.

She bent slightly sideways for my plate, slid it in front of her, and then lifted up her empty hands as she looked up and straight into my eyes. Her whole face radiated with a smile of recognition as if to say, "Hello. You are finally here." Suddenly I had no more words, no more thoughts, there was no more world, no more anything. There was no beginning and no end. A warm energy flowed through my body. I knew instantly that we had met before, that she knew who I was, and that she knew everything about me. I had never been so certain of anything. I had just met my real Mother. I had met The Mother, who knew only how to give and who didn't ask for anything in return. She communicated a total acceptance of who I really was, with no judgment, just pure love and compassion. I was stunned, speechless and, later, overwhelmed with gratitude.

It was explained to me later that I must have been ready to meet my true teacher and that I had been given a glimpse of my True Self. Amma was mirroring my True Self. I did not understand this language. What was my True Self? Immediately I wanted to know more about Mother, whose full name is Mata Amritanandamayi, meaning Mother of Immortal Bliss. She was also known simply as Ammachi, or Amma. I bought her autobiography and read about Mother deep into the night, learning about her troubled childhood and her unbelievable devotion. Fortunately, Amma had been born in India, because her unusual behaviour in a Western country would surely have ended in her institutionalization in a psychiatric hospital.

Amma, or Sudhamani, as she was called as a child, was born on September 27, 1953, in a small fishing village in the state of Kerala in the south of India. Her father was a simple fisherman. She was one of the middle children in a family of thirteen, five of whom died in infancy. It is said that upon her birth, Sudhamani didn't cry but instead had a beaming smile. Although her parents were light coloured, Sudhamani's skin was of dark, bluish complexion, a physical characteristic that was disdained by her family and relatives. Her dark complexion was the main reason why Sudhamani was forced to leave school (her other sisters had a lighter skin colour) in the fourth grade to be the family servant when her mother became chronically ill. She assumed the responsibility, and the servitude, without complaining. That she had been singled out to work and serve her family and other relatives like a slave simply because of her dark skin, was puzzling to me, although while travelling in India, I had already noticed that very dark-skinned people were often treated with scorn and that they occupied the more menial jobs.

During her childhood, the customs of the caste system frowned upon touching people from a lower caste, but from an early age Sudhamani showed an immense compassion for the poor and she was not afraid to touch or hug anyone. She often fed the hungry from her own family's meagre supplies, an act for which she was repeatedly beaten. She also had an unusual tendency to constantly chant the name of Krishna. While carrying his picture and chanting Krishna's name, she would often faint in ecstasy, behaviour her parents did not understand.

Reading about Sudhamani's compassion for the poor and her steadfastness in practicing what she believed at such a young age gradually opened my heart. While reading her biography, what stood out for me was that no matter how badly she was mistreated by her family, relatives, and the other people who negatively judged her curious behaviour, she never harboured any bad feelings toward them.

However, despite my profound experience upon meeting Amma and reading about her childhood, I was still suspicious and guarded. When I received my first darshan—a hug—from Amma, Martine cried and hugged me. She told me that she had been praying for years for me to come and get Amma's darshan. I hadn't expected anything from the darshan and all I took away from it was an awareness of the firmness of Amma's hug and her wonderful, sweet smell.

A few days later, there was talk amongst the ashramites about the many people who would soon be arriving for Devi Bhava, an event at which a guru embodies the energy of a goddess.

They explained that during Devi Bhava, Amma embodied the energy of the Divine Mother, which in the Hindu tradition was an expression of her love and compassion for all forms. My curiosity was really aroused when I looked down from the apartment building's balcony to see canoes filled with families, dressed in their best clothing and laden with suitcases and bags, being transported across the water to the ashram. I wondered where they would all sleep and eat. Several times I went down and wandered through the crowds, watching in astonishment as everyone sat, ate, slept, or waited wherever there was space on the ashram grounds or in the hall or temple. No one was in a hurry or seemed concerned about what was going to happen next. The event was supposed to carry on through the night and continue well into the morning.

Numbered tickets were being handed out by Indian women devotees in yellow saris to the long lines of local people on the steps of the temple. For some reason, all the Westerners in attendance were given their tickets in the hall. I thought this was a good opportunity to have a close look at how they counted people. It seemed impossible to me that any human being could hug 10,000 to 15,000 people without getting up, eating, or going to the washroom. In addition, it was said that Amma hardly ever slept. This information made all of the activities appear even more mysterious, and my scepticism and suspicion increased. The event was to happen in the big hall and would go on all night until the last person received Mother's hug.

In the early morning hours, one of Martine's friends asked me if I would like to help give prasad, which is normally something edible that has been blessed by the guru. She showed me several devotees sitting directly behind Amma who were rolling candies into small sealed paper bags of sacred ashes blessed by Amma. Other devotees placed these little bags into Amma's hand; she then handed one to each person she hugged. I sat down and was shown how to roll the candies into the little bags. Although the task seemed to be very easy, there was a kind of nervous energy involved in this duty and the women who were teaching me were solemn and exacting about how it should be done. Finally, I seemed to get the corners tucked in correctly and was shown how to give the prasad, three little bags at a time, into Amma's hand. I was instructed not to lean on Amma's hand when giving her the bags. It should be effortless. I moved right next to her and when her hand opened up I put a cluster of three little bags in it. Then I heard the woman sitting behind Amma's chair say, "She is not doing it right." I also heard the woman who had just taught me how to give Amma the prasad say that I was doing it wrong. It reminded me so much of how I had tried endlessly to please my mother, hoping for some affection, and yet it had never come. I began to feel nauseated and suffocated, like a heavy weight had descended upon my chest and I had trouble breathing. All I wanted to do was run off the stage, but then I suddenly felt a warm feeling flowing through my whole body and heard a loving, warm, and clear voice in my heart say, "My child, whatever you do for me is right." I knew immediately that this was Amma's voice.

I cannot remember how I got off the stage but apparently I stumbled into Toni's arms and cried for hours. A huge weight had drained out of me. Later on, I returned to the stage and watched Amma from a distance as she continued hugging and wiping away the tears of the thousands of crying people, all of whom were pulling and hanging on to her for dear life, needing and wanting. While standing there, the realization struck me that this human being called Amma could not possibly be a normal human being. What she was doing seemed humanly impossible. Amma kept hugging until about 11 o'clock the next morning. She had hugged over 17,000 people. I had seen it with my own eyes, and I was awestruck.

Toni and I stayed at the ashram for an extra three days until Amma left on a North India Tour with her many devotees, including Martine and her partner.

Forty-Two

After we left, Toni and I took taxis through the countryside and into the mountains, visiting the many temples in Madurai. Then we boarded the train to Tiruvannamalai, where we sought out the ashram of Sri Ramana Maharshi (1879–1950), to whom I had been introduced by Gangaji, my spiritual teacher from California. Here, I bought many more books about the teachings of Sri Ramana Maharshi. We walked around the holy Mountain of Arunachala and explored the caves in which the guru had lived and meditated for many years in silence.

We headed up the East Coast to Mamalapurum and watched as street-side sculptors pounded large rocks and carved statues of the Indian gods and goddesses. We stayed in Sri Aurobindo's ashram in Pondicherry and visited the Aurobindo community. Finally, we relaxed in a hotel on the beach for a week before flying off to Thailand. During all this time my mind was continually focused on Amma, and I wanted nothing more than to find a quiet place and read her books.

After leaving Amma's ashram, I noticed I had lost interest in sightseeing. All I wanted to do now was read about Amma. For Toni's sake, I went through the motions when we visited interesting places, but my mind was elsewhere.

When we arrived in Bangkok, I went through culture shock. Toni loved it, but I hated the city and promised myself I would never return. The Thai people seemed to possess innumerable tricks to cheat or rob us of our money. While I realized many of them were poor, I could not become comfortable in such a society. We decided to sign up for sightseeing tours to get away from it all. But the tour operators stopped, whether we wanted to or not, at jewellery stores and attractions not mentioned in their brochures. One couldn't even take a taxi or rickshaw to a specific place without the driver trying to stop somewhere so they could get a commission or a free tank of gas from a shop owner.

The crowds and traffic, the pollution and noise of Bangkok made me want to hide in the hotel until our departure, when we were scheduled to fly to the island of Koh Samui and meet up with friends. I ended up by the hotel's swimming pool with my books and Toni went off sightseeing by herself. Instead of travelling through Thailand, we stayed for several weeks on the island of Koh Samui. We were both tired and content to relax on the beach and soak up the sun.

Upon our return home to Canada, I had two dreams that made a deep impression on me. As a rule, I did not focus on my dreams and forgot them by the time I woke up. These two, however, remained vivid in my mind. In the first dream, I was in a garden picking up some soil with both hands. I closed my hands and when I slowly opened them again an exquisite light-green, spring lettuce started growing in my palms. It grew to a beautiful, full-sized lettuce. I woke up.

In the second dream, I was in a place I did not recognize and I was told to get on bus 18A. When I got to the bus loop, I saw a bus with that number and bought a ticket. I asked for a map of the area. The bus left and after a while I opened up the map to see where I was going. The map was blank. I woke up. I did not know the meaning of these dreams, but I was struck by their clarity.

Forty-Three

A short time after this, at a party in early 2003, I met Denise, an astrologer who was also a healer and counsellor. She agreed to do my very first astrology reading. At the outset of the reading, I asked Denise about my two dreams. She told me that the first dream explained the present transformative process I was going through. The dirt represented the earth on which we live. The lettuce was the earth's creation; a higher existence, a higher frequency, and I was creating it by opening my hands and allowing it to flourish. The process of transformation was in my hands.

About the second dream, she said that the number 18A was a numerological nine, meaning an initiation. The blank map explained that I was not supposed to predict or strategize on this journey nor be permitted to know the outcome, which was contained within the process of the journey itself.

I needed to be patient, and because I was a "doer," I needed to know that this time the doing was taking place on an entirely different frequency. All I had to do was learn where that frequency was and tune into it. She explained that my impatience stemmed from a fear that I was not going to reach an outcome or complete my journey. But here we were talking about the soul's purpose. At this stage in my life, said Denise, I was perfectly on time and on schedule, completely into my rhythm. My chart showed that.

I was in this life to find justice and beauty. If I saw unjust situations I became angered and would fight for justice. She explained that I was a very strong person. I spoke my mind and people would have to take it. I asked her pointedly if I had much more to accomplish. "Yes," she said, "but you have to work in a different way this time. You are looking for a new way to find deep, inner security, and it is spiritual security you seek now. It

217

has to be found in a 'deep letting go' as opposed to holding on. But it is energy we are talking about, not 'things.'"

I then asked Denise about my relationship, as I sensed that Toni and I were growing apart. She replied, "It is true—you are. You may be able to hold on in a different way, or stay connected in an entirely different way, and you may not. But if it happens, it will be an easy transition."

Denise said that I was a triple air sign, connected with metal. That seemed to validate my big metal sculptures. While sculpting was decidedly a stepping-stone to the awareness of my spirituality, she said, my interest in it might be short-lived.

I questioned her about my relationships with people. She said, "People around you will evolve as they are supposed to. Learning to detach will be important in the journey you are about to undertake. That is always the hardest lesson for anyone going into that journey, because we are all attached. Detachment is actually very loving," she added. "You are not trying to change them or tell them what's good or bad, what's right or wrong. You're just giving them respect by letting them go. I think that's very compassionate."

Finally, Denise said, "You will be completely immersed in your purpose in this lifetime by the time May arrives."

Forty-Four

It was now early June 2003. Toni and I decided to take our motor-home to meet up with Amma's tour of the United States. Her two-month tour would include many different cities all over the country. We had other engagements, so we intended to join the tour at its first two stops, in Seattle, Washington, and San Ramon, California. Several of our friends, now curious about the new spiritual teacher in our lives, came along and attended the public meetings in Seattle. Some stayed for the two-day retreat.

Seattle had a large following of long-time Amma devotees. They had regular satsang and bhajan practices and were involved in different charitable activities in the city. Many devotees from various parts of British Columbia travelled regularly to Seattle to attend these different events.

About 6,000 people attended the free public event in the downtown core of Seattle. During my darshan, I asked Amma if I could come to India for her 50th birthday celebrations, and she agreed. I asked her if I could join her European tour in the fall and she said, "Yes, yes." I had been told that the European tour was already full, but Mother's "yes" could change everything.

During the event, two German devotees asked me if we were heading to San Ramon after the retreat. If so, could they join us? I checked with Toni, who was fine with the idea of extra passengers, so I gave them a key to the motor-home and invited them to settle in after Devi Bhava.

At about 7 a.m., close to the end of Devi Bhava, a young American devotee, Sarvaga, approached me and asked if she could also join us on our trip to San Ramon. This time I was inclined to say no. I did not really relish the idea of having five people in the motor-home all the way south. As this feeling passed through me, I saw Amma lean over and gaze at me while she was giving darshan to someone. I answered that we might not have enough seat-belts for so many people, but Sarvaga just nodded and said, "Don't worry. Amma always finds me a seat at the very last minute." She left and sat down on the stage. I could already see the end of the darshan line and wondered how she was going to find a seat in time. Guilt overcame me. How could I refuse to take her? I turned around, intending to head to the motor-home to count the seat-belts. But before I left the hall I looked back to the stage and again I saw Amma leaning over and looking at me as she gave darshan.

Our motor-home did have five seat-belts, so I had no reason to say no to Sarvaga. I returned to the hall's stage and invited Sarvaga to join us. Again Mother looked straight at me—and I laughed. She was ensuring that her devotees, her children, were all taken care of.

When Toni and I returned from breakfast, all three of our passengers were spread out on the beds laughing and counting their good fortune in being able to sleep all the way to San Ramon. They asked if we could try to be in San Ramon by the next morning for their 10 a.m. seva (selfless service or duty). I promised to do my best but had no intention of speeding. Normally we drove the 15-metre motor-home and car at between 85 and 95 kilometres per hour.

The three devotees had worked all night and were exhausted, and soon I had a motor-home full of sleeping women. I had slept a few hours and the trip south on the US I-5 freeway was going well. Driving, even large vehicles, was relaxing to me. Having been a professional driver for years, I was tuned in at all times to what happened on the road. A bhajan tape was playing and I was settled in for the long haul. For a long time while I drove I smiled to myself about Mother's clear message to me to be more generous. Then I noticed something unusual. Our motor-home was passing trucks at a speed of over 110 kilometres per hour without feeling any pull. The motor-home drove unusually smoothly at that high speed the entire day. It made me laugh even more. Mother's presence was right there; I could feel it. The next morning when we arrived in front of the ashram, Toni unhooked the car and drove the devotees to the front of the hall, where they arrived at exactly 10 a.m, just as Mother walked in. As I drove back onto the highway and passed some trucks, I could feel our vehicle's usual pull once more. Mother's children had been dropped off and I was to pay more attention and slow down again.

Forty-Five

During our 10-day stay in San Ramon, I decided to ask Amma for a spiritual name; suddenly it became important to me to have one. To this day I'm still not sure what my desire was all about at that time. Perhaps a part of me knew a new life lay ahead of me.

Normally, three lines lead to Amma. The fastest line, where regular devotees or new people gathered to obtain her famous hug or ask a simple quick question, was in the middle. It headed straight to where Mother sat. The other two lines approached Mother from her sides; one was the question line and the other was for special needs people. These lines were monitored. When I asked the person in charge of Amma's question line how to go about getting a spiritual name, I was told that Mother hadn't given any new names lately. For several days I continued to ask, until finally I was told to line up after the question line and perhaps Mother would give out some names.

Finally the question line was over and soon I was kneeling next to Mother's chair. She gave no hint that she knew I was there; she just kept on giving darshan. Kneeling was not easy for me—I had developed osteoarthritis in my hip and knees some time ago—but I was determined to stay there.

In my heart, I kept asking Mother for the one thing I most wanted: to help me to see the Divine in everything. I also vowed to her that I would keep asking the same question until my last breath. And I knew I would. For a time it seemed she would not give out names that day. But after what felt like about half an hour she turned toward me and gave me a loving smile. Very gently, she pinched my cheek, and gave me the name of SitaLakshmi. I had an idea what the name meant but wanted to be sure. I asked Swamini Krishnamrita, who smiled and said that it was a very beautiful name. Sita was the consort of the god Ram. She was known for her patience and loyalty. The goddess Lakshmi was known for providing abundance, wealth and spiritual liberation. Since then, I have carried my new name with much happiness. It has reminded me to be more patient, more forgiving, and more generous. Receiving my new name also made me feel like I was undertaking a new beginning. I knew that from now on a life with more gentleness lay ahead of me.

Forty-Six

In August of that same year, I left for India again to join Amma's 50th birthday celebration. Later that fall I would travel straight from India to Europe to join Amma's European tour.

As soon as I walked through the check-in points at the airport in Vancouver, I got my tape player out and played bhajans, the musical chanting prayers. Although I still understood very few of the words, it connected me to something. There was something very familiar about the sound and music. Amma's voice calmed me, and automatically focussed my attention inward.

I had decided that, if I was going to India for a few months to stay in Amma's ashram, that I would also visit another well-known avatar, Bhagavan Sri Sathya Sai Baba. I would travel to his birth town, Puttaparthi, about 180 kilometres north of Bangalore. Worldwide estimates suggested that Sai Baba had over 10 million devotees. I had read several books about him and was intrigued. His messages were very similar to those of other avatars, or self-realized people. He was known for his miracles in healing people from all kinds of diseases. He also produced all kinds of trinkets such as mallets, stones, and statues seemingly from nowhere into his hand, and then gave them to his devotees. I could not really understand why he did that. But then, some people found it unusual that Mother hugged everyone day in and day out.

Instead of miracles in Sai Baba's ashram, I saw huge crowds of people from all over the world. Each day it took hours for everyone to be searched and seated in the hall for darshan. Everyone was required to pass through a metal detector, and other stringent rules were enforced. If you were not wearing the proper scarf or your money belt was too big, you were refused entry into the hall. For some reason, my small meditation cushion was found offensive; it was taken from me and I never saw it again. When Sai Baba finally arrived, he was slowly driven into the hall in a golf cart. He looked thin and frail. I was told that he had recently fallen and was still recovering. He smiled, waved, picked up letters from outstretched hands, and nodded at a few people who then followed him into his meeting room. It took a total of three minutes, and then bhajans followed. One meaning of darshan is "meeting the guru." However, with Sai Baba it appeared to mean that the guru passed you or the guru looked at you, or you might be lucky enough to be invited for an interview. So far, I had not met anyone who had ever been invited for an interview. I reflected on what this darshan meant to me. I did not feel anything, but observed people as devoted and touched as when others met Amma.

I did get into the line at 3:30 a.m. to attend chanting the Omkar, meaning twenty-one Oms, at 5:00 a.m. The small temple could accommodate only a limited number of people. Once the door opened, it took some jostling to find a cramped space to sit. The energy was so strong that one morning my body started to shake uncontrollably. I was not afraid and let it happen. The shaking did not stop until I rose and left.

After five days I decided to leave for Amritapuri, where Amma's ashram was located. After my latest experience, I missed Amma more than ever. I kept saying over and over, "Amma, thank you for hugging us. Thank you for singing and talking to us. Thank you for spoiling us and letting us sit so close to you." Mother had always made it clear that we should not attach ourselves to her form, but I was in a hurry and took a flight, not a train, to Cochin, a large city north of Amritapuri.

During the plane and taxi ride, I pondered my meetings with the two different avatars, Amma and Sai Baba. I knew I was not able to appreciate to the fullest who they really were. Could others? Here I was in a country with a completely different culture and form of devotion, meeting what they called avatars, Godlike people, they said, who came into this world to lighten the dark energy in which many of us lived and functioned. They left when they decided to. After some thought, I concluded that their existence was beyond what my mind could understand. I accepted this and became quiet inside, yet I was aware of a force in me that needed to learn even more. I seemed to have no other choice but to follow this instinct. Would this trip give me the answers I sought?

I took a taxi from Cochin airport to Amritapuri. The taxi driver was talking as fast as he was driving. The torrential rain, typical of August, had caused the taxi's windows to steam up, but the driver must have had radar in his head because he was leaning rather heavily on the gas pedal. Driving in India was a special experience, the thrill varying depending on the state of one's nerves. I usually thought it better to look out of the side windows instead of straight ahead. There seemed to be no road rules—drivers kept to the middle of the road and only swerved at the last minute to avoid oncoming traffic. They loved honking. Signs on all the trucks read PLEASE HONK. The noise was constant. Perhaps the drivers released their frustrations in this way—they rarely yelled at one another. There seemed to be a system or secret honking language between them because most of the time they managed to avoid each other just at the last moment.

Forty-Seven

Amma's 50th birthday was on September 27. Plans had been made to hold a four-day celebration in Cochin, and people from all over India and around the world were expected to attend. Mother agreed to celebrate this birthday because her devotees wanted it; as for herself, she said she would rather we come to pray and chant for world peace. She said that the present situation in the world needed more positive energy, and with hundreds of thousands of devotees praying and singing for peace, universal energy would change for the better. I would not have wanted to miss this special celebration, but I also felt some inexplicable force pushing me to attend and I needed to find out what it was all about.

When I arrived at the ashram at 6 p.m., the registration office was closed, so I had to wait to register until after bhajans. Amma came into the hall. Children surrounded her as she walked toward the stage. I was always surprised at how tiny she looked, while her presence felt so very big. After bhajans, dinner was served and I was assigned to a room. There were already a Belgian and a Croatian woman in the room. It was tight, and I was told that eventually we would be four in this little space because the ashram was so crowded. The others soon left and I got the only real bed in the room. The remaining space was filled with a small kitchen with a sink but no cooking facilities, and a toilet and cold shower. There were no cupboards; I would keep my clothes in my suitcases and on lines hung across the room.

Within a few days, I became ill, suffering from stomach aches and migraine headaches. Soon after their arrival, many other people also became sick. Some attributed our illnesses to Amma. Others believed it was meant to happen so our defences would be down and our cleansing could begin. Whatever one wanted to believe, we were sick, our defences were down, and our cleansing took place. In this way we could start our inner work.

Sick or not, it was wonderful to be surrounded by Amma's energy, see her smiles, and receive her darshan. In my first darshan she had held me for some time and stroked my back. Now I knew what that meant. She opened up my channels and thus helped me connect better with her and with myself. While in her lap I recognized her scent. Sometimes when I was at home in Canada or, say, out for a walk here at the ashram, I would suddenly get a whiff of her scent, and it confirmed that Mother was right there with me. I had spoken to many other people to whom her scent had also suddenly manifested.

Surrounded by devotees that by now I knew, I enjoyed being called by my new spiritual name, SitaLakshmi. I began to trust that Mother would take me where I needed to go. I had a very clear image in my mind and heart of a little three-year-old blonde child—me—in a white dress and shoes that I recognized well. The child held Mother's hand and we walked into the light. Briefly I wondered why I envisioned myself at the age of about three. But then I realized that at that age, I was not yet conditioned to the realities of life. I was innocent and pure, ready to be shaped and guided. I felt that way now.

I did not know how to express my gratitude for meeting Amma. I just kept repeating, "Thank you, Mother." I tried to work hard on what she was teaching. I failed over and over again, but here and there a glimmer of it got through, and I just kept trying. I now had a deep knowing; it was that I would continue to try until the end of my life. I did not seem to have a choice anymore. This path was giving me a richness and fullness I could not explain. It was not an easy path. I was repeatedly confronted with my impatience and my tendency to be critical—of both others and myself. I had to let go in so many different ways. My new journey had troubled some of my family and friends. I experienced much sadness through the loss of these old-time friends, some of whom I had known for 20 to 25 years. Some were disturbed by the expression of devotion and ceremonies in and around Amma's presence. For instance, why was it necessary to wear white clothes during

Amma's visits to the West? I was constantly reminded to be careful—"They are after your money, Clasina." My sadness also came from having to question the sincerity of those friendships. Amma said that our attachment to other people mostly brought suffering.

I had now accepted Amma as my true Mother, my guru and my teacher. I was committed to do my work on myself to the best of my ability, to try to overcome my endless worldly desires, to open my heart to all people instead of only those in my daily life, and to be more patient and forgiving. Mother said that eventually, one day or another in one life or another, we all had to follow the spiritual path to realize the Self. It was now my understanding that to realize the Self was the reason why we were born into a human body.

The task of realizing the True Self was to undertake a journey toward being One with "All That Is;" being One with "That" which resided in me and could not be removed, "That" which would stay when my body dropped, "That" which was not conditioned. The task was to become One with Divine Energy. My simple mind could actually understand that nothing in our lives was real. If I looked at any solid object on this earth, I knew that in reality it was not as constant or as solid as it looked, as each object could be pulverized and made smaller until it finally became pure energy. And there existed pure consciousness. After that I could simply acknowledge only that there was faith.

I got glimpses of what this might be all about, even while I did not understand it. I simply had to let it be. Mother's messages and teachings were simple and very clear, but to do the work was extremely difficult. How could I surrender and still work on my impatience, doubts, desires, or anger? The ashram was the perfect place, and even better would be to go on tour with Mother, where I would be confronted with these things continually and surrounded by support. Mother would place me in many situations to help me practice what I needed to learn as long as I remained open and willing to confront myself. Mother loved chaos as a teaching tool, and would put me right in the middle of it over and over again. When I say that she put me into these situations, I mean that I had to believe she was beyond what I could imagine, that she was the

Divine incarnated, or totally One with the universe. Otherwise, none of it would make sense.

If I compared Mother with anyone I seemed to understand better, I thought of Jesus Christ. I was not very familiar with the Bible, but Jesus did promise to come back to earth. Did He say when, how, or what He would look like? How would people recognize Him? What if someone came up to us and said, "Hi am Jesus, I am back now." The person would be ignored or treated gently, as people would think of him insane, or on drugs or alcohol. Who knew? Jesus might or might not be in a physical body at the moment. I believed that Jesus had been back on this earth already many times, but in different forms, and that is why we did not recognize Him. I think that in truth, Jesus never left this earth – His spirit has always been present for those who desire to connect with Him, and I believed that Jesus and Mother and many other Mahatma's, or Avatars, were and are One and the same Being. They were and are what I called the embodiment of Love and God, as we all are, but we do not have the capacity to see the spark of the divine in each other or ourselves. I believed that Mother was an incarnation of "All That Is" – an embodiment of unconditional love.

Amma did not claim to be anything. She only gave of herself. It was her incredible humbleness and her tireless outpouring of pure love and compassion that made me fall quiet and believe in her divinity. Her purity was as spotless as the white sari she wore. I was in awe of her all the time.

People ask me, "But how do you talk to her?" There were times when I could physically ask her questions, but my prayers and silent talks with Amma worked as well as standing right next to her, no matter where in the world I was. One day I heard a devotee ask her, "Mother, if you are connected with millions of people, how can I get through to you? Your line will be constantly occupied!" She laughed and answered that her line to us was always open, that she could hear us perfectly well, but the static we might hear on the line depended on us. Another person asked, "Mother, am I on your list?" Her swami interpreted the question, and she responded, "You are always on my list, but you just need to be sure that I am on your list."

When I was not sure of what was going on within me, I just went and watched Mother give darshan. I watched her for hours and my heart never failed to open up. My questions were answered, often immediately. The osteoarthritis in my hip did not allow me to sit close to Mother on the floor like many devotees did. But when I started feeling a little deprived, occasions would always arise to allow me to meet her. She would touch my hand while walking by, or give me a certain look, or something else would happen to give me the extra bit of attention I needed at that moment. One day, for one reason or another, we were told not to reach out when Mother emerged from her apartment and headed for the temple. But when she came out and arrived in front of me she stood still, stretching out with her open hand and looking at me. She waited until I reached out to her and then she touched my hand. Her touch felt like a soft breeze from the ocean, but it had a strength that I found unfathomable.

During my time in the ashram, I wondered many times how following my spiritual path would unfold. Would I live permanently in the ashram, or continue going on tour with Mother? Would I stay home in Canada and pursue my sculpting and just see Mother now and then? Would I build the spiritual retreat centre that had been on my mind for several years? Would I pursue a quiet devotional path of meditation and selfless service, or would my service involve work in one of Mother's charities? Denise, my astrologer, had told me that by the month of May, 2004, I would know what I would be doing for the next 12 years. One day I watched as Mother, full of pain after giving darshan for many hours, descended the steep, narrow temple stairs. Her sari was black with the natural oils and dirt from people's faces. In that moment, I knew I could not just go off and have a quiet life somewhere while Mother did all the work. I knew that it was my duty to help her wherever and with whatever I possibly could.

Before leaving Canada, I had wondered what to give Mother for her 50th birthday. Several ideas went through my head before I remembered that she either gave everything away or sold it and used the money for her charities. Then suddenly, I remembered visiting the children in Mother's orphanage. They would certainly

be attending her birthday celebrations, and I thought about giving them all new clothes and sandals. I became so excited about
the idea that I immediately e-mailed Brother Dayamrita in San
Ramon and asked what he thought of my idea. He responded immediately, saying that it was a great idea, and that I should ask
Mother for permission when I got to India.

When my businesses were doing well, it had always been a
pleasure to donate to charities, but something was different now.
This time I was aware that I was not only giving to Mother and the
children, but that I was ultimately giving to myself, that the giving
would come full circle. When the time came to ask Mother, and
after my question was translated, she asked, "All?" I nodded and
said, "Yes," and then she smiled and said, "Okay." I signed up for
the next orphanage visit to see the children again.

The orphans were always excited to see visitors arrive from
the ashram. The girls would immediately take everyone by the
hands and lead them to the main hall for a show of dancing and
singing. The boys, always a little shyer, stood in the background
waiting to perform on their drums. Before I left the orphanage, I
met with Mother Saraswati and the Swami in charge to discuss the
logistics of getting the new uniforms made. We calculated the cost
and set everything into motion quickly, because over 500 sets of
clothes had to be made before Mother's birthday, now only two
months away.

Forty-Eight

The first time I arrived in the ashram I was astonished at the high-rises and various other buildings crowded onto a small, long and not very wide peninsula in the middle of nowhere. On one side of the ashram were the famous Kerala backwaters, and on the other side the Arabian Sea. Most of the devotees stayed in two very tall buildings of about 17 stories each. Many owned apartments that they occupied when they were in the ashram. As soon as they left, the apartments were rented out. The rental money went toward the ashram costs and Mother's charities. There were also several lower buildings that housed the swamis, bramacharis, brahmacharinis, and the renunciates. At any given time, several thousand people lived in the ashram. There were buildings for the printing presses, shops, and kitchens, and a hospital, not only for the many people who lived in the ashram, but also for the people from the surrounding villages. A hall for large gatherings stood directly beside the cow shed (I could sometimes hear and smell the cattle when we were singing bhajans). There was a small store where we could buy things for our daily personal needs. Finally, the ashram's temple rose up, noble and serene, and next to it was Mother's apartment. The main floor of the temple was used for daily prayers, meditation, satsang and darshan with Mother. The second floor housed the offices, a computer and e-mail room, a travel office, a registration office, and a few small shops.

Across the backwaters lay the small village of Vallickavu, where we could find taxis, a large college run by Mother's organization, and many small shops. For the price of one rupee each way, it was easy to cross the backwaters in the long canoes that came and went throughout the day.

Life in the ashram could be as busy as one wanted. Each day began with Archana, the chanting of the 1,000 Sanskrit names of the Divine Mother, as early as 4:30 a.m., after which chai (tea) was served and people practiced yoga and meditation. Depending on the day of the week, Mother would arrive at the temple at 10 a.m. for either satsang or darshan. Satsang with Mother began with meditation and a speech. Some time was spent discussing ashram affairs, then there were questions and answers followed by, on Tuesdays, a lunch that was blessed by Mother. Finally, there was darshan for the new arrivals and those who were leaving. As well, Mother always welcomed anyone who felt homesick or troubled for any reason. Darshan normally ended at about 4 p.m. Mother came back to the hall at night from about 6:30 p.m. to 8:30 p.m. for bhajans.

Most devotees dressed in white, but there was no specific dress code. Women were encouraged to cover their legs and shoulders. Devotees and visitors who stayed at the ashram were expected to help out for at least two hours per day with seva, which entailed assisting with cleaning, food preparation, office work, and other such tasks. There were several educational courses happening at any given time, including ayurvedic treatments, massage, Reiki, and Sanskrit. We also had access to both a children's and an adults' library.

Soon, I found my own rhythm in ashram life. Each day I arose at four, took an enforced cold shower (there was no warm water in the ashram), and tried to do Archana in the temple. I was having a lot of trouble with it. Even though the names were printed in a little book and were chanted by a lead singer, she often went too fast for me. It seemed an impossible language to learn. I asked other devotees about it and they encouraged me to keep trying. "It will get easier," they would say. I was told that the sound of the chanting of the 1,000 names created a special energy that benefited the world, and that a devotee would never go hungry because of the daily chanting of the Archana.

Next, chai was served. It was mainly black tea with milk and sugar in it, but because it contained caffeine I could not drink it. Afterward, I joined the yoga group. My yoga mat went everywhere with me, and I practiced it several times a day by myself to keep my body as flexible as possible, despite the osteoarthritis in my hip.

Breakfast at the ashram offered three choices. One was Indian food that was included in the cost of my US$3 per day food and accommodation. This food consisted of rice with a vegetable sauce or iddlis—rice patties. Indian food in the ashram was too spicy for my delicate intestines and I was thankful I could afford to eat in the Western restaurant, where breakfast started at nine. Most of the time I had porridge with milk and sprouts or yogurt, hardboiled eggs, bread, butter and jam.

In addition to the restaurant, there was also a Western-style café, which opened at seven or eight o'clock. There they served pancakes, toast, omelettes, muffins, cookies, coffee, different types of herbal teas, and even soft drinks. People washed their own dishes after their meals.

There were many renunciates in the ashram: men, women, and couples. Mother did not ask that anyone renounce everything they owned. If someone did want to spend the rest of their life in the ashram, they needed special permission from Mother. There were times that she might approve right away, but at other times she would let people wait for years. People could live in the ashram without ever becoming renunciates. Right now I could not see myself living in the ashram, let alone becoming a renunciate. There were many other, different ways to serve in the world.

Because this was my second time in the ashram, I did jobs for seva as diverse as cleaning vegetables, interviewing people for Mother's new television station, serving food, helping with the dishes, and sweeping floors. When Mother came into the temple at 10 a.m, if I was not doing seva, that is where I wanted to be.

After lunch, which was served from 1 to 2 p.m., I either performed seva again, walked back to the temple to sit with Mother, or had a nap. Most of the time I would nap after Mother left the temple at about 4 p.m., and then I would do some yoga or reading. Soon it was time for bhajans, followed by dinner at 9 p.m., and the day's activities concluded.

Bhajans with Mother was a very special time, and the hall was always full. Sometimes during certain celebrations, special events happened during the day and in the evenings at which people performed dances and sang, often with Mother in attendance.

When Mother left the hall after bhajans at night, it was fun to follow her toward her apartment where Ram, the eight-year-old ashram elephant, was waiting to be fed. Ram used his trunk to pick up flower petals that had been thrown onto the cement floor and then he gently showered Mother with them. He bowed to her, beautifully and gracefully. She fed him with her hands, first elephant food and often other treats. After she had washed her hands, the holy water was given to Ram to drink. When he'd had his fill, he took the remainder into his trunk and turned around to shower everyone who stood nearby, but being very careful to avoid spraying Mother. No one minded getting soaked. Finally, Ram and the devotees played tug-of-war with a towel. He always won. A gate had been installed just before the stairs that went up to Mother's apartment, as Ram often did not want to leave Mother after his feeding time. Ram missed Mother so much when she was away on tour that when she arrived home he would try to follow her up those tiny stairs.

Children were very much a part of Mother's ashram. Some families lived there full-time. The children either went to the schools close by or were home-schooled by their parents. The ashram also had a swimming pool that the children used daily, as swimming in the ocean or backwaters was not safe. When Mother walked around the ashram, toward the hall or to special events, the children always ran beside her. Often they sat on the stage right next to her during bhajans, depending on how long they could sit still.

At the approach of each weekend, crowds of people, dressed in their best clothes, arrived at the ashram from the surrounding villages. Many arrived from far away to receive Mother's darshan. People were given free food, and they slept everywhere. It was interesting to walk through the main kitchen and see many people bent over low burners and drenched in sweat, stirring huge pots of rice, curry sauce, and vegetables. On weekends, the ashram would often feed between 12,000 and 17,000 people, three times per day. When the rooms were filled, people would sleep on the floors in the hall or the temple. I was always amazed by how people could just lay down on cement floors and fall asleep, often with only a few pages of a newspaper underneath them for padding. Before seeing the ashram I had been skeptical about the numbers of such crowds, as I just could not imagine they could be possible.

Darshan went on all night and often would not end until Monday morning at 10 or 11 o'clock. During that entire time, Mother never ate or used the washroom. Sometimes she would sip some coconut milk. Toward the end of Devi Bhava, she would baptize and bless the newborn babies and give the older babies their first solid food. To the children who were going to school for the first time, she taught the alphabet, holding their little fingers and writing in the sand. People received mantras and spiritual names and some got married. After all that, Mother would arise, glowing. No matter who one was, whether it was someone's first or 20th time watching Mother during this special time, their hearts would melt and they would be awestruck and silent.

My apartment was on the 12th floor and I enjoyed sitting on the balcony overlooking the backwaters and the Arabian Sea. The view was spectacular. The vegetation around the ashram resembled a thick green jungle with palm trees and a wonderful variety of birds. Fishing nets were set out on the backwaters while the fishermen waited for night to set in, when they would light their oil lamps to attract the fish. Long, narrow canoes travelled back and forth between the ashram and the village. It was remarkable how many people could fit in those canoes, and still they didn't capsize. When the operator had a large load, the passengers had to stand so more could be loaded on, which brought in more rupees, of course. Other canoes sailed graciously by under power of colourful sails made from stitched rice bags. The ocean was too rough for swimming, but all day I could see little dots on its surface—people fishing from their ocean canoes.

In the distance I could hear chanting from the loudspeakers at other temples. Here and there a few cows made it known that they needed milking. Sitting on the 12th floor, I basked in a pleasant breeze that cooled me down. Sometimes at night I would sit there when I could not sleep, either because I was too hot or because I needed to work something out.

Forty-Nine

My diary read, "pay attention—pay attention—pay attention. Divine energy is everywhere. Move with this energy. Give your worries to Amma." I was fascinated by this divine energy. Mother said that God was within us. I still had a lot of trouble with the word God and the thought of having God inside of me troubled me even more. I reflected on this often. Where was God when I needed Him, or Her, or Whomever? I had so much trouble with God being a Him in the Bible. Somehow it gave me a feeling that the Him the Bible talked of was more sympathetic toward men than women, and that men knew it. Perhaps that was another explanation for why men generally hold more power than women in the world. This had bothered me for decades, and I needed to move beyond it.

If God was in me then "It" was in you and in Mother and in everyone. But Mother said, "No. It is not only in everyone, it is in everything." For some reason that I did not understand fully, hearing that made me feel better. After some time, I began to focus on God as Divine Energy and that worked better for me. Mother suggested that we did not need to use the words God or Him, but could use a different name that felt comfortable to us. Then I heard the following question asked of her: Is God a man or a woman? She answered:

> *Neither—God is That.*
> *But if we must give God a gender,*
> *God is more female than male,*
> *For he is contained in She.*
> *Amma*

My mind was preoccupied with another question for Amma. My question was, "If we do have to come back in a next life, can we at least take this lifetime's spiritual knowledge with us?" I did not want to have to start all over again. The answer came a few days later when someone asked Mother the same question during satsang. Mother reassured us that we would indeed take our spiritual knowledge with us into our next life if we needed to come back, and we would repeat only those lessons that we had not fully learned in this life.

It was clear that we were all in the ashram to work on ourselves and to grow spiritually, so it was very important to spend a good deal of time alone, even when surrounded by family and the many devotees one knew or became friends with. There were so many different ways to work on oneself. Just watching myself and others functioning and resolving issues in different situations could teach so much.

What were we to do when the behaviour of another person irked us to the point that we lost our temper? Surrender. Amma said anger was a sword with two sharp edges.

She also said that we had "monkeys" in our heads jumping around frantically and that they needed to be quieted. On my first visit to India, I learned that it would be helpful to ask Amma for a mantra, a personal chant that is connected to divine energy and helps to quiet the mind. Without really understanding the seriousness of what this was all about, I asked her for a mantra. She agreed. We were not to tell anyone what our personal mantra was; it was ours, and would become our direct line to Amma. At any given time, when we all followed one another in one line toward her for darshan, she whispered our mantra in our ear three times while she hugged us. To that point, I had not taken the ceremony very seriously. But when Amma placed her handful of flower petals on my head to bless me, I felt myself shaking. I knew then that this was very serious.

Using my mantra became an important part of my life. When my thoughts went off somewhere or engaged in useless worrying and negative thoughts, it became increasingly easier to catch myself and use my mantra right away. After a few seconds I would not even remember what I had been thinking about. If I sat in traffic or waited for anything, my mantra surfaced automatically. It calmed the monkeys chattering in my head and helped me to turn inward and focus when too much was going on around me. It also helped me to fall asleep. I'd had no idea that my mantra would become so important in my life.

Fifty

Rumours circulated that on her birthday Mother would announce the creation of a new charity that focused on prostituted children. A French documentary video entitled The Day My God Died was made available for those of us who were interested. We were asked to read some literature on child prostitution before we signed up. I went to the office and read through some very extensive reports on the subject, finding myself shivering at what I read. We had been warned that the video could evoke many strong feelings and that, if we needed it, we could stay afterward to talk and receive support.

The video made me physically ill. It showed seven- and eight-year-old girls who had been lured away or kidnapped from their villages and forced into prostitution. What they had to endure was horrific. The children were drugged, beaten, gang raped, put into solitary confinement in dungeon holes, and deprived of food and sleep to break them down and make them compliant. One child, aged about 12, told about being raped by 14 men when she had arrived at a brothel several years before. She was allowed only one shower a week while she "served" a minimum of 30 men a day. She had become pregnant several times, but had given birth to only one child, whom she was told would be taken from her if she did not bring in enough money. The video revealed how these children were forced to behave in an overtly seductive manner to attract men for business. Men visiting the girls were interviewed and asked why they were engaging in sexual activities with girls who could be their own young daughters. They answered, "Look at them—how they are provoking us. They are asking for it." When asked what they would do if their own daughters were violated in that way, the men responded that they would kill those men who touched their daughters.

241

The children were not allowed to use any protection against sexually transmitted diseases; thus, many eventually contracted AIDS. They were kept working until their health deteriorated irreversibly, and they spread the disease to the many men with whom they were in contact. These men subsequently went home and infected their wives. Eventually, the girls were thrown out into the street to die. If they were somehow rescued, they were returned home to their villages, but their parents wanted nothing to do with them—they now brought only shame on the family and the entire village.

The video showed a prostituted teenager who had been rescued by a shelter and was slowly dying of AIDS. She had returned with the video crew to the place where she'd worked, trying to convince other teenagers to get out and come to the shelter. The girls had been deceived so many times that they did not know whom to believe anymore. At the same time, the madams of the brothels avoided responsibility when asked questions. They either denied involvement or stupidly smiled into the cameras as though they did not understand what they were being asked. When the video was over, there was not a dry eye in the room. A heavy silence hung in the air as we all got up to leave.

I watched the video while I was still feeling very weak from a fever, and its content hit me violently. I was angered, sickened, and extremely sad all at once. The sight of seven- and eight-year-old children being so abused was appalling; they were innocent. I became physically ill again. Yes, where was this God? And where was this God when I had needed Him myself at the age of seven when my father was beating me nearly to death?

While I'd watched the video I felt such empathy it was as if I were there with these children. I was livid as I thought about my own parents, who had certainly done nothing to nurture me as a child, and had instead only heaped abuse. But what choice had I had? The accumulation of years of confusion, anger, and sadness welled up inside me. I could not sleep, and cried most of the night. In my heart I questioned my sense of Amma's love for us. I felt angry with her and decided that at the next satsang I would ask her about this God. Her devotees, myself included, saw Amma as

God, so I would have this God in front of me and be able to ask Her straight out: "What is wrong with this stupid world that this great God created? As far as I'm concerned, He hasn't done a very good job at it. Look what is going on—how do you explain it?"

Meanwhile, I continued to rage against God, whoever and whatever He or She was supposed to be or represent. At that moment, I did not believe in anything. How could there be so much beauty created—nature, flowers, animals, and loving people hand in hand with so much horror? At least give the suffering to those who deserve it, not to innocent children. I was so upset that I wanted to head toward Amma's apartment and demand answers immediately.

I barely had enough patience to wait for the next satsang. I thought I wouldn't care how many thousands of devotees were there; whether I was asked to speak or not, I was just going to stand up and insist upon an answer. If it meant I got kicked out of the ashram, so be it. This was going to be my chance. I recalled Amma had said something like, "Your need to know something must be so urgent that it is like trying to escape from a burning house. Then the answer will come." And that was how I felt. For over 50 years I had been begging God for an explanation, and it was time to get one.

As I thought about this, I found some solace in my intentions to question Amma during the next satsang, and eventually I dozed off from pure exhaustion. When I first awoke, in that state of semi-consciousness, I seemed to have a new understanding of what I would never be able to fully articulate: in my mind I saw the little girl—me—as the victim, fusing and becoming one with the male perpetrator. There was no longer a duality, just a single entity. During the blending I felt all the anger and sadness slowly seep out of my body. At last some understanding was revealed to me of what had gone on, and I was stunned at how vividly it had come, and in such a brief moment. Things were now much clearer to me and I felt I needed no further explanations. The Oneness had been shown. I would be forever grateful. Now I understood why I had become so sick and weak. My defenses had been broken down so that through my suffering I could see what I needed to learn. Having the opportunity to see this video ultimately showed me that it was now time to address my deep need for clarification. That was also why Amma had whispered in my ear not to be afraid during my last darshan. With her grace and wisdom, I was able to see that what I had endured as a child had been necessary in order to better understand what this Oneness was all about.

Fifty-One

Volunteers were urgently needed to clean and prepare the stadium in Cochin for Amma's birthday celebrations, where hundreds of thousands of people were expected daily for four days. Physically, I was not that well, but decided to go anyway and just work as much as I could. When we arrived we saw people busily setting up the stage and constructing kitchens, restaurants and outhouses, but I was surprised to see how much there was still to do. My group was to clean out the meeting rooms and washrooms. The stadium had not been used for seven years, and dirt had been accumulating over that time. There were layers of it—in some places thick soil and grime—and broken glass windows and garbage were piled up everywhere. The washrooms were filthy—I had never seen anything like it before. Our cleaning equipment was so inadequate that I almost laughed. There was no electricity and the rooms were so dark that we could barely see what we were cleaning. The only long hose we had was riddled with holes and water seeped everywhere before we had a chance to scoop and sweep the garbage out. I could see that this was not only a cleaning task, but it would challenge our patience and tolerance as well.

When we were finished cleaning on the first day, we returned to Mother's school, where we had sleeping space assigned to us, ate dinner and fell on our sleeping pads on the floor, totally exhausted. We headed back to the stadium the next morning.

The broom I was using would have been in the garbage long ago at home, and during the work I had visions of importing decent wheelbarrows and cleaning equipment on the next ship to India. Everything was so disorganized that it became funny to me, although some people didn't think it was funny at all. It took me a little while to see the meaning of this work party's exercise.

But then I could see Mother's humour at play: at this task we were learning humility and how to relinquish control. I relaxed, did the work as best I could and stopped when my body said "no more." I even enjoyed getting dirty; it made me feel youthful again. How could we possibly keep white clothes clean with this kind of job?

As soon as we returned to the ashram, my friend Jane from Vancouver arrived and moved into our apartment. This was her first time in Mother's ashram and in India. Before her arrival she had also traveled to Bangalore to meet Sai Baba. We were happy to see each other and I got her acquainted with the ashram as soon as possible. She settled in very quickly, becoming involved in all kinds of programs and seva duties. She seemed to be doing seva for both of us, and there was no way I could keep up with her. Our apartment was already pretty crowded with three people, but the arrival of many thousands more devotees was still expected. I brought in one more sleeping pad for my friend, Jennifer, who would arrive soon from California. We put all of our big suitcases high up on the only shelf available; the others went into the kitchen, and only the essentials stayed close to our beds. Having the only real bed in the room, I kept everything I had with me underneath it. My body did not like the rainy season and I was happy that no one else was claiming the bed.

I was still very moved by my vivid experience of feeling the victim and the perpetrator become one, and continued to explore what the idea of God meant for me. I could not help but go back to my memory of being nearly beaten to death, and I wondered how, as a little girl of seven or eight years old, I had come to my sudden realization that death did not exist and that only the body died. And why had my father stopped beating me at the precise moment of my realization? During the beating, I was aware that I was watching the event as if I were outside of my body. I could see my father hitting me and kicking me with his wooden shoes while I huddled on the kitchen floor, but who was the "me" who was watching? Then again, while I was watching I knew that there was yet another observer watching me, so who was that? Was it my sister's spirit? Was it God or Amma? Amma said that she had been in our lives long before any of us had known about it.

My thoughts also kept returning to the time on my kayaking trip on the West Coast when I gave up paddling in the storm, ready to die. When I saw that my arms kept moving, I knew that it wasn't me controlling my body. How had I been able to feel the trees grow on that trip? How had I felt the air pressure warning us of bad weather to come long before it actually arrived? How had I sensed danger from afar and saved a baby's life in England when I was only 16 years old? Who had done those things?

With the first two experiences, I'd had a sense of total surrender. With the others, I could understand that there may have been a strong intuition at work. I'd been very tuned-in to the baby; we had bonded very strongly. I decided to ask Amma about these things during a satsang. I knew that it was a little selfish to ask personal questions during satsang, but I had written them up in such a way that other devotees would benefit as well. And so far, I hadn't asked anything during satsang, nor had I been in the question line before.

Too many people had arrived by now to fit everyone into the temple, so the satsang was moved to the big hall. Because I could not sit on the floor, I took the closest spot on the chairs, so I could run to the front when Mother asked for questions. I was so nervous that it was impossible for me to meditate. But when question time came, three devotees sitting close to Mother got there first. She used up all her time to hear and answer their questions. I had been in considerable pain sitting on the ground for so long and got up to return to my chair. While I was walking to my chair Mother gave me the answers to my questions. Although she did not speak aloud, I heard her clearly. I could not believe it! I pushed Jane, who was sitting next to me, and laughed, saying, "I got it, I got it!"

It was so simple now that I fully understood. During my ordeals, it had been my sister's spirit I felt, it was God, it was Amma, and it was me, because we were all One and the same. The situations in which I found myself had taken me to other levels of awareness and shifted my sense of my connection with the Power, the Divine Energy. On those other levels of awareness I had new and different strengths and intuition. Mother spoke of the amazing powers we have within, explaining that most of us did not know how to tap into them. Her infinite grace helped us connect with these inner powers.

Devotees from all over the world, including my friend Jennifer, were now arriving at the ashram at all times of the day and night. This was also Jennifer's first time in India. We were now four women crammed into one small room. We constantly had to walk over each other's bodies and luggage to get anywhere. Thank goodness Jane, Jennifer and I were close friends, but we felt compelled to confront our German roommate about her cleaning duties, and not allow her to switch off the fan in our stuffy room. Tempers flared between her and Jennifer. It was a perfect opportunity to practice tolerance. It was now also very hot, making this exercise even more interesting.

Amma was giving her last Devi Bhava before her birthday celebrations. We were told that her Western devotees would not get darshan during the celebrations, which was why she was giving darshan and spending some time with us daily before we all left for Cochin. The ashram was busy and lively. Amma was in a fun mood and told us, through her interpreters, how many trucks of rice had been ordered to feed hundreds of thousands of people, the amount of drinking water that would be needed, etc. She seemed happy to have her devotees from close to two hundred different countries all together in the ashram. She told us that over 20,000 Indian devotees had volunteered to direct traffic, cook, clean, and attend to the multitude of other essential tasks, leaving her Western devotees to simply enjoy the festivities. She was aware that her devotees from abroad had made extra efforts to attend the celebration and that some could stay for only a few days. Therefore space close to the stage, and Amma, had been reserved for us.

The organization of this event had been going on for months and we could feel the excitement mounting. The logistics of transporting thousands of devotees with their luggage from the ashram to the arena in Cochin were mind-numbing. How it was successfully achieved was nothing short of a miracle. Devotees would stay either in hotels or for free in the schools.

When we got to Cochin, we were astonished by how much the stadium had changed in such a short period of time. Hundreds of people had been working day and night for weeks to build the hall, finish the stage, the sunroof, Mother's little house, food stands, bookstores, kitchens, and washrooms. The new cement statues decorating the entrance were still wet. Everything was colourfully decorated. Masses of people were moving around in all directions without any panic or confusion. Everyone seemed to be in a festive mood.

I had never seen such crowds before; the swarms of people were controlled by thousands of police officers from the district and the military. There were people standing, sitting, sleeping, and eating everywhere. I saw no one fighting or arguing; the only disturbance I ever witnessed there was some pushing when Mother arrived at, or left, the stadium. Busloads of people were driven in and out of the area day and night. The volunteers directing traffic were all dressed in uniforms and easy to recognize. Even after standing in the hot sun for many hours each day, directing traffic and giving information, their constant good nature impressed me.

In the large kitchen areas, hundreds of cooks prepared food for the masses of devotees and volunteers attending the celebrations. Piles of uncooked rice and vegetables stood at least three metres high. Dozens of men stirred huge steaming pots with wooden paddles, cooking the rice. The rice pots were so large that six or seven individual burners were needed beneath each one as it rested on large square rocks. Sweat poured down the rice-stirrers' semi-clad bodies. Hundreds of women and men sat peeling vegetables, and constant streams of people passed by with plates to get their meals. Observing this scene, my mouth was agape in amazement. Certainly they knew how to throw a large party here in India. I was sure that most of the devotees working in the kitchen had dedicated themselves to do this seva for the entire four days and probably wouldn't see anything of the festivities.

Speakers from around the world had come to join in a three-day segment of the event called Amritavarsham 50 – Embracing the World for Peace and Harmony. Those days were filled with workshop sessions and speeches given by India's president and prime minister, Christian ministers and priests, professors, rabbis, swamis, business CEOs, actors, and activists. Subjects under discussion included Promoting Universal Values; Freedom of Expression and Respect for Essential Human Rights; Reflection, Dialogue and Service; Embracing Universal Motherhood for Peace and Harmony; Exploring the Potential for Change; Healing the World Through Universal Motherhood; Embracing Selfless Service for Peace and Harmony; Transformation for the Individual; and Transformation for Society.

The messages of the speakers clearly expressed and examined the world's most pressing needs. The need for peace and harmony in the world was more urgent now than ever before. The disparity between rich and poor was overwhelming, despite the fact that the vast resources of the planet we lived on could provide for the essential needs—food, clothing, shelter and education—of all human beings. And we were capable of living in peace and harmony, if each human being would just try to put aside his or her greed, anger, and selfishness, and instead focus on helping and respecting others and looking after the earth with more loving care. I believed that, increasingly, more people in the world were becoming tired of the extreme violence, the corporate greed and corruption, and the noise, pollution, and poverty they saw daily, and were already seeking alternative ways to live in more harmony and peace with one another.

My favourite speaker was Ms. Yolanda King, daughter of the late Martin Luther King. The subject of her speech was "Inauguration of Women's Initiative." She was a precise, charismatic, and very motivating speaker.

The afternoons were filled with ceremonies and the evenings with cultural dance and music performances given by people from the many different cultures and countries in attendance. It was impossible to attend all of the workshops, speeches, and events.

My friends and I stayed in a hotel in town about 20 minutes by rickshaw from the stadium. Joined by Cory, another devotee from Vancouver, we were all ecstatic about sleeping in beds with sheets, and having hot and cold showers, air conditioning, and laundry service. Ah, how we become attached to our material comforts!

A small, simple house had been constructed on the site for Amma to rest and to receive dignitaries. Jane was interviewing many of these dignitaries for a special television program and I only saw her when she came to the hotel to shower and have a short sleep. Between the programs, Jennifer and I needed breaks from the crowds, the noise, and the heat, and we returned to the hotel several times a day. And we overindulged eating Western food in one of the nearby hotels.

During one of my afternoon breaks at the hotel I received a call announcing that a truck loaded with the orphans' clothes and slippers had arrived. I was asked to come to the school to hand out the new clothes. By the time I got to the school, the children were already asleep on the floor.

The older girls were told to wake up the younger ones. Mother Sariswati called out their names; I gave them each their bag of clothes and had them try on their sandals. Although I already knew a number of them, now was my chance to see each child individually. Again and again, I looked into their dark brown faces and huge beautiful eyes. Half asleep, they smiled shyly and said while thanking me, "Namah Shivaya," which meant "The Divine in me greets the Divine in you."

My view, or perhaps it was my awareness, began to change. I was not sure of what was happening, but slowly I began to see myself in each child. Soon there was no difference between us; I could feel what they were feeling. I felt as if it was me accepting the clothing. I was in awe as I became aware of what was going on inside of me, and I wondered how long the insight and sense of connection would last. In fact, it lasted until about 4:30 a.m., when the girls had all been given their outfits. Now the boys were being awakened. I protested when I saw a six-year-old stumbling toward me. He could barely open his eyes. I said that the older boys could surely help the younger ones get dressed in the morning. Everyone was very tired. We stopped.

During the one-hour ride back to the hotel, I was still in awe and speechless. What a gift I had been given. What a fabulous, incredible gift to be able to see myself in these children. I had discovered, completely, the true meaning of giving - that giving to others was ultimately giving to oneself, making it full circle. Then the most incredible thing happened. Totally exhausted I began to prepare for bed, my mind and body were barely functioning, while staring at the floor in a daze, I saw a bright golden light surrounding my feet. Its meaning flashed through my mind and as my stare came into focus the light disappeared. I had heard Mother mention this golden light and understood it to mean being in touch with the Divine within oneself at that moment. At last, I'd had a glimpse of what I had been seeking. What a beautiful gift!

September 27, the last day of the celebrations, was Amma's birthday. The day began with meditation and yoga, followed by bhajans, Amma's Pada Puja (a ceremonial fire and worship) and her closing speech, with her translators standing nearby. These were followed by several presentations by various government officials and the inauguration of Amma's future social services and charitable projects, including a group of 1,008 lawyers who committed to offering service to the needy at no cost. Symbolically, Amma handed over the keys to several of the recipients of the newly built free houses—part of a project to build 100,000 free houses for the destitute and homeless throughout India within the next 10 years. Next were dedications of both a new care-home for the elderly and a charitable hospital for tribal people, followed by 158 free marriages in Amma's presence, the release of some new books and the distribution of 15,000 saris to the poor.

That morning I saw several busloads of "my children" arriving at the stadium. Some of them noticed me on the side of the road and were waving and yelling "SitaLakshmi! Come!" In tears, I saw them entering the stadium, proudly wearing their new clothes. They all looked clean, with hair perfectly combed and faces smiling. The children were put right in front of the stage close to Mother. I left my friends and joined Mother Saraswati and the children as they watched the festivities. What a day!

Mother spent the rest of her 50th birthday giving darshan for 23 hours to over 50,000 people. That was what she wanted to do. A television set was placed in front of her so that, now and then, she could watch the performances taking place behind her. I would never forget the remarkable feeling of togetherness I shared with these other hundreds of thousands of people as we all chanted for world peace:

> *Om lokah samastah sukhino bhavantu – Om santi santi santihi,*
> *May all beings in the universe be peaceful – Om peace peace peace.*

Fifty-Two

One and a half million people attended Mother's birthday event over the span of four days. They had come from all over India and from close to 200 other countries, and now they all had to get home. Most planned to leave immediately after the celebrations. Jennifer would return to the ashram for a few days and then on to the United States, while Cory, Jane, and I hoped to rest an extra day and then try to get seats on the train to Tiruvannamalai to visit Ramana Maharshi's ashram and climb to the top of the holy Mount Arunachala.

When we reached the train station, we could see that there was no hope of getting even standing space on any of the departing trains. Half–jokingly, we implored, "Please, Mother, we need three sleeping couches for tomorrow's train." We stood in line for tickets and, lo and behold, when we reached the wicket, there were three seats available. We stared at each other, and then laughed and laughed as we thanked Mother. At the train station the next evening, the platforms were filled with both Indians and Westerners. It looked as though the big party was continuing. When the train departed, several groups of people got together to chant the Archana.

Before leaving India, I decided to visit the Nadi Readers in Madras. I'd been told about them by a devotee at the ashram. The word Nadi means "destined" in Tamil. The Nadi readers—also called the Palm Leaf readers—used leaves approximately 2,000 years old. Apparently people from all over the world and from all religions who were destined to look into the leaves would come exactly to the readers when they were supposed to.

When I arrived, a man took my left thumbprint a few times and put me into a waiting room, where about 20 people sat, including one other Westerner. Surprisingly, the man came back to get me within half an hour. We went into a little room, where the Nadi reader and a translator were sitting.

In the small room I was shown into, there was a small pile of palm leaves in front of the reader, each one about four centimetres wide and 50 centimetres long. He chanted the writing that was on the leaves and the translator asked simple questions. All I needed to do was answer yes or no. The process took some time because the reader had to go to his library to find the appropriate palm leaf for each set of questions. Finally, he asked if I was born in October or November. When I confirmed this, he gave me my precise birth date. He told me my first name, and the first names of my father and my mother. He could see by reading my thumbprint, he said, that three gods protected me and that nine planets surrounded my birth, which seemed a lucky sign. The reader said I was born to a respectable family; I raised my eyebrows at that. Later on he said that although my father was very violent, he had a good heart.

I was told that this birth (in 1944) was a very important one for me. This lifetime was meant for spiritual work and to serve others. Because of my many experiences during childhood, I had an aura behind my head. I wondered, "Don't we all have one?" The reader said there would be many turning points in my spiritual life and I would experience much joy in serving people. I would have a long life, and enjoy peace of mind. I had done well in business, where I'd had many people working for me, and I now had a comfortable and luxurious life. However, I did not wallow in this comfortable life but showed more interest in serving people.

I now also had a female guru in my life named Mata Amritanandamayi (Amma); she had given me the spiritual name of SitaLakshmi. Now my mouth dropped—could the Nadi reader read my mind? I was informed that Amma would lead my spiritual life and take me where I needed to go. In my 60th year, I would have an unexpected accident but I was not to worry; this had to happen because of a previous birth. (I had this accident on my North India Tour several months later as predicted.) I was told that I'd had a previous birth in India in the state of Kerala, the state where Mother's ashram is. I was also given some details about my bad karma from this previous life.

The reader talked about the health problems I had now and would have later. He said these problems mainly had to do with my intestines and certain pujas should be performed to protect me from them. I would be exposed to certain dangers and I should be doing pujas for those, too. Then the reader told me that a plane had been in danger and lives were saved because of my prayers. I immediately recalled the flight from Vancouver to Amsterdam on my way to India, where I had identified a man behaving very strangely and drew this to the attention of the airline authorities. Consequently he was not allowed onto the plane.

I had time to do one puja in the Nadi reader's puja room. The assistants left to get the puja materials—fruit, flowers, coconut, sweets, and typical clothing for an Indian couple, including a sari, pants, and shirt. I gave them money for food and sweets for 59 orphaned children and another charity in order to pay off my karma money debts from a previous life. I had never done a puja before so they led me through the ceremony. They encouraged me to pay for a 240-day puja for my health, and promised to mail me some of the ashes so I could carry them in a talisman around my neck for protection. I decided that I had done enough and would do other pujas in Mother's ashram if I needed to do more. I trusted that Amma was protecting me just fine. Just before I stood up, understanding that the reading was over, the reader told me at what age, on what day, in which month, and in what physical position I was going to die. It took my breath away.

The reading had taken the entire day. I was tired and did not know what to believe anymore. I returned to the hotel, picked up my luggage, and left for the airport.

Fifty-Three

To travel with Amma, devotees entered the darshan line from nine months to one year in advance of the specific tour and asked Amma herself for permission to accompany her. If we had gone on a specific tour one year, we would likely not be able to join the same tour the following year.

The cost to each devotee for the six-week European Tour was about US$1,400, which included food, accommodation, and transportation by bus. The accommodation was usually at the houses of local devotees, on the floors of the halls where the events were taking place, or in simple hotels. We brought our own sleeping bags and sleeping pads. We might "work" 12 to 16 hours a day, depending upon what tour we were on and what seva we had been assigned. Many of those long hours were spent in constructing and taking down the bookstore and information booths. Our travel schedule to so many different European cities and countries allowed us just enough time off to sleep and do our laundry, but we had long breaks so we could sit close to Amma. I would learn to sleep under the bookstore tables while 6,000 people were singing bhajans or going through the puja ceremony, or on the floor in the aisle of the bus, or sitting up while travelling. Often we had a resting room available to us to take a quick nap between programs.

The large inventories of books, CDs, jewelry, and clothing, along with the kitchen equipment and sound system, travelled with us in huge trucks. Our cooks attended to the Indian cooking, while local devotees took care of Western meals and snacks. Everyone who attended the events, including volunteer staff, was fed at least three times a day, while snacks were available as long as Amma was giving darshan, which was often well into the morning hours. A rotating system of touring devotees was set up to assist the local devotees with crowd control and help with the darshan lines and prasad so that the thousands of people coming to see Mother would move along as smoothly as possible.

In the European cities, as soon as Amma was finished with Devi Bhava, we had already packed up the kitchen, the bookstore, and our personal belongings. After the last person had been hugged, we had breakfast and were off to the next city to set up again by nightfall. By this time of day, we had been awake and busy for 40 hours or more. We were totally immersed in serving and there was no time for any sightseeing whatsoever. Most people on staff were not interested in sightseeing anyway, myself included. We would go off shopping for our basic needs, or go out for walks whenever possible.

Before I joined Amma's European tour in Paris, I stayed with my dear friend Jannie in Amsterdam for a few days. I had lost a lot of weight in India, and Jannie spoiled me royally with my favourite Dutch goodies, including stuffed almond cookies, dark chocolate, raisin buns, homemade apple pie with real whipped cream, all kinds of Dutch cheeses, raw herring, and dark heavy breads. Her tables were always full of flowers. We had a lovely time catching up with each other on our long walks with her affectionate dog, Daisy. It was a real treat.

In Paris, it felt wonderful to be back in familiar territory, especially after I discovered a little café close by the hall that served marvelous café latte with enormous chocolate and almond croissants. After returning to the West following a long stay in India, many Western devotees, me included, went a little wild eating all the food we had missed and dreamed about. It was said that a true spiritual person should not only be detached from worldly desires, but also from tasty foods and treats. I understood that even while I ate this delicious food, the taste only lasted a very short time and I knew that tomorrow I would want it again. But at that moment I was revelling in it.

Upon reaching the hall I joined the other devotees, who were already setting up for the upcoming event. My seva would include setting up and taking down the bookstore. Because I had travelled and lived in Europe, I would also translate when needed, as most of our group spoke only English.

The first day of darshan in Paris was October 7, my 59th birthday. Normally, the devotees who volunteered on a tour could go for darshan only when invited by Amma, or if it was one's birthday, or if one was not feeling well. During my birthday darshan, Amma offered an apple and held it as I took my first bite.

At the end of the Paris tour, Amma left for Finland with a group of devotees who had paid the extra flight costs. The buses took the rest of us to the ashram in Pontguin, close to Chartres. This ashram was an old castle in the middle of the country, surrounded by farmers and crop fields. We had extra time to rest, do our personal chores, and go for long walks in the fields. Most of us had come straight from stays of several months' duration in India and the weather in France was much colder. We all bundled up in our fleece jackets and hats. Not even attempting detachment, we revelled in the food, including wonderful soups, different types of breads and cheese, salads and desserts. I still loved French cooking.

After several days we headed off for Barcelona, Spain, where we joined Mother and the rest of the group for the three-day program. There, we slept in the hall where the event took place, which was situated right next to the ocean. Some of the European devotees, who were following Mother's tour on their own, camped in the parking lot in their cars, vans, and tents in the strong, howling winds. We all enjoyed some extra time off and it gave me some precious alone time to amble along the beach and visit some of the many famous outdoor sculptures in this beautiful city. In Spain, about 6,000 people per day came to see Amma for darshan.

After visiting France, Spain, Switzerland, and Germany, we arrived in Holland. I called my eldest brother, Jan, from the hall where Amma's three-day program was being held. I had no time to visit him during my current stay, but promised to see him after the program in London ended. I had made plans to return then and stay with my friend Dickie for a week before heading back to Canada. I asked my brother if he and his wife were interested in visiting me at the hall, but he accused me of being "in a cult" and said he wasn't interested. I didn't respond to that, but promised to call him when I returned.

When my long-time friend, Dickie, came to the hall, I took a few hours off to have lunch and a walk with her before she went for darshan. When she got close to Mother, I joined her from the side and we approached Mother together. I told Mother that we had been friends for 43 years. She gave Dickie an apple and asked us, "Happy?" Later on, just before leaving, Dickie took me to the side and said, "We've been friends for so long, and I've never told you how much I love you." She hugged me and repeated, "I love you." "I love you, too," I said tearfully. To have spent this time and gone for darshan together with my dear old friend was a true celebration and blessing.

I had a wonderful time staying with Dickie. I believe our friendship had lasted for so many years not only because we cared about each other, but also because we felt a deep mutual admiration and respect. We lived our lives thousands of miles apart, but it felt as if we lived in the same city. It never mattered who called or wrote first after some silence. We were always able to accept and support each other without any judgments or expectations. The mornings of my visit were spent chatting together, reading the paper, and drinking coffee in our pyjamas.

I had left Holland close to 43 years earlier and my brother, Dirk, had neither phoned nor written me a card or a letter in all those years. Nevertheless, he found it completely normal that I called him or wrote him birthday cards. But during my mother's funeral over two years before, a serious rift had developed between me and Dirk. We hadn't spoken to each other since.

As well, there was so much animosity between Dirk and Jan, my other brother, that they hadn't spoken to each other for many years. Dealing with the inheritance from my mother had made the situation even worse between them. The last time I had seen either of them was during my mother's funeral.

Dickie knew my family very well and offered to join me when I went to visit Jan and his wife. During the visit, I gave Jan a Dutch translation of a DVD about Mother called "Embracing the World." One day, if he was interested in what his sister was doing, I suggested, perhaps he would have a look. He put it aside without a word.

The next day, I gathered all the courage I had and, with a heavy heart, called my other brother. It had taken a lot of soul-searching, but I finally decided it was my job, no matter the reason for the rift, to make a gesture and try to change the negative energy between Dirk and me. Dickie and I had talked about it and she encouraged me to reconnect with him. When I called, my brother sounded surprised. He thanked me for calling him—he would have never done that before—and invited me to his apartment. Because he smoked, I said I would rather meet him for coffee somewhere else. He promised not to smoke when I visited and would also open his windows several hours before I arrived. I was shocked, to say the least.

The morning of our visit, while I was buying flowers for an old friend of my mother's, Dickie encouraged me to buy some for my brother, too, and I listened to her. Part of me couldn't believe I was doing this. When we got to Dirk's place the windows and even the front door were open. He made us coffee and talked incessantly. By the time we left two hours later, he hadn't asked anything about why I was in the country or what I had been doing during the years we hadn't spoken. But that did not matter to me. All that mattered was that the energy between us would become positive. We would never be great friends, but he was still my brother.

The next day, Jan and his wife visited me at Dickie's, and as he handed me back Amma's DVD he said, "We have a lot of respect for that woman." When I told him of my visit with Dirk, he was visibly surprised. I explained that my life with Amma gave me the courage to do these things, that in my own way I was trying to make this world a better place. Jan did not know what to say.

One morning before I left, Dickie came down from her attic with a box full of letters. "These are the letters you've written to me since we met in England 43 years ago," she said. "I've kept them, hoping that one day you would write a book." I told her that I did not know how to write. She said, "You are special and many people could learn from your experiences." "You are such a wonderful, loyal friend," I said. As I was preparing to leave for the airport, I decided to leave the box and my old letters behind. But back home, one week later I began to write.

Fifty-Four

Christmas in Canada was over, and having recuperated somewhat from Amma's European tour, I had a strong sense that I needed to return to India and join the North India tour.

By this time, after 17 years, my relationship with Toni had moved into a different direction. Although we were still in contact on a daily basis, we now lived in separate homes and were exploring our own needs independently. Toni was living with Amma's teachings in her daily life in a well-balanced fashion, while my mind was totally focussed on Amma and my spiritual life. I had to find out what this was all about now and would worry about balance later.

I exchanged e-mails with Jani, my contact at the ashram in India. Jani was one of the main tour organizers and presently on the South India Tour with Amma, but she replied faithfully as I inquired about departure dates and whether there was space on the "comfort bus." I knew that sitting with three people on the cramped wooden seats of the ashram buses just wouldn't be possible for me with my osteoarthritis. Not only were those ashram bus seats filled to capacity, but the aisles were crowded with cooking pots, bags of rice, and luggage.

The plane arrived in Trivandrum in the middle of the night and I took a taxi to the ashram. It turned out to be a nightmarish ride through a torrential downpour. It began about half an hour into the drive, and I suggested a few times that we stop and wait it out, but the taxi driver preferred to struggle through it despite being able to see almost nothing. He was resourceful and wiped both the inside and the outside of the windows with anything he could find in his car. More than once we found ourselves off the road, and we hit a few things left and right. Although it seemed as if it would fall apart at any time, the Indian taxi proved to be as amazingly resilient as its driver. Throughout the entire ordeal, I was not afraid, and let go, willing to let destiny take its course. Little did I know that the entire trip would be an exercise about learning to "let go" in a way I had never comprehended.

After several hours, my taxi arrived at Mother's ashram. The tall, strong, bare-footed driver was clearly exhausted, but relieved that we had arrived safely. His eyes were red and he was not very stable on his feet. He still helped me find and awaken the people in charge of the night arrivals before he dropped my suitcases in front of the elevator.

Typically, arriving at the ashram on a Saturday night meant arriving in the middle of Devi Bhava. I had planned it that way and even hoped to go for darshan that night, but Mother had cancelled it. Some hours after my arrival, I woke up to the sound of noisy seagulls and thousands of Indian devotees and their families standing around the temple in line for breakfast and darshan.

As soon as the Western Office opened, I was assigned to a room on the 17th floor of the tall, D building. Two women were already rooming in the flat. When I unlocked the door, I could hardly get in as the small space was occupied by three mattresses, some suitcases and, although the flats normally had no furniture, a table with four chairs. The beds were unmade and clothes were strewn everywhere. It wasn't dirty, just very messy. I could see immediately that neither housekeeping nor maintaining any order were priorities of the occupants. My automatic response was to shut the door again without even going in, and return to the office to get another room. Then something stopped me; I did walk in. I looked around and cleared out a corner to put my mat down. I piled my suitcases into the kitchen and got dressed to line up for darshan.

My roommates turned out to be lovely women, thoughtful and sensitive. Murielle was a young, energetic, French woman in her late twenties who had trouble saying no, and kept herself busy with a lot of seva. Kirsten, about my age, was from Sweden. She stayed busy running from one program to another. What I liked most about them was that we could share experiences, yet each go about our various activities independently. When we had a few free minutes and did meet together in our room, we sat around dressed in our most comfortable clothes, drank tea, had some treats, and exchanged news. When we attended the same programs we smiled at each other, but avoided small talk. Life in the ashram was very simple, and I settled in to my past routine quickly. Since arriving, my feet had swollen and even walking in open sandals was painful. I decided to walk barefoot for a while. I'd had swollen feet before, but not with this much pain. I increased my water intake and hoped for the best.

One morning after breakfast, I was on my way back to the flat. As I walked past the temple I clearly heard a voice within me telling me to turn around. I stopped and looked back. There, standing near the area where the Indian people gathered to wait for darshan, was an elderly Indian woman. Into my mind came the clear message that she needed food. For a moment, I thought I was imagining it and took a few more steps forward. Then I decided to turn around and investigate. Otherwise, I knew I would just keep wondering about my impulse all day.

I approached the woman, who had a kind-looking, simple face. Her thin body was dressed in a simple but clean sari. She smiled at me shyly, but when I asked whether she had eaten, we could not understand each other's words. I resorted to requesting help from a young student passing by, asking him to translate for us. It turned out that the elder had just walked six kilometres from her village to get Mother's darshan and had no money to buy any food or a bus ticket. I asked the young man to tell her that I would get her some breakfast and request that she please sit down. When I returned with her food, the woman's smile was even broader and I saw that she had no teeth. Before leaving, I indicated that I would be back at 1 p.m. to buy her lunch.

When I returned, someone had already given her food. We smiled at each other and I headed for the Western canteen. After my lunch I passed by the temple again on my way to the flat and saw her lying asleep in the fetal position in some shade on the cement floor. I guessed that she was resting during the hottest time of the day before her long walk home. She looked so frail sleeping on the hard cement. I wondered what I could give her to take home. Suddenly it came to me, and I walked to the area where

Mother's pictures were for sale. I bought a small standing picture of Mother and put it close to the woman's head, so that when she awoke she would immediately see Mother. Close by, an Indian woman who had been observing the scene gave me a large smile of understanding, then indicated that she was keeping an eye on the sleeping woman as well. So over and over again, in these small ways, I learned that Amma watched over all her children in many different ways, and I was reminded again not to take for granted the voice that spoke to me from inside.

Life consists of only two events; performing an action, and experiencing the result(s) of that action.

Amma

***

About 190 devotees from 26 countries showed up at the pre-trip orientation meeting in the main hall. Combined with the numbers of Indian devotees from the ashram, the group totaled about 400 people. Our travels would begin in Amritapuri, where Mother's main ashram is, include programs in 17 cities, and take two months. Among many stops, the big cities would include New Delhi and Calcutta. At each stop the events would last from one to three days.

With such a large number of people travelling from event to event, the organizational aspect of the tour was mindboggling, but the organizers seemed to know exactly what needed to be done. We were given homeopathic malaria pills and we went over a few other medication requirements that might be needed on the tour. Mother was not keen on us sightseeing while we were on tour; it diverted our concentration from our spiritual quest and it also seemed to create confusion. We were each to prepare a "sleeping roll" consisting of everything we might need overnight, since in certain cities we would stay only one night and leave immediately after darshan. At those events our large suitcases would stay on the roofs of the buses. Inside the buses we would each carry all we needed for travel, including edible treats, water, extra clothing, and small pillows for the long rides.

No Western clothing was permitted. Because of the many men we were travelling with, women were told to be fully dressed in the sleeping and bathroom areas of the ashrams or schools where we stayed. That meant our shoulders and legs were to be covered at all times. Men, on the other hand, were permitted to walk around bare-chested, or in T-shirts and shorts. Because we represented our ashram and Mother, we were asked to have our clothes as clean as possible at all times. Water was in short supply, but laundry services would be provided whenever possible. Only the brahmacharinis and the renunciates were allowed to wash their own saris. We were told that we each needed eight changes of white clothing—two sets for travelling, two for seva, and four to wear when we appeared on or near the stage during the programs with Mother. Upon hearing this news, I and a few other devotees took the canoe across the backwaters and headed to the tailor's shop to have a few more sets of clothes made. I even purchased a small sari blouse and a swimming dress in case Mother decided to go swimming with us, although she hadn't done that for a few years. Apparently the swimming dress was also practical for sleeping. While I tried on the clothes, I had a good chuckle imagining what my friends at home would say if they could see me.

There was one more tour of the orphanage offered before we left, and I signed up eagerly since I just loved spending time with "my" children there. I also looked forward to seeing Mother Saraswati again. The focus of her life was the welfare of the orphanage's more than 500 children. It was clear that she loved each of them equally, and she doted on them. Her patience and calm, easygoing disposition was admirable.

On the day of the tour, the organizer had taken ill, and she asked me to lead the tour because I knew the orphanage's history and had assisted her before. The tour group consisted of 25 men, women, and children from several different countries. The orphans were in school that day, but as soon as they had a free moment, they ran over to initiate play, chanting, and dancing with us. There was lots of laughter, and the orphans had no shyness in climbing onto laps and holding hands with the tour participants. It was amazing to see how they motivated each other. Mother

Saraswati prepared our lunch while the children kept performing. At our departure I wanted to give her a gift—as a renunciate she owns only what is given to her—and just before we boarded the bus, I made a sudden decision to give her my favourite bracelet, one that Mother had worn for five months. She protested, but I showed her a bracelet on my other wrist, letting her know that now we both had one.

Before we left on the North India tour, there was one more Devi Bhava, and Mother gave darshan for 13 hours straight. I thought it had given me a taste of what the crowds would be like on this tour. I hadn't seen anything yet.

Fifty-Five

Men who walked easily along the roof edges with the heavy suitcases were packing our luggage on top of the buses. It was evident that they had done this many times before. Devotees looked for their assigned seats on lists at the buses' doors. I was assigned to the back seat near the window in Mother's old, 16-seat camper-van. It looked comfortable and others looked with ill-concealed envy toward the little bus.

The North India tour was supposed to depart at 4 a.m., but after several delays we were finally told we might not leave at all that day. I decided to remove my watch and simply let things unfold as they would. We finally left at 2 p.m. the following day and travelled until we reached our first stop in Kannur 13 hours later. We couldn't believe our good fortune in having a camper-van with air conditioning; we were able to keep the windows closed during the hottest time of the day and keep the dust, wind, and smells out. I kept my swollen feet on a special meditation cushion; still, the long bus ride made the swelling worse.

The tour convoy included seven buses and one camper-van for the devotees, a large truck carrying the sound system, several cars, including a vehicle carrying the swamis, and Mother in her own small camper-van. The luggage of about 400 people and huge kitchen pots and burners were all loaded atop the buses and covered with big blue tarps. One bus had several hundred plastic chairs stacked together on its roof. On several occasions the buses had to be rerouted, as in certain places their heights prevented them from passing under electrical wires or through underpasses. At one place, a bus broke the overhead wires, creating great sparks. Sometimes, the large buses and trucks in the convoy ahead of us leaned over to the side so much I was amazed that they were still upright and moving forward.

En route, our convoy was often joined and escorted by several armed police vehicles. Depending upon which areas we passed through in North India, Mother's camper-van was attended day and night by a number of police cars with blinking lights on their vehicles. Often when we spent time with Mother off the road, the rest of us were also surrounded by many armed police officers. I counted 36 of them one day. Mother's popularity did not only extend to millions of ordinary Indian people, but included many important government officials such as the prime minister of India, chief ministers, ministers, and governors, who all wanted to protect her on her journeys. Mother herself didn't pay too much attention to the anxiety others felt about her safety. When a devotee expressed concern that a crazed person might kill her, she replied that we were not to be afraid. She had chosen when to enter this world, and she would also choose when to leave. She said she would be with us for many more years.

The air-conditioned camper-van that had looked so comfortable at our departure turned out to be just the opposite. Sitting in the back, I was thrown into the air each time it hit a pothole, drove over rocks, or made a sudden stop. There are very few smooth stretches of road in India. For many hours we lurched around on the uneven roads; there were potholes everywhere and most dirt roads had uneven shoulders because of floods, overuse, or construction. My hip was not happy and I had to resort to taking painkillers. Keeping my arthritis inflammation down became an art. The benefit of the van's air conditioning was short-lived, because on the second day of the tour Mother ordered it turned off, explaining that it was too expensive to run. Some people had paid for air conditioning and they were promised a refund. Now hot dust and pollution settled into the van. In no time our eyes were sore and our faces covered in grime; it was no use trying to keep our clothes clean, and we had no choice but to become drenched in sweat and dust. My two seatmates, having been on this tour before, had wisely brought some masks, and they loaned me an extra one. During the ride, they swathed their heads and faces in towels. The dust was so bad that out of our entire convoy we could often see only the two

buses directly ahead of us; the third, more distant bus was completely enveloped in clouds of dust.

After stops at several cities, some devotees began to take
the train on the longer hauls. People ventured from the other buses
to occupy the empty seats on ours, thinking they might be more
comfortable, but they quickly and silently disappeared again back
to their own transportation. Some of us took turns lying on the
floor—two people could just fit stretched out. When we did not
know how we could possibly sit any longer, it was a small blessing to stretch out, but then we had to deal with more dust coming
through the floor. It was also much hotter down there, although
the entire van felt like a furnace. When the sun hit the windows
we covered them with cloth or towels.

The buses had no toilet facilities so we had to stop every
three or four hours to look after our personal needs. The drivers
were very reluctant to pull over for any emergencies because the
whole convoy had to stop whenever one vehicle did. It was almost impossibly uncomfortable for those who had diarrhea or for
women having their periods. Whenever we eventually did stop,
we had to rush. The men disappeared to one side of the road while
the women retreated to the other side. Needing more privacy than
men, the women required more time to find places that provided
cover. It was quite a sight to see a convoy of 400 people trying to
find a little private spot to do their business. Our drivers had no
understanding of the women's hygienic needs, so we developed
a few ways of pressuring them to stop. One woman was quite attractive and knew how to sweet-talk them. One woman gave them
no option, but threatened them with a mess if they did not stop
for her, and sometimes the three men on our bus would add their
support to our cause when we complained too loudly, or if they
also had to go badly. During one of the stops with Mother, she addressed the issue and promised to look into buying some potties
for the buses. For such a large and mostly efficient operation, I
found the primitive travelling conditions somewhat appalling.

One of the main reasons Westerners joined Mother's tours
was to be able to spend time close to her. Not only did we get the
best seats close to the stage during the programs, but Mother also

stopped en route to eat or have tea with us. If we were lucky that might happen twice a day while we travelled. Suddenly, we would see Mother's camper-van stop, often in an open field in the middle of nowhere, followed by the cars carrying the swamis, who got out to scout the area. If the area was unsatisfactory, they would get into their cars again and the caravan would take off, trying to find a better spot. Sometimes our stops were planned—at a devotee's home or a government official's estate. When Mother stopped en route, we forgot our fatigue and it no longer mattered how many hours we still had to suffer in those horribly uncomfortable buses before we got to the next stop. Mother would answer our questions and listen to jokes and stories, and together we sang bhajans. Then off we went again.

There would be competitions between the buses as to which one could stay closest to Mother's camper-van and which devotees got out first to run and sit closest to Mother. It was quite something to see all the devotees running about, trying to discover where the swamis would put Mother's chair so they could crowd around it. I carried my own little stool around and was happy to sit at the back.

Fifty-Six

In Kannur, the local devotees had organized a procession that would travel from a point in town to the stadium. We were asked to join them and, before we knew it, we were walking through the streets followed by thousands of people, musical bands with loudspeakers, and decorated wagons. It was searingly hot and we scrambled to find sunscreen lotion to protect ourselves. It looked as though not a soul was at work; the sidewalks were crammed with people viewing the procession. As I observed all the activity, I imagined my family and friends at home looking upon all this, and I giggled to myself. I would never have dreamed I would be doing this. My love for Mother made me walk there on my aching, swollen feet with deep affection. I smiled at the people on the sidelines. I was certain these people had never seen so many Westerners in an Indian procession. That evening, when I looked down from the stage, I saw a great mass of heads. The stadium was totally packed. I became quiet and reflected on how it could not be humanly possible for anyone to give each one of these people a hug. Mother was so physically tiny that we could hardly see her, surrounded as she was by throngs of people. My mind was not capable of understanding what she could accomplish or who she really was. I once asked a few other devotees if they had any idea, but they shook their heads and had no answers either. Amma was beyond what my human mind could understand. And when my mind could not understand, it had to surrender.

It was impossible to find any quiet time alone. On tour, we could not just go off for a walk and meditate; there were always so many people around. Mother asked us to avoid small talk, so we became accustomed to having only a short conversation and then walking away. At home in Canada, I lived a very secluded life in the country, so being around people constantly was difficult for me. There were several ways in which I learned to separate myself from people in the same room, such as meditating or reading, sitting facing the wall, or lying on the floor and closing my eyes. Some people wore a small "silence" sign. When walking somewhere we looked at the ground to avoid eye contact. We greeted others by putting our right hands on our hearts for a moment but saying nothing. In the beginning, that felt strange because I knew the people that I passed so well. But I learned quickly that not speaking was not a personal slight.

Sometimes we stayed in ashrams, sometimes in school classrooms, and sometimes in the private homes of local devotees. I had never travelled with such a large group of people nor shared sleeping space with 80 to 90 women, often all in one room with two toilets and meagre washing facilities. Most of the time, there were no showers; we just used a bucket and a little container to scoop water over our bodies. In the schools, we moved school desks to make extra sleeping space, and then had to clean our filthy "sleeping facilities." Those tasks became increasingly difficult depending on what time we arrived and how exhausted we were.

Getting up in the middle of the night became a normal way of washing and cleaning up, even if it meant going back to sleep with wet hair. Alarm clocks went off throughout the night because people either wanted to get up to meditate, do seva duty, or join Mother, who always did darshan through the night, no matter where we were. Most of the little travel alarm clocks looked and sounded the same, so it always took some minutes before a person realized that it was her alarm clock ringing. When devotees came in during the night, they had to use flashlights to navigate the room. Airline sleep masks came in very handy. I had to learn to sleep under all kinds of conditions, with a good deal of noise, often during daylight hours, and with people walking over me since space was frequently cramped. I might get a few hours of sleep during the day because I arrived or worked at such awkward times during the night. I knew that if I was going to survive this part of the tour, I needed to take things as they came.

In Talassery, I and two other devotees stayed with a local family in a room on the main floor of their simple home. The family included the father and mother, two teenaged children, and the father's sister. The boy was somewhat shy, but the young girl, about 13 years of age, would come and sit next to us and practice her English whenever we sat down. Her father, a mechanic on sick leave, spoke English a little better and often got called upon to translate for us. Even when we pulled our books out or wrote in our journals, the young girl would stay beside us. We could see that she was used to sitting still for long periods of time without saying anything. She had no qualms about looking at or questioning me about what I was writing. Several of the family members would stand directly in front of us and stare intently. Perhaps they wondered if we might need something, or perhaps they were just curious about us. The father did not hesitate to walk into our room without knocking, even if we were sleeping or in the middle of dressing. It was clear that our Western boundaries were very different and despite the heat, we finally had to resort to locking ourselves inside our room.

The real treat our host family provided was the clear water from a deep well next to their house. In their bathroom we could open the window, lower the bucket, and fetch lovely, cold, clean water. It was a real pleasure to be able to wash our clothes in clean water and hang them outside on the line to dry. The neighbourhood women also came to get their water from our host family so there was constant socializing going on outside the house. Everyone was curious about the family's guests, so we were on the receiving end of much pointing and smiling.

Our host's sister was in her late 40s; she was living with them because her husband had died. For this reason, she was not allowed to go out at all. Her brother even bought all her clothes. We could see that she was used to being constantly thankful for whatever she was given. When, at the end of our stay, I invited everyone for lunch at a nice restaurant, she was forbidden to come. She was very surprised when I asked what kind of food I should bring back for her. At the restaurant, our host was adamant that I not bring any food home for his sister; however, this time I did not listen to him. I also bought a large box of different kinds of sweets for us to try at home, but there seemed to be a misunderstanding, as the family disappeared with all the treats as soon as we got back to the house. When I gave his sister her food, she bowed deep and touched my feet. Her humility moved me at the same time as it made me feel uncomfortable.

Usually, we needed to be ready and on the bus at 5:30 p.m. to head to the stadium or whatever other large, public area was reserved for the public program. Amma normally walked into the stadium at about 7 p.m. Each program began with the local VIPs greeting her with beautiful, elaborate garlands and long speeches. Then she gave her satsang, which was translated into the local language. At about 10:30 p.m. bhajans started. From the moment we walked into the stadium at 6:30 p.m. until bhajans started at 10:30 p.m., no English was spoken or translated. The crowds often numbered between 40,000 and 50,000 people. The loudspeakers were so loud that sometimes I had to put my fingers into my ears on top of my earplugs. Just when I began to think about escaping this routine, we got the message from Amma that she expected each of her Western children to attend these public meetings. This was a good time to meditate, she said, and to cultivate patience and surrender, no matter whether we understood a word of what was being said or not. I thought to myself, "Well, this is very hard for me to do, but I am here to learn, and if Mother really wants me to do this, I will, and see what comes of it." It was a real struggle for me. I admit that sitting through those programs was one of the most difficult tasks of the tour, but I did attend all but one of them. Ultimately, I learned how to let go of the waiting and to be in the moment, so I had no more struggle.

After bhajans, we were offered a dinner that had been prepared by the local devotees, and then we assisted Amma on the stage. Stage duties consisted mainly of either making the prasad or helping the local volunteers hand the prasad to Amma. While she was giving darshan she would often give a signal that a certain person was to sit close to her for a moment. There were also quite a number of devotees who assisted the people in line as they approached Mother, and helped them leave after they'd received their hug. That was a big job. Often many male and female police officers tried to organize the line, beginning at quite a distance from the stage. Indian people could stand or sit in line for hours at the hottest time of the day, so close that their bodies touched one another. Their quiet endurance was admirable, yet as soon as Mother began to hug people, they would become impatient and wild. Droves of people would then approach the stage together in a horizontal line as though they were first in line, even when their darshan ticket number read 20,000 or higher. One night, just as things were becoming totally out of control, I watched Mother simply look up from giving darshan and somehow the tension ceased immediately.

When things did spiral somewhat out of control, we had to get out of the way quickly, otherwise we might get pushed over and trampled upon. At the beginning of the tour, I was afraid to be caught in the middle of these huge, unruly crowds as they cried, begged, and even kissed our hands or feet to persuade us to get them closer to Mother. I knew that Mother would give them all a hug, until the very last person had received one, but somehow they each wanted their hug now. Many of these people were so very desperate. An opportunity to see and touch Mother meant so much to them; they saw her only once every year or two and they desperately hoped she would give them some relief from their suffering and need. After a while, I could understand and feel their desperation and urgency.

I felt guilty about leaving Mother at midnight while she was still giving darshan to many thousands of people. When I looked at the crowds, I often wondered how she would manage to see them all. But she just continued hugging people one by one, wiping their tears, listening to their sorrows and desires. They leaned their bodies on her, pushing and pulling and wanting, wanting, wanting. And she smiled, talked to them, cajoled them, giving, giving, giving. Her body moved forward to each person as she gave them a full hug and her complete attention for a moment. When she let the person go, they were immediately pulled away from her by the devotees assisting the "out-line," to make space for the next person. This was done very rapidly and sometimes with some force because people did not want to let go of Mother. As always, during these 20 to 23 hour-long darshans, Mother would not get up to stretch or go to the washroom. She would not eat and only now and then did I see her drink some tea or coconut milk. When she did finally get up to leave, she looked absolutely beautiful. Her face was flushed dark-coloured and her eyes were radiant.

A few times I stayed on until the 3 a.m. bus left for our sleeping facilities, but my body needed a minimum of six hours of sleep. I had to decline most after-midnight stage duties, no matter how appealing they sounded. Once, I asked an Indian woman next to me if she also felt guilty when she left during Mother's darshan. Her eyes filled up with tears. We talked about our vulnerability and our smallness for a while and admitted that our bodies just could not keep up with Mother's pace. Although some others were able to stay up all night with her, we couldn't manage it, and we just had to accept that. Another devotee overheard our conversation and also began to cry. The darshan number sign was at 7,600 when we arose to leave, knowing Mother's work would go on for many more hours. Her sari was soiled with sweat and oil from the many heads that had already been on her shoulder. We walked toward the bus in silent contemplation.

Fifty-Seven

In six cities out of 17 on this tour, following the public programs in the stadiums, we stopped at Amma's Brahmasthanam temples—puja temples—where three days of programs and special pujas were offered. She would come into the hall to give darshan at around 11 a.m., darshan would continue until about 4 p.m., and then she would return for pujas and bhajans at 6:30 p.m. Following that, she gave darshan again until well into the morning. As I have mentioned, it was known that Amma did not sleep, but apparently she dozed a little every now and then. Often after 18 to 23 hours of darshan, Mother made private visits to people's homes, met with dignitaries in her room, and answered mail. She was fully aware at all times of what was happening in her many charities and ongoing projects around the country and abroad, and was in constant contact with them.

After close to 10 days on the road, I realized the real tests were just beginning for me and the other devotees. We were suffering from fatigue, the heat was hitting us hard, and the pushing and shoving of the large crowds was almost intolerable. We lived with incessant loud noise and lack of sleep. Patience was running short; people were getting irritated with one another. My feet were still swollen and the pain did nothing for my own disposition. My mind said that if I wanted to survive seven weeks of this, it was time to start practicing detachment, tolerance, and patience. My mantra became my greatest help.

It had taken me a long time to learn to use the mantra properly, but now I silently intoned it throughout my waking hours. When I was in conversation or busy interacting with people my mantra kept going like a pot simmering on a small burner; as soon as I was finished it returned to a full boil. Whenever my mind slipped away to unimportant things, my mantra popped up as though my spirit was saying, "Okay, that's enough; stay in the present." It was not possible to read in the bus, so I watched what was going on outside, listened to my bhajan tapes, and used my mantra.

Practicing detachment was another difficult task for me. At first I was reluctant to do it, as I had always thought that detachment made us appear aloof and uninterested. I discovered that in reality it created freedom, the freedom created space, and the space created a way to be able to look at things objectively, until finally, in the end, the freedom and space of detachment created love and compassion. Amma says:

> *Compassion is not something one person has for another, but rather something that arises when one begins to see all others as one's own self. As real compassion develops within, the sense of "other" begins to lessen.*

But then something happened that made me fail terribly. In Bangalore, I woke up one morning to find that my suitcase, which I had placed at my feet, was gone. I looked around and found it thrown near the door. My tape recorder and bhajan tapes, as well as some of my clothes, had spilled onto the floor. I was stunned and angry and asked if anyone had seen anything. It turned out that one of the devotees had tripped over my suitcase when she returned in the middle of the night. She had picked it up and thrown it wherever she could. The same devotee had complained about a long clothing line I had strung for hanging wet clothes, and she had grilled me several evenings earlier for leaving the stage before my replacement came when I was doing seva. I had been in too much physical pain to remain and argue at that time. Now I was simply not going to let her get away with her behaviour, and after she woke up I told her angrily that if she ever touched any of my things again, she would find her own belongings in the toilet. I said that since we all had to constantly walk over luggage and bodies perhaps she should invest in a flashlight. I added that the clothesline she was complaining about was mine and it would not be a good idea for her to touch that either.

I also grilled her about her constant negative behavior. Her response was that I could have waited to talk to her about these things in a more adult fashion, not when she was just waking up.

I thought that confronting her would make me feel better, but it didn't. Amma said anger was like a sword with two sharp edges. It created and spread negative energy on both sides. Over the next two days, I attended three pujas, and took some of the prasad to the devotee's bed with a little note that read, "Please accept my prasad." With this gesture it was over for me and although she didn't talk to me for some time, I felt I had done what I could to make amends.

Perhaps the best thing about the tour environment was that most often when tempers did flare up, each person tried to put the incident behind them as soon as possible. People would talk things over and apologies would be expressed and quickly accepted. Being a devotee and having the desire to grow spiritually included following Amma's teachings to forgive, forget, and try to do better next time. It worked wonders when everyone involved in the community had the same attitude.

One morning in Mangalore, I returned to the stage for a while to watch Amma give darshan. For a few days I'd been feeling that she was ignoring me. She did not look at me even when I was on or near the stage. Nothing was translated into English and Amma seemed to be exclusively focused on her Indian devotees. And rightly so: we were on tour in India and we Westerners got all her attention when she was in the U.S. or Europe. Truth be told, we got much more attention on those tours than any Indian typically got on this tour.

She often said "I am not the body," which meant that she was teaching us to detach ourselves from her body. She also said, "Child, I reside right inside you." But at that moment I did not feel inclined to think that way. I felt sad when I looked at her. I could see her, I could hear her laugh, I could nearly touch her, and I still felt sad. Although I had a great spot close to Amma, I gave it to a brahmacharini who had been slowly pushing me to the side. I walked away in tears.

What was I doing here, enduring all of this discomfort? What was my purpose? Then I wondered where I would rather be. At home in Canada? No, I didn't want to be there—that's why I had come here. With my friends who were on a cruise? No, I did not like cruise ships; all one did was eat and eat, and sit around amongst loads of other people. I found them tiresome no matter whom I was with. Would I like to be in Europe with my family and friends? No, I had just been there. I ended up wanting to be just where I was, with all the discomfort and with Mother ignoring me. Deep inside I knew she was not ignoring me and that she was completely aware of what was going on. But that is not how I was feeling just then.

So what was this lesson all about? I was still in tears while I made my way toward the area where I was supposed to do my seva. I bought a cup of tea, sat on a rock, and watched what was going on. We were on a hill and I could see quite far into the distance, where there were many small cement houses surrounded by countryside. My eyes turned to the huge refuse pile where garbage from the event had been dumped over the past three days. A small brick wall separated the dump from the main kitchen, where thousands of people had received food. An elderly woman was rummaging around in the dump, trying—in vain, I thought—to find something useful. For a moment, she stood still with an empty plastic bottle in her hand. Nearby, a line of people were leaving the kitchen with plates of breakfast in their hands. I had no desire to eat, I was too upset; instead, I decided to give my plate of breakfast to the woman. I walked over and we smiled at each other; I moved my hand toward my mouth and pointed at her. She understood and nodded. I ran to the kitchen and returned with a plate full of food. When I handed it over something happened as we looked at each other. There was no hint of begging in her eyes, no request for anything; we were meeting on an equal level, woman to woman, human being to human being. We were the same, experiencing the Oneness Mother talked about. She gave me a little smile and only three teeth showed in her mouth, but she still looked beautiful with her dirty sari and skinny, bony body. As I turned around and walked away, I heard Amma's voice loud and clear in my heart saying, "My child, this is where I am." What an emotional and beautiful lesson that was. How quickly I had forgotten that Amma was omnipresent and how I needed to be reminded again and again. It was now time for my seva duty and while I squeezed lemons and peeled fruit, I asked Amma to firmly hold on to my slippery hands.

During satsang in a field a few weeks later, Amma asked for stories. I finally put up my hand. She invited me to come closer and I was handed the microphone. I told the story of my sadness, my search for meaning, and my encounter with the woman at the dump and my discovery that the Divine is everywhere. As I told the story, Amma listened intently and looked straight into my eyes. When I stopped, she turned to a swami to hear his translation. The swami then translated her response back to us. She said that it was a beautiful story and that my sadness was a sign of pure devotion; my meeting with the woman on an equal level was a sign of our One-ness. Later on, many devotees, including some men, approached me and thanked me for my story, saying it had brought tears to their eyes. It seemed that many had very similar experiences of feeling separated from Mother and had been very sad about it.

Fifty-Eight

People on the tour were now seriously complaining about chronic diarrhea. I had no idea, and really did not want to know, how the Indian devotees were handling this problem without toilet paper while we travelled. I also heard people coughing a lot during the night and I guessed it was due to the pollution and dust. Some people were getting sick with viruses and parasites. The fatigue of the tour and the long hours we spent in the "square wheeled buses," as they were called, were especially hard on the sick people. Some people with diarrhea were obliged to spend a night in the hospital where they were given an intravenous saline solution to rehydrate. Some devotees had to stay behind in other accommodations to get well, and then take the train to the next city on the tour. Some would travel a few cities ahead, where they stayed in a hotel and waited for us. All these health problems worried me, and I washed my hands more than usual. I also washed my feet with diluted chlorine before I went to bed. I was determined not to lose weight on this trip, so I ate a lot of sweets, cookies, and bananas, as well as rice three times a day. As a result, I experienced the opposite of diarrhea. I drank three or four one-litre bottles of water every day and took some electrolytes. I decided that as long as I could bear it, I would continue the tour as programmed. Only if I became really sick would I make other arrangements. I knew that it would be very difficult for me to undertake this tour again—it was both mentally and physically very hard for me.

At about 1:30 a.m. on our way to Bangalore, our camper-van was suddenly rear-ended by one of the tour's other buses. The driver had been following us too closely, and when our van made a sudden stop he lost control and rear-ended us. I was asleep when we were hit. I heard a loud bang as I felt the impact and then I was

283

unconscious for a moment. When I returned to my senses, I had no idea where I was, and then it slowly became clear that we had been in an accident. The rear end of the van was completely mangled. All of its rear windows as well as some side windows were shattered and ceiling panels lay on the floor.

Because I was in the rear of the van I was smashed up pretty badly. The seat in front of me had been torn from the floor and had hit me on my side. Just prior to the accident, the devotee who had been seated next to me decided to lie down sideways on the floor. She had to be pulled out first. She told me later that, moments before we were hit, she had placed a small pillow in front of her face for protection in case the driver had to stop suddenly. When she moved to the floor, I decided to sit sideways and give my legs a rest. If I had stayed in a sitting position, my body might have been crushed. Also on the back seat was an Indo-American man; he had to be pulled out as well.

I felt nauseated and my head, neck, and shoulders were beginning to hurt. We were about two or three hours out of Bangalore. A decision was made to get me to the nearest hospital, so I was put on the floor in the aisle padded and covered by blankets and cushions. I was amazed that the van was able to continue driving. From my vantage point on the floor it was quite a sight to see the wind flying through the van, the devotees curled up on their seats dressed in all the layers they could find. It looked like a hurricane was blowing through the bus while it drove on. On the floor I was able to find some composure and relax a little.

When we finally arrived at the closest hospital, I got up to go inside. Surprisingly, my head was perfectly clear and my shoulders and neck now felt fine too. The others in our van were also okay, their major complaints being only a few bruises here and there. When we were able to look at the total damage to the van, we became very quiet and thankful to be alive. The doctor confirmed that I had a cracked or broken rib and advised me to rest for 18 days. But I needed to continue, I said, so she ordered me to sit on the front seat of the camper-van for the remainder of the trip. Amma did not say a word to us about the accident. Her words were not needed; we knew that we were blessed.

Later on, I discovered from others that this had been an inauspicious time to travel—accidents were bound to happen. Some time ago, my initial response would have been, "How could something like this happen when we were travelling with a Mahatma? Isn't she supposed to protect us at all times?" Now I knew much better. My astrological chart had predicted I would have an accident in my 60th year, and now I had. It may sound strange, but I was certain each person in that van was supposed to have something happen in connection with their karma, and Amma had made sure it happened close to her so that we would be protected. If I had not been in India, an accident would have happened to me somewhere else and it could have been much worse.

At first I did not believe that the van was repairable, but while we were in Bangalore for a three-day program mechanics worked on it day and night. It was fixed by the time we were ready to leave for Devanagere, our next stop. From Bangalore to Devanagere we had to move to a different bus. I was in excruciating pain and had trouble breathing. Each pothole made me cringe, and for the first time, I had serious doubts about being able to make it through the tour.

Back in the camper-van again, I had a new Australian seatmate. She had serious trouble with her neck and also needed to sit in the front. Valsala was about half my age. She was fun and attractive, and she took on the job of cajoling and charming the two male Indian devotees in charge of getting the driver to stop for our washroom needs. She was very good at it.

The road had neither marked lanes nor street lights, and most of the driving was done during the night when it was pitch dark. Many vehicles had only one or no taillights and, in many cases, no brake lights, so unexpected surprises came at every turn on these long hauls. In addition, a great number of heavily loaded tractors and carts pulled by cows, bulls, horses, or camels travelled during the night, and they had no lights at all. Because our windows were open at all times, our travel was accompanied by a continuous barrage of honking.

During the most harrowing events of the drive, Valsala and I would scream, "Amma" or "Krishna" and duck for cover. It was important to call the name of the Divine with our last breath in order to benefit our rebirth. When the danger passed we would giggle out of nervousness, surprised that nothing had happened.

One night en route to Puna, we had satsang with Amma. After a time, I left the group, just to be alone for a few minutes before getting back on the bus again. Sitting on my little stool and watching the stars, I gently touched my swollen feet, silently complaining because they hurt so much. Then, for some reason, I took out a little bag of sacred ash Amma had given me at darshan in Hyderabad and gently covered my feet and ankles with it. It felt inexplicably soothing. When we continued our journey I fell asleep. Several hours later when I awoke, all the swelling and pain were gone. I could even see the veins. My feet were completely healed. For the rest of the trip I had no swollen feet or ankles. What could I say? I could only be thankful because these things were so far beyond what my mind could understand. And when my mind could not understand something it just became quiet. I recalled that my dictionary said faith meant, "unquestioning belief that does not require proof or evidence" and another dictionary defines faith as "a firm belief without logical truth." How else could I explain these happenings?

Fifty-Nine

As with everywhere else, the programs in Mumbai were packed with thousands of people. The streets were impossibly crowded and the begging was becoming more aggressive. Until now, people had asked us for money and things, but they had not touched us. Perhaps in Mumbai the desperation was even more intense, because begging people followed us longer and pulled at our clothes, or they just walked in front of us while touching our arms. Although Amma discouraged giving money to the beggars, she also said to use discrimination. In certain cases it was all right to give a few rupees. I did give away money now and then, especially to the very elderly. I grew to have a sense for who truly needed it. The problem was that once we started giving, they always wanted more. Initially that irritated me, as if what I gave was never enough, but when I placed myself in their situations, my heart melted and overflowed again.

The thin young children who boldly begged around the ashram had a certain charm of their own. Their brashness indicated that they were used to rejection but must have had some success in perseverance as well. I recognized those qualities of boldness and perseverance quite well; they were what I had needed for my own survival. Many of the begging children ran around half-naked and dirty. We gave them small tasks, such as cleaning up the garbage, and they did a good job. When they were done we gave them plates of food. I could see that they enjoyed working for their meals—after eating they would laugh and tumble about playfully. Watching them, I was saddened to think that these children were denied the very basics in life—decent food, clothing, and shelter. Going to school was not a possibility for them.

One night, about halfway through the program, I suddenly couldn't bear the chanting any more. The Archana was chanted continuously during the pujas. Devotees chanted during seva, in the bus, in our sleeping quarters, everywhere. At every program there was constant chanting on the loudspeakers. Even the bhajans irritated me. Ordinarily, I loved the bhajans.

On top of my irritation with the constant chanting, I began to notice how many devotees intoned, "Mother said this," or "Mother wants that." They would interrupt conversations or make subtle disparaging remarks about what the rest of us were doing. They gave the impression that Mother was busy all day meeting with them in order to put restrictions on the rest of us. It was confusing because these remarks often came from long-time devotees and renunciates, yet I felt the need to be on guard against them. I began to think I was being brainwashed. Then I had to laugh, especially about the word brainwash, as that was indeed what was happening, and it was also precisely what I wanted. I really wanted Mother to wash all those years of conditioning from my brain so that I could experience stillness and peace of mind and grow spiritually. People were so afraid of the word brainwash. Someone deciding to become part of an unfamiliar spiritual community made others so quick to judge. But what did things like getting an education, attending church, watching television, or reading newspapers do except train people to think certain thoughts and form certain opinions, to behave in certain ways? In any case, it was my brain; I was close to 60 years of age and I could do with it what I liked. Amma says:

> It is not the surrender of one's personality but rather the handing over of one's limited self to one who will change it into the infinite Self.

More and more things irritated me. I turned inward and tried to figure out the reasons for it. All I could think of was that I needed to surrender and detach even more, so things that happened around me would not affect me. When that answer came to me I knew it was true, I truly knew, but at the same time I craved some space away from people, some quiet, a decent meal—like a real salad with cucumbers and nuts. I wanted slices of heavy, dark, wholesome brown bread. I longed for a clean room with a bed just for me, so I could sleep, hide, and read for a whole day. A warm shower would be the ultimate pleasure. Ah, I was missing my material comforts. But I was determined to stick to the program and I very well knew why. Next to my bed at home there was a little note I looked at frequently. It read:

> *True spirituality is to go beyond all desires, to go beyond the mind and its thoughts. This is what a true aspirant longs for.*
>
> *Amma*

The words "longs for" stayed with me and made me smile. Mother used such simple words, but they were so very difficult to live by. It took constant mindfulness and constant trying. It was through constant trying that I had accomplished so much in my life. It had always paid off. I could be very persistent, to the point of being obsessive. This time, trying meant something totally different, because instead of acting and doing, I had to let go and surrender—something exceedingly difficult for me.

The night before we moved on from Mumbai, our suitcases were loaded onto the buses' rooftops. We were told to hand in our bedrolls at 3 a.m. and be ready to leave by four. I got up a little earlier than everyone else to have a last-minute shower. Then I packed my bedroll and took it to the bus. Mine was the first one outside and I made the terrible error of leaving it there, thinking the loading would begin soon. I went back upstairs and started waking up the women on the balcony before stacking the chairs and cleaning up the room and toilets.

When I went down to the buses afterward, the loading was done and I had no idea my bedroll had been stolen. I only discovered it when we unloaded in Surat. I did not know if I was receiving a sign to "let go more and more," but my new sleeping bag, silk liner, fleece jacket, toiletry bag, two sets of clothes, towel, and mosquito nets had disappeared, and I could not fathom the lesson in this. I was upset for a while, but then became grateful that it had been only my possessions that were stolen, because once home I could easily buy new things. All the same, it was very inconvenient. Fortunately I had carried my yoga mat, sleeping pad, small pillow, and thin blanket into the bus, so I could at least lie down in the aisle. I borrowed some shampoo and soap until I could get to a shop, and just did without the rest.

Sixty

The days went by and I was aware that things were getting much tougher for me. I was slowly moving to the edge of my endurance. I became increasingly quiet. Each day I thought I could stand no more, but I did—I simply endured. One day, as we travelled on a 23-hour ride to the next town, I became so uncomfortable that I could do nothing but repeat my mantra for hours. Both my arthritic hip and injured rib were causing such agonizing pain that I did not know how to sit, stand, or lie down any longer. The temperature must have been well over 40 degrees Celsius. Pollution, heat, and noise saturated the bus, and I could feel the dirt between my teeth and in my nose and eyes. It was impossible to keep my glasses clean, and by now they were thoroughly scratched. All of it was pushing me further and further away from my hold on clarity, control, detachment, and sanity—closer to some precarious edge. It felt like any leftover strength was draining out of my body and mind. Then, very slowly, I realized that, as I was being pushed to the edge, I let go, and in letting go, my ego was letting go as well. It could not hold on. I watched things disappear, bit by bit, as though they were being left at the wayside, until nothing was left except awareness of the moment. And then, when nothing was left, the "I" left me as well. Then there was, at last, real peace. A peace and a quiet that I could not, and still cannot, explain. But the awareness was there.

Control had been so important in my life in so many different ways. I had tried to cling to it during my childhood years of abuse and troubled family life, as a teenager being away from my home and country with only a limited education, trying to establish a life of my own, then struggling for years to keep my businesses afloat. It seemed I had always lived my life in survival mode. But what had I really been holding on to? Now that it had all drained out of me I felt no need to hold on to anything. There was nothing to hold on to, except a knowing that there was no time as I knew it, that I was not the body I carried, and that ultimately I was just energy, awareness, consciousness. A peace and a lightness overcame me that I had not known before. This feeling is with me now when I go inward and connect with that part of myself where everything is perfect and nothing is needed, or when I am in nature, while meditating or listening to bhajans.

One day in Pune, a Dutch devotee who wrote on the Internet about Mother's many charity projects invited me to visit some new apartment buildings being erected next to the slums. We were shown around the project by the swami in charge of all of Mother's housing projects for the poor. It was Mother's wish to build 100,000 houses within 10 years, and this swami was running several projects at the same time. He explained that Mother's goals were on track with this project. Immediately I could see that he not only knew exactly what he was doing, but he did things well—quickly, efficiently, and with good humor. His perpetual smile was attractive and contagious. When he had given us all the figures and facts about the project, he excused himself and disappeared to attend an appointment.

We moved away from the new buildings into the slums with some other devotees who translated for us. Soon we were surrounded by the many children and adults who lived there. They were visibly amused and curious about our visit. I was the only Western woman present on this visit, and the little girls automatically took my hands, held onto my clothes and asked lots of questions. They wanted to know my name, where I was from, if I was married, if I had children. It made them laugh to hear that my Indian name was SitaLakshmi.

The worst slums in this area had already been destroyed and a new building was being constructed in its place. The people now surrounding us would be the first to move into the finished building. The construction was happening in several stages, and they had already moved from the worst living conditions into a more habitable part of the slums with small huts. Some even had electricity and fans, but none had running water, and many women with their young children in tow had to wash their laundry at communal taps installed elsewhere.

When we asked to see their living quarters, they happily invited us in and offered us tea. I was impressed with how well organized and resourceful these people were, considering their limited resources and space. Sometimes nine or ten family members lived, cooked, and slept together in a small space the size of my bedroom at home. One small building served as a toilet facility for the several thousands of people who lived there. It was evident that the sewer trenches in front of the dwellings were also used for those needs. I wondered what this would look like during the rainy season and the floods. Something interesting occurred while I spent time with these people in their small living spaces. We laughed a great deal and photographs were taken, and gradually I became aware of a distinct familiarity, as though I had been in some of these places before. I seemed to know exactly how they lived and managed. I also felt that if I were left behind here, I would know exactly what to do.

When I returned to our sleeping quarters, my three roommates asked where I had been. They each looked at me with such curiosity that I finally asked what was going on. I looked different somehow, one of them said, much younger, that my eyes were brighter and bluer than she had seen them before, and that I was radiant and glowing.

According to Mother, there were many different ways of reaching the goal of finding our True Self, and thank goodness for that, because on this trip I was not getting up at 4:00 a.m. to do Archana and then meditate as most other devotees were doing. When I awoke each day at 4 a.m., my first thoughts were of Mother, and I silently talked to her for some time. I had no trouble hearing her answers to my questions. Most of the time I would then fall back to sleep for a little while. Thinking about Mother had slowly become a natural part of me, no matter where I was or what I was doing. I went to bed listening to bhajans and fell asleep while repeating my mantra. I expressed my gratitude to

Mother continually and took nothing for granted, perhaps because lately I was so much more focused and aware of my thoughts and what was happening around me. Somehow the feeling of gratitude filled me up so much that my thoughts frequently went to what more I could do for others. My cup seemed full and overflowing. Still, one of my most difficult tasks was to try and see the Divine in each person. I was so grateful to have had some experiences in being One with nature, animals, and children, and with some adults. Being One with All, I believed, would be the same as finding my True Self.

"Think of God as your own Self," Mother said. That phrase was very important to me, because it took me away from all that I had been taught to believe before. Mother also said that neither she nor God needed anything from us. What we did, we did because of our own needs. I believed that ultimately we prayed and meditated to the Divine in our own selves. I believed that the energy we created through prayer, chanting, meditation, good or bad thoughts, and good or bad actions became part of the total universe and was reflected back to us in one way or another. The law of Nature, the Universe, or the Divine, whatever we might want to call it, was not random and made no mistakes.

One frequent question for Mother was why was there so much violence and disharmony in this world and what could we do about it? Conflicts have always existed, she said, and they still do and will in the future—such is the nature of this world. Prayers for the welfare of the world, for peace and harmony, are not just empty words. They really do have an effect. Prayers send out strong positive vibrations, weakening the intent of the negative forces that create discord and disarray in the world.

This really hit home for me again when I read Masaru Emoto's very interesting little book called The Hidden Messages in Water. In his book he says, "The entire Universe is in a state of vibration, and each thing generates its own frequency, which is unique. This is the fundamental principal of the Universe. Everything is eternally moving and vibrating—on and off, at an incredible speed."

This Japanese scientist takes photographs of water crystals to illustrate his compelling theory about the effect positive and negative energy has on water. His pictures show deformed and unclear crystals of dirty water and their transformation into beautiful clear crystals after they have been influenced by prayers and sweet words, even if these words are just written on a piece of paper taped to a glass jar. The book shows his photos of opaque water crystals from a dirty lake and their transformation into clear, well-formed crystals after being subjected to a monk's prayers.

Mr. Emoto also writes about experiments with jars of cooked rice. After three jars were filled with rice, one was spoken to daily with gentle words, the second was scolded, and the third was ignored. After one month, the first jar began to ferment with a smell of malt, the second turned black, and the one left ignored rotted. I thought it fascinating that the rice in the third jar, the one that was ignored, had rotted. That experiment made me think of my childhood. It seemed that being abused, horrible as it was, was not as damaging as being totally ignored. I was also reminded of some devastating television footage of babies and young children left alone in orphanages in poor countries around the world and how they slowly wasted away physically and mentally. These experiments showed me the incredible force of negative or positive words, either written or spoken, and their repercussions.

Sixty-One

Ahmedabad was one of the most depressing and badly polluted cities I had seen on the tour so far. Filthy dust hung in the air like smoke. I was afraid to breathe and kept my mouth covered most of the time. I felt indescribably sorry for the people living there; it was no wonder that so many people in India had serious lung and hearing problems. Our journey to Bhopal would take 19 long hours, so we left immediately after Mother finished giving darshan.

On the journey to Bhopal, it was interesting to see the many billboards in the places we passed. The advertisements showed only happy and laughing Westerners and Indian people with light complexions. In this society, the whiter their skin, the higher status they were accorded. One day after the program when we were waiting for Amma to pass by, some light-skinned Indian VIPs were also standing in line. They pushed the poor aside heedlessly in order to be able to secure the better spots for themselves. But what good did it do to smile at Mother while treating other people this way? Mother often melted the hearts of the wealthy so they would be more open to sharing with the poor. She simply said, "What is not given is lost." It was known that India had many wealthy people now—the newspaper recently reported 11 billionaires—and that if they would share with the poor in their own country, poverty would cease to exist.

In Jaipur, I had a wish fulfilled. The owner of a hotel had given Mother four rooms and I was fortunate enough to share one of them with an Irish woman. We couldn't believe our luck—just the two of us in one room. For one night we had a room with a small balcony, a real bed with a sheet, a warm shower, a television, and laundry service. The hotel had a restaurant and we were within walking distance of the stadium. What a wonderful treat.

This was Mother's first visit to Jaipur and over 50,000 people were patiently awaiting her. The police were in control until she began to give darshan, but when the crowds moved to the stage en masse, the police could not restrain them. As usual, Mother was not disturbed and continued to hug people well into the afternoon hours.

We were all spoiled that evening as a wealthy devotee and one of the local organizers invited all the volunteers and devotees travelling with Mother for dinner. And what a scrumptious dinner it was! We had a choice of North or South Indian dishes followed by an exquisite dessert and chai tea. I had wished for a decent meal, a normal bed, and some space. Mother had given me what I asked for, and so much more.

In New Delhi it was hot during the day, but it could be very cold at night. The floors were carpeted in our sleeping hall and some blankets had been left from a previous event. Each devotee had the sleeping bag they had brought on the tour, but as mine had been stolen I resorted to using one of the blankets I found there. That was a mistake. In the morning the woman sleeping next to me asked if I had the measles. When I looked in the bathroom mirror I saw that my face was covered with flea bites. They were everywhere. At this point I had gone through so much that I no longer cared. My mirror had been stolen too, so I did not have to look at myself.

With another devotee, I went into town for breakfast and to visit a bookstore, where I bought the book, "Mother Teresa," by Navin Chawla. The tour would finish in Calcutta and I planned to stay an extra two weeks to volunteer at Mother Teresa's Home for the Dying in Kalighat, Calcutta.

In the night I was hit with a great headache, and diarrhea and nausea. I vomited and felt wretched. The next day there was no program so I lay on the floor, close to the bathroom. By now so many people were sick that our two bathrooms, for about 90 women, were occupied constantly. Those who were able found a different floor or quickly got out of the way when they saw a sick person running toward the bathroom.

During that day on the floor I pondered the True Self and karma. If the True Self was pure could it be touched or influenced by karma? After considering the question for a long time, I came to the conclusion that our True Self has always been pure and immortal. Our karma was connected to our physical identification with our body and worldly accomplishments. It also depended upon our belief that these things made us who we were, and the things we did in response to our senses. All of our actions and lessons in our previous lives and the life we lived at the present time resulted in either positive or negative energy that we called karma. Ultimately, there was no duality between good and bad; they only existed in our physical incarnations. Whether we suffered or were content was connected with our physical identification, ego, desires, or karma, and we had a choice to embrace either extreme, no matter how challenging that might be, especially when the body or the mind was in pain.

We were all here to learn. I also had faith that Amma kept a close eye on the burden of her children's pain and suffering, and that through her grace she carried the heaviest loads. For some reason coming to that conclusion made me feel blissful—even though my body was not so happy.

For the rest of the day I read the book about Mother Teresa. The stories of such deep human suffering and the compassion of those who really cared melted my heart and made me cry. Mother Teresa shared so many similarities with Amma. Their selfless work for humanity was done with such humility and their love was so unconditional. I saw that this was true power.

Sixty-Two

For the Brahmasthanam Festival we went to Amma's ashram. Attending the programs there made it obvious that in New Delhi, a very different type of people came to visit Amma. Most of them seemed to be from the middle and upper classes, and they wore Western clothes. Not one man wore a dhoti—a cloth wrapped around the waist. Some young girls were in shorts. Most children wore American-style clothing and carried around junk food. Some of them were overweight—a thing I had rarely seen in other parts of India. Everyone, including the women and teenagers, seemed to have a cell phone and they loved using them. While the ceremonies and speeches were taking place on the stage, they had no qualms about making and taking calls. Large families sat together and had long conversations even while Amma was talking. I thought their behaviour was quite ungracious and wondered why some of them had come here. Was it just a casual outing for them? The difference was also noticeable in the parking lots; here far more people owned cars. In other cities, people would arrive on the local buses or other organized mass transportation. I wondered if people here weren't overly influenced by the materialistic lifestyles of people in the Western world.

To get to Lucknow took us 17 hours. During a stop en route, Mother talked about the control of the mind, and how different parts of our minds often give conflicting messages. We needed to learn to heed and act according to the good part only, she said, and not succumb to the negative part or allow it to manipulate us. Only a few minutes later I was being put to the test. I was seated upon a small mat on the ground. In pain and unable to sit any longer, I decided to get some tea. As I walked away, an Indian devotee, a woman, immediately moved onto my mat. I turned around and said, "Excuse me." She did not respond and did not move. I decided to deal with it when I returned. While I was pouring myself some tea, I heard Amma loud and clear in my heart, saying, "Bring her some tea too!" I was somewhat angered and certainly not in the mood to be generous, but then I heard Amma's message again. Not only did I hear it, but it changed my mood and I thought it was an excellent idea. I returned with two cups of tea and handed one to the woman on my mat. She was very surprised. She smiled warmly and said thank you, and moved over so we could share the mat.

Varanasi, the city of Shiva on the bank of the Ganges, was one of the holiest places on our tour and perhaps in all of India. It was an auspicious place to die. Many elderly pilgrims came to live here as they waited to be relieved of the cycle of life and death. This was the place many devotees on the tour had been waiting to visit. Even devotees who had restricted themselves from sightseeing now headed to the Ganges for a swim and to see the famous burning ghats where bodies of the dead were cremated. I threw my wish out onto the sacred river in front of me: "May I one day be able to come back and stay for a little while. And may I see the Divine in all Forms." Then we walked down to the ghats, where we watched in awe as bodies smouldered in the fires. Canoes were paddled out into the middle of the river to drop off the forms of dead babies who had been wrapped in cloth and tied to a rope and a large rock. Babies did not need the purification of fire.

Durgapur was a one-night stop. After the buses were loaded the next morning we all relaxed in our rooms, awaiting Amma's word to leave for the short trip to Calcutta. Many local women had come to see Amma because they had missed her the night before. They waited for hours and, kissing our hands and touching our feet, begged us to take them to Amma's private room. Amma finally appeared; she talked and joked with them, and began to give them darshan. They were ecstatic. I could never get enough of watching people receive Amma's darshan. In tears after receiving a hug, a young woman approached me, repeating, "Amma gave us a home and now my son is going to school. I am so happy." She introduced her son, who was unable to talk, but he was beaming with joy and used some sign language to demonstrate what he had learned. The two of them jumped up and down in excitement and clung to me. It melted my heart, and I wondered what I could give them to remember this wonderful event. I rummaged through my bag and found a picture of Amma I had bought the night before.

On her way to the camper-van, Amma saw people's garbage from the event still strewn on the ground, and she asked why it had not been cleaned up while we were all waiting for her. During the entire tour, at every place we had visited, after they had eaten, people would just drop their leftover food—and plates, napkins, empty bottles, and cups—on the ground wherever they happened to be standing or sitting. If there were any garbage cans, they were often neither used nor emptied. Crowds of 40,000 to 70,000 people generated an enormous amount of garbage and sometimes we had to be careful not to slip on the wasted food. Ordinarily the local volunteers would clean up after the event, but in this case it hadn't yet been done. Perhaps they were waiting until Mother left. But Mother leaned down and started picking up the garbage herself. Suddenly, everyone joined in.

Sixty-Three

We arrived in Calcutta, thoroughly exhausted, at 1 a.m., to find that our ashram was in a derelict area of the city. If it was possible, these were the worst sleeping facilities of the trip so far. Our floor was so filthy that I was tempted to take a taxi to the nearest hotel. Some Western men came to our floor seeking their wives; the excrement and urine was so bad in their quarters that they were not willing to remain. I discussed what to do with two other female devotees. We felt too unsafe to leave the building at that time of night and decided to move out the next morning as soon as we woke up. Those who stayed behind had no choice but to clean up the mess.

I was installed in a room where the stench of the washroom was so overpowering that I simply had to move into another room. They were all cramped but eventually I found a spot. I left my clothes on, put in my earplugs and pulled on an eye mask, and pretended that I was sleeping in my own bed. It worked, and I woke up at 6 a.m. One of my roommates had already moved into a five-star hotel as soon as the dawn broke. She'd chosen not to wake us up or wait for us. I decided that since I had come this far I was not giving up now. My other roommate also decided to stay at the ashram for the remaining two nights.

We had a few hours before the programs started and some of us took a taxi to Mother Teresa's Home for the Dying, right next to the famous Kali Temple. When we arrived there, I spotted Diane, the nurse from Australia whom I had met in the ashram in Amritapuri. She was sitting on the stairs in a large plastic apron, smoking a cigarette. She was working here now, bathing the new arrivals who were picked up from the street. She found the job difficult, but very rewarding. She said that many of the people who were brought in were extremely dirty and malnourished, and in such pain that they did not want to be washed. They would often even spit at her; nevertheless, she found it fulfilling work.

Diane invited us inside for a little tour and explained how the volunteering worked. Volunteers from all over the world dropped by to help, donating whatever time they had. Everyone met at Mother Teresa's main house for either the 7 a.m. or the 3 p.m. shift and people were dispatched to the job they wanted and were able to do. A group of Japanese women had just arrived and were feeding the very sick. There was one room for the male patients and another for the women. Separated by a wall, they laid on stretchers, keeping the nuns and volunteers very busy. The atmosphere was calm and joyful even though people were dying. Diane, like many other volunteers, was staying at the Salvation Army while she worked at the Home for the Dying. Also an Amma devotee, she would see her while the tour was in town.

In Calcutta the begging reached its peak. Amma was asked whether such extreme poverty was a result of people's karma, and she replied that it was our karma to help and take care of them. The opportunity to move around the city a little provided me with a chance to see the living conditions of the street people. Most of the time it felt unreal. Literally hundreds of thousands of people lived on Calcutta's streets. Some lived behind a plastic tarp against a wall, while many had absolutely nothing to give them shelter. Many large families slept together on newspapers or pieces of carton on the bare ground, often with no blankets to cover them. Some had a few cooking pots and cooked whatever they could find. Wherever there was a single water tap, we saw crowds of people washing themselves, their clothes and their cooking pots while life went on around them. People's washroom needs were attended to in the gutters a few feet from where they slept. Buses, trucks, and rickshaws spat out diesel fumes; the air pollution was horrific and thick as fog. My eyes and throat burned, no matter what I used to cover my face. The constant honking of all the moving vehicles was deafening and I was sure that thousands of these people had hearing problems. The air temperature was 42 degrees Celsius.

Once again, as when I was visiting the slums in Mumbai, I experienced a feeling of familiarity, a special connection as though

I had been here before. I could feel people's suffering and a pain that touched me to the core. I had a strong push-pull feeling. This was the last place on earth I would want to stay and at the same time something was pulling me here. I could not fathom it, and at times, all I could do was watch in helpless sorrow, softly weep, and pray. I was overwhelmed into silence by all that was going on around me.

Finally, the last day of the tour dawned and after the public was gone, Mother gave all of us darshan. She was in a cheerful mood, joking with everyone.

The next day we were all invited to have lunch with her at the estate where she was staying. A special tent with views over the Ganges had been set up in the garden for this occasion. Mother reflected with us on the time we had spent together on this tour. What had we learned? It was up to us to take every opportunity to grow. This had been a two-month-long journey, but to me it felt like a lifetime.

That night I moved into a simple hotel with a devotee from South Africa. It was our intention to take a few days of rest and visit the Krishna Temple and the Museum. Then I would move into the Salvation Army and start work at Mother Teresa's homes, while my roommate would return to the ashram in Amritapuri. However, I became seriously ill with vomiting and diarrhea and several days later, I still felt entirely depleted of energy. I realized that my body, if not my spirit, was insisting that it was time to head home so I could recuperate properly. This journey had taken a heavy toll on me both mentally and physically.

During the evening of my departure I wanted to do something for the beggars in the street where I had been staying. So far I had refused to give them any money. I thought that perhaps the kitchen in my hotel could make a few pots of food, but how was I going to distribute it without getting mobbed? There were so many of them!

Finally, on a street corner, I glimpsed a food stall where the vendor was cooking noodles, vegetables, and eggs in a large wok. I approached and asked him to prepare nine bags of food for me. It took some time before he understood what I wanted, and then he laughed and rounded up some friends to help him as he began cooking in a frenzy of activity. I used the time to scour the part of the street closest to my hotel a few times and to figure out to whom I would give the food on my way back. It worked perfectly. I gave food to several families with small children who had no cooking pots. Some handicapped people who sat together got a bag, food went to some cycle rickshaw people who desperately needed something to eat, and I gave a few small bags to some elderly people who sat on their own. Everything was handed out by the time I reached the entrance of the hotel.

My taxi was waiting. On the way to the airport I watched the evening light mix mysteriously with the dark pollution in the sky. The noise of the traffic was deafening and crowds of human bodies mingled among the dark buildings. It still all looked unreal as I said goodbye to Calcutta. I was leaving, yet I wasn't. I was part of this world, yet I wasn't.

Epilogue

So many phases of my complicated life have felt unreal as they unfolded, and they still feel unreal—my abusive childhood, my family, my time as an au pair living in different countries, immigration to Canada, my businesses struggles, my intimate relationships, and even my spiritual journey. This is what we call the "past," but is there really a past? It seems as unreal as what my mind can plan for the future. Is there a future?

It seems that nothing is real, that everything around us is changing relentlessly and at great speed. Today it is popular to use the phrase, "living in the now." The word *now* is as simple as the word *love*. However, when everything is said and done, *now* and *love* are all that there is. We have free will to choose what to do with them, and that may be as real as it gets for most of us.

Amma says that we are asleep, that we live in a dream, and that only the total surrender of our ego will awaken us. For me, some tough life experiences were needed to finally be ready to find and follow the path that leads me inward. There are no shortcuts to that path, but there is always opportunity for grace.

I would have never thought that one day I would be thankful for my abusive parents. Being born into my dysfunctional family knocked me down repeatedly, but it also taught me to fight for a better existence—one I knew was out there somewhere. My years of au pair work exposed me to some decent families, where people showed they cared about one another, and my time with children allowed me to begin to heal and re-nurture the child in me who hadn't had a childhood. At the same time my growing fluency in several foreign languages provided me with a skill that opened many doors for me.

Dickie came into my life to be my long-time true friend and confidante. From Hayati I learned about love, intimacy, and trust.

In his presence I was able to say what I felt, and laugh wholeheartedly about nothing and everything, confidently, for the first time in my life. My work with Club Méditerranée gave me the opportunity to travel to foreign countries and learn about different cultures. Martine provided me with a stable, happy family life in my younger years and ultimately our friendship led me to Amma. Creating the Vancouver Outdoor Club kept me connected with nature and gave me the means to help others discover their own potential in the outdoors. Toni's love and encouragement helped me believe in myself when I needed it most. My businesses taught me how to fight for justice, not only for myself, but for others as well. They helped me become financially secure so that I can now share with those in need. Sculpting gave me an extra gentle push to expand my creative horizons, and opened the door to a new place of self-awareness. All along the way, I needed all of the hurdles I faced to guide me along the course that finally led to my spiritual path. Ultimately, there was no other course I could have taken.

I had always thought that happiness was somewhere out there in a place I couldn't reach; that it was meant for other people. I had to discover that what I was looking for was part of me, in me. Once I was on my true spiritual path, my desire for anything else faded into obscurity. All I was looking for was already inside me.

I am created as pure love, to be pure love. If I lose my connection to the boundless love inside of me now and then because of my worldly needs and involvements and ties, I need only to find a quiet place and go inward to discover it again and again. When I do find the true happiness that resides inside of me, my heart overflows. As Amma says so clearly, over and over again:

"When the heart flows over you automatically start to give."

Appendix A

Flowing

1. Three panels, each approximately two metres by half a metre, represent the flowing waves of the ocean, streams and rivers, the flow of energy of the trees and flowers, the flow of our lives on earth, and the flow of the universe's energy that we will join after our physical bodies die. Each panel is of slightly different size, length, and form, but they fit and flow perfectly together. The three panels also represent the three stages of life. First, childhood, with its eagerness to learn, explore, and rebel against rules and customs. Then adulthood, trying to put into practice what we

'Flowing' Bridge Housing Building.

have learned, and seeking purpose, stability, and security. Lastly maturity, the exploration of spirituality and letting go of life's and our own expectations and demands.

A circle in the left-hand corner situated between the two lower panels also has a slow movement of energy, and represents the sun and the moon. Warm energy from the sun is needed for all growth on earth; the presence and light of the moon keeps an eye on everything while we rest, surrounded by darkness.

Finally, there are two metal bars of different lengths across the three panels, holding them all together. The longer one crosses all three panels and represents passing boundaries and limitations during the waves of life. The shorter line represents staying within certain boundaries. The piece is spray-painted black.

Looking at it and Looking from it

2. We are all able to look at both the bright (yellow chair) and the dark (black chair) sides of life. We all have that choice: young or old, rich or poor. Each side will take us in different directions. Being able to balance the bright and dark sides of life may bring the harmony we seek in life. Being able to view life situations from different perspectives may bring growth, understanding, and compassion.

These chairs may provide a sanctuary for the body to rest, to take nourishment, to listen to our loved ones, to laugh and cry together, to give us all the freedom to express ourselves and to explore our lives and others and the wonderful world in which we live.

Could you imagine yourself sitting in one of these chairs? Which one would you choose? In which chair have you been sitting most of your life? Are you able to move from one chair to the other? With whom would you be sitting?

Each person will have a different way of viewing these chairs, just as they have a unique perspective in life.

Glossary

Archana – A ritualistic chanting of the 1,000 names of a particular deity.

Ayurveda – The ancient traditional system of Indian medicine.

Ashram – A residential community where spiritual discipline is practiced; abode of a saint.

Avatar – Divine Incarnation—ava-tarati—to come down.

Bhajans – Devotional songs.

Brahmachari – A celibate male disciple who practices spiritual disciplines and is usually undergoing training by a spiritual master.

Brahmacharini – The female equivalent of a brahmachari.

Chai – black tea boiled with milk.

Darshan – An audience with or a vision of the Divine.

Devi – Goddess. The Divine Mother.

Devi Bhava – "The Divine Mood of Devi." The state in which Amma reveals Her oneness and identity with the Divine Mother.

Dhoti – A piece of cloth wrapped around the waist, usually worn by men.

Ego – Limited "I" awareness, which identifies with limiting attributes such as the body or the mind.

Guru – A spiritual teacher. Remover of darkness, gu = remover + ru = of darkness.

Karma – Action or deed. Also the chain of effects that our actions produce.

Mahatma – Literally, "Great Soul."

Mantra - A sacred sound or group of words with the power to transform.

Namah Shivaya – "The spirit in me greets the spirit in you" or "The Divine in me greets the Divine in you."

Omkar – A chanting ritual, 21 Oms.

Prasad – Blessed offering or gift from a holy person or temple, often in the form of food.

Puja – Ceremonial worship.

Renunciate – An individual who renounces all worldly things and lives in celibacy to serve a guru and humanity.

Sanskrit – Ancient Indian language, said to be the language of the Gods.

Satsang – A spiritual talk or discussion; the company of saints and devotees.

Seva – Selfless service, the results of which are dedicated to God.

Swami – One who takes the monastic vows of celibacy and re-nunciation.

Swamini – The female equivalent of a swami.

AMME SARANAM
Retreat Center for Women
Education and Healing Center

Amme Saranam means "Mother's Refuge", a safe haven where women can grow and heal mentally and physically.

AMME SARANAM, a non-profit society, will offer women a place to explore their inner spirit and outer worlds through educational and spiritual programs. It is our intent that by living with this balance, a more peaceful and compassionate world will naturally evolve.

Through the creation of this Center, there is an opportunity and an invitation to return to the Mother's unconditional love and compassion qualities. When there is love there is no effort, no division, no greed, no hunger for power, no need for violence.

The inspiration for this very special project comes from my devotion and gratitude for my spiritual teacher Amma. By witnessing the unconditional love she is constantly showering on humanity, she opened my heart. Her humility leaves me in awe.

All net proceeds of this book are dedicated to AMME SARANAM an Education and Healing Retreat Center for Women.

AMME SARANAM
For more information: www.amme-saranam.org

Acknowledgements

Writing this book would have not been possible without meeting my spiritual teacher Amma. I constantly feel her presence. Her inspiration and spirit follows where ever I am and what ever I do, day and night. I am especially grateful for the encouragements and comments on various drafts of the manuscript from my friends, Dickie, Shirley, Caffyn, Maureen, Cindy, Chris, Jane, Allen, Laurie and Toni. Thanks to my editor Arlene Prunkl for going the extra mile - you are a gem.

To protect the privacy of certain persons, some names have been changed.